*M*emories
of *W*ar

Memories of War

Micronesians
in the
Pacific War

SUZANNE FALGOUT
LIN POYER
LAURENCE M. CARUCCI

University of Hawai'i Press
Honolulu

Library of Congress Cataloging-in-Publication Data
Falgout, Suzanne.
    Memories of war : Micronesians in the Pacific War / Suzanne Falgout,
Lin Poyer, and Laurence M. Carucci.
        p. cm.
    Includes bibliographical references and index.
    ISBN 978-0-8248-3130-1 (pbk. : alk. paper)
    1. World War, 1939–1945—Social aspects—Micronesia (Federated States).
2. Memory—Social aspects—Micronesia (Federated States). 3. World War,
1939–1945—Personal narratives, Micronesian. 4. Oral history. 5. Micronesia
(Federated States)—History. I. Poyer, Lin. II. Carucci, Laurence Marshall.
III. Title.
    D744.7.M54F35 2008
    940.53'966—dc22

                                    2007022048

This publication has been financed in part with Historic Preservation Funds from
the National Park Service, Department of the Interior. The contents and opinions
do not necessarily reflect the views or policies of the U.S. Department of the Interior.
Additional funding for this publication was provided by the University of Hawai'i-
West O'ahu, the University of Wyoming, and Montana State University.

University of Hawai'i Press books are printed on acid-free paper and meet the
guidelines for permanence and durability of the Council on Library Resources.

Designed by Josie Herr

CONTENTS

PREFACE

We are very grateful to the Micronesians who granted us interviews during our oral history project in 1990–1991, which was funded by the National Endowment for the Humanities. Neither our earlier book, *The Typhoon of War,* nor this one could have been written without their help. Those participants who wished to be named are listed in the Appendix. In direct quotations in this text, we have identified most speakers by name. In a few cases, however, we have masked the identities of contributors to protect their privacy.

Numerous others participated in the research, analysis, and writing of this work. Suzanne Falgout gathered accounts in Pohnpei and Kosrae; Lin Poyer in Chuuk and Yap; and Laurence M. Carucci throughout the Marshall Islands. In each area, the authors worked with Micronesian research assistants (also listed in the Appendix). Furthermore, the assistance of local Historic Preservation Officers in each area (also listed) was an invaluable aid to our success. They guided us to people known as particularly good raconteurs or who had interesting stories to tell. We are indebted to our two historical consultants, Dr. David Purcell and Fr. Francis X. Hezel, and to James West Turner for insights on cultural memory. We also thank University of Hawai'i-West O'ahu students Tara Moorman, for assistance in selecting interview material, and Kari Lynn Harumi Nishioka and Jennifer Hackforth, for assistance in selecting photographs. We also thank those at University of Hawai'i Press, especially Masako Ikeda who, along with two anonymous readers, offered comments on our manuscript. Masako Ikeda and Yoko Kitami kindly offered assistance translating Japanese terms. We are also indebted to Cheri Dunn and Robert

Kelly for their work in the production of this book. All errors, of course, are our own responsibility.

For materials from Guam, the Northern Marianas, the Republic of Palau, Kiribati, and Nauru, we depended on existing literature and oral history accounts, especially holdings at the Hamilton Library at the University of Hawai'i and the Micronesian Area Research Center at the University of Guam. We are thankful to many colleagues who granted us permission to use information on World War II in Micronesia they collected. For some of these materials, we have only limited contextual information. We refer the reader to our colleagues for additional information. We wish to especially acknowledge the excellent work conducted by Wakako Higuchi and Dirk Ballendorf on Palau. We have also greatly benefited from recent work on Micronesian history and the Japanese colonial era—especially the work of Mark Peattie—and from published and unpublished materials at the Micronesian Seminar on Pohnpei, U.S. military archives, anthropologists who have worked in the Micronesian area, and a few interviews with American veterans of the Pacific War. Our access to Japanese perspectives was limited to information published in English. We sincerely hope that more Japanese-speaking researchers will pursue that line of research in the future.

We have also benefited from the recent multidisciplinary rethinking about the Pacific War, especially the work of Geoffrey White, Lamont Lindstrom, and others in their examination of Islander perspectives on the war in Melanesia as revealed through oral histories.

Funding for the field collection of oral histories was provided by National Endowment for the Humanities Grant RO-22103-90, "World War II in Micronesia: Islander Recollections and Representations." The East-West Center provided an opportunity for us to meet following our fieldwork. Additional funding for Poyer's travel to archives and research support was provided by the Taft Memorial Fund of the University of Cincinnati.

We dedicate this book to all those who helped us in our work, and offer it as a memorial to all Micronesians who suffered through the "typhoon of war" in Micronesia.

ISLAND NAMES

PACIFIC ISLAND NAMES and their spellings have varied throughout the historic period. Even today, Islanders often prefer different spellings from those recognized as "official" by their national governments. This table lists names and spellings of islands and island groups mentioned in the text. The first column is the spelling used in this book. The second column is the spelling most often used in U.S. documents during World War II. The third column lists other variant spellings, including the official standard name (if different from the first two columns). Asterisks (*) indicate currently accepted official spellings.

Text spelling	WWII-era spelling	Variant spellings
Banaba*	Ocean Island	
Chuuk*	Truk	
Enewetak*	Enewetok	Brown's Range
Eten (Chuuk)	Eten (Truk)	Etten*
Ifaluk	Ifaluk	Ifalik*
Jaluij	Jaluit*	
Kiribati*	Gilbert Islands	
Kosrae*	Kusaie	
Mili*	Mille	
Mokil	Mokil	Mwokil,* Mwokilloa
Parem* (Chuuk)	Parem (Truk)	
Pohnpei*	Ponape	

Text spelling	WWII-era spelling	Variant spellings
Puluwat*	Enderby Island	
Ronglap	Rongelap*	
Sapwuahfik	Ngatik	Ngetik*
Toloas (Chuuk)	Dublon Island (Truk)	Tonoas*
Tuvalu*	Ellice Islands	
Weno* (Chuuk)	Moen Island (Truk)	

Note: We use the English spelling of Palau and its islands. The local name is Belau, and each of the islands has a different Belauan spelling.

INTRODUCTION

SOME SIXTY YEARS after the end of World War II, Micronesians still speak about their wartime experiences, and those of their parents and grandparents, as a time of profound transition, "the greatest hardship" that they and their societies have endured. These islands, ruled by Japan for decades before the war, contested in the bloody Central Pacific campaigns of 1943–1945, then governed by the United States, play a key role in the military history of the conflict. Yet the many volumes of Pacific War history based on Allied or Japanese sources scarcely mention the Islanders across whose lands and seas the fight was waged. The story of the northern Pacific theater, and most of that global war, is archived as the record of the major combatants' experiences. Micronesians, like other indigenous peoples, are "missing in action" from the written accounts of World War II.

MICRONESIA'S "MISSING IN ACTION"

Our ethnohistorical research on Micronesians during the war years set out to fill this gap. During 1990–1991, we collected approximately four hundred oral histories from Micronesian elders. Our field research, conducted with the help of Micronesian research assistants and translators, focused on the Marshall and Caroline islands and included accounts from men and women of different statuses, educational backgrounds, and wartime work assignments. We also used existing collections of oral history by other researchers for Palau, Guam, the Northern Marianas, Kiribati, and Nauru.

Our interview design was intentionally simple. We explained our project, asked permission to record and use the interview information, and invited consultants to share their war-related memories. Interviews were conducted in the speaker's first (or preferred) language and later translated into English. Interviews were largely, though not entirely, open-ended. We asked people to talk about the war within a chronological framework: the Japanese colonial era, war preparations, the conflict itself, war's end, and initial American occupation. At the conclusion of the interview we invited their reflections on the entire era and asked what they would like others to know about their wartime experiences. Interviewers provided guidance when needed and asked follow-up questions for clarification or elaboration. Otherwise, we allowed speakers to follow their own inclinations in focusing on what they felt to be important.

Despite the passage of so much time since the war's end, we were not disappointed with what we were able to learn. Because so little had been written about indigenous experiences of the Pacific War in Micronesia, the first book resulting from our research provided a historical overview of the circumstances and impact of the war years (*The Typhoon of War: Micronesian Experiences of the Pacific War,* University of Hawai'i Press, 2001). In that book, we combined information from documentary sources with oral history, using the historians' work to set the context of the military events that controlled the circumstances of Islanders' personal experience.

The use of extensive short passages from our interviews in the first book helped convey—through the voices of Micronesian survivors—the presence of Micronesians during the war, the detailed knowledge, the thoughtful reflection, and the feeling tone contained in their stories. In collecting and analyzing these accounts, we were struck by the wide range of Micronesian experiences. Indeed, one of the challenges we faced in writing the first book was to portray this diversity. But we were also struck by certain regularities in what storytellers had to say and in how they said it. Although people's memories of wartime experiences were varied, they were also distinctively Micronesian. Our goal is to acknowledge the importance of these memories and their links to Micronesia's present and future.

PLAN OF THE BOOK

Whereas our first book was an ethnohistory of the war in Micronesia written primarily for specialists in Pacific Islands studies and military history, this book aims at a wider audience, looking at the common (though not uniform) ways in which Micronesian individuals and communities think about, retell, commemorate, and otherwise represent the war today. Our focus is not so much on the events of the war as on the remembrances themselves—the ritual commemorations, stories, dances, and songs that keep memories alive through a process that social scientists call the "construction" of cultural memory. Keeping alive a community's memory of an event or experience is not automatic or simple. Instead, it is an ongoing process of social interaction and cultural creation through which people tell themselves, and others, stories about their past. We wish to identify distinctively Micronesian cultural memories of war and to learn how and why they are selected, formed, and perpetuated from one generation to the next.

We begin the book with background information on Micronesia, starting in chapter 1 with some of the underlying similarities but also important differences across that region of the Pacific. We offer an overview of the Japanese colonial administration and of the Pacific War (as told from the perspectives of the two major combatants, the Americans and the Japanese), a summary of postwar conditions of the region, and the modern political statuses of the islands. Chapter 2 offers a short introduction to the idea of cultural memory—how cultural expectations shape personal experiences into recollections that are conveyed to the future. We also discuss how Micronesian cultures encode and transmit memories—in the landscape and in various types of performances—with particular focus on memories of World War II.

The rest of the book presents Micronesians' memories of the war years largely through their own words in narratives and songs, showing how Micronesian cultural and historical backgrounds help them understand, cope with, and share their wartime experiences. At the same time, the dramatic, novel, and even discordant nature of those experiences created new frameworks for understanding themselves and the wider world, as well as new motivations and methods to use in telling their stories of war.

Part 2 presents Micronesian understandings about war, and the Pacific War, in general terms. In talking about the war, what do Micronesians select as important cultural memories? What do these cultural memories say the war was about? Chapter 3 discusses the fact that Micronesians' approach to the meaning of the war has little to do with the military strategies of the combatant powers. Instead, their war memories focus on local conditions and certain themes that recur throughout the region. Chapter 4 presents the shock of the war's arrival for Micronesians, chapter 5 the hardships and suffering they endured, and chapter 6 their sense of overwhelming fear in combat situations.

Part 3, on Micronesian vantage points, asks how narrative form conveys Micronesian experiences of war. It considers how the way the war was fought in the islands—the facts that Micronesians were caught by surprise in a war that was long distant and then abruptly a part of their lives; found themselves in the middle of a foreign war but marginal to its instigation, prosecution, and resolution; were in a largely fixed position within a war characterized by great mobility across a global expanse; and attempted to understand and cope with two sets of foreigners (one close at hand, one largely unknown)—helps to shape the manner in which wartime narratives are told. Chapter 7 explores the Micronesian perception that "it was not our war," and chapter 8 discusses the war as a "typhoon." Chapter 9 examines Micronesians' continued reassessment of the character and motivations of major combatants—especially the Japanese, but also the Americans—as the war progressed. Chapter 10 demonstrates strategies Micronesians used to cope with wartime stresses.

In Part 4, we examine some dominant Micronesian cultural themes. Every culture has its own key symbols or particular emphases, and as we might expect, when people remember the war years, they tend to remember and to talk about the subjects of greatest interest to them. Chapter 11 considers topics of perennial interest to Micronesians—happiness, harmony, and abundance; romance; and chiefly culture—that are also frequently found in wartime stories and songs. Chapter 12 examines the culturally and historically important farewells and welcomes to the Japanese and Americans that accompanied the war's end and the transfer of colonial rule.

Part 5, the book's conclusion, steps back to take a wider perspective on how Micronesian remembrances of the war fit into the broad scope of their vision of history and identity in the modern world. Chapter 13 reveals that, although the war resulted in major dislocations and realignments of Micronesian economies, societies, and cultures, it is only one part of the entire span of Micronesian pasts and futures. How are wartime experiences kept relevant and memorable? How have Micronesians today changed their view of World War II, war in general, and their place within the modern world? Finally, chapter 14 provides the full text of "The Great Airplane," a song composed on Fais Island, Yap, shortly after the war. This dance song covers the entire wartime period and includes many of the themes we present throughout the book.

We hope readers will take from this book a sense of cultural memory as an active, shaped reality. Students of history know that the past is not concrete or fixed, but is understood anew by each population in terms of its own experience and by each generation in terms of its own needs. In learning about how Micronesians remember the Pacific War, we can learn something about how all groups of people sift, evaluate, commemorate, and rely on their vision of their past as they construct their future.

PART I

Backgrounds

Chapter 1

"MICRONESIA"

THE ATTEMPT TO PORTRAY Micronesian cultural memories of the war is a more ambitious task than it may at first seem. Micronesia—which includes the Marshall, Caroline, Marianas, and Kiribati islands and Nauru—is a vast area of the world and one that embraces much geographic, cultural, linguistic, and historical complexity.[1]

"MICRONESIA"

"Micronesia" is a Western label given to the area; it means "little islands." While generally smaller than those elsewhere in the Pacific, the more than two thousand islands in this area range from tiny sand spits covered at high tide to Guam's relatively large land area of 225 square miles; they extend over an area larger than that of the continental United States. The islands differ in composition and resources as well as size. The western islands of the Marianas, Palau, and Yap are continental in origin; those to the east are volcanic, either high mountainous peaks (including those in Chuuk Lagoon, Pohnpei, and Kosrae) or low coral atolls (including those found in Outer Island Chuuk, Outer Island Pohnpei, the Marshalls, Nauru, and Kiribati). Different island sizes and types, along with climatic and other factors, set variable conditions for productivity, population sizes, and sociopolitical complexity.

Peoples in this region speak more than twelve indigenous languages. Micronesian languages and cultures are historically related, descending from Austronesian speakers who voyaged from maritime Southeast Asia beginning almost five thousand years ago to settle the Pacific Islands. Yet the differences

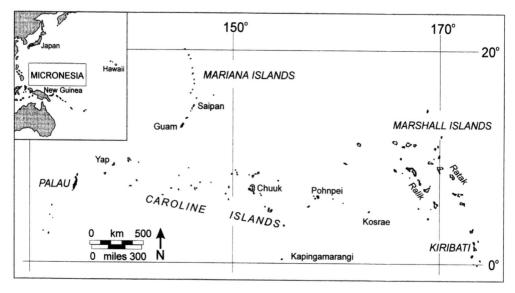

Micronesia

are great: the archaeology of western Micronesia reveals some of the earliest Austronesian settlements in the Pacific, while the rest of Micronesia reveals some of the latest Austronesian settlements. In addition, the region contains two Polynesian outliers (Kapingamarangi and Nukuoro). Adding further complexity, peoples of Micronesia were great seafarers, and the islands saw repeated interisland contact, population movement, and political realignment throughout prehistory.[2]

The islands also differ in their experiences during several centuries of European and Asian contact. The first European landfall in the Pacific was that of Ferdinand Magellan on Guam in 1521, and for more than two centuries Guam served as a port for the Spanish galleons sailing between the Philippines and Mexico or Peru. The Spanish galleon route led to Spanish sightings and occasionally visits to other islands. However, the rest of Micronesia experienced little European contact until the nineteenth century, when proximity to whaling grounds and to the route of the China trade spurred the development of several important ports of call. These served primarily for reprovisioning ships in transit, but a small trade in such Micronesian produce as copra, bêche-de-mer, and tortoiseshell also developed. The establishment of these new sea-lanes and trade centers was quickly followed by new missionary activities, mostly by American Protestants, who dominated eastern Micronesia, and Spanish Catholics, who dominated the western islands. Whaling, trading, and missionary activity gave most of Micronesia some familiarity with European and (in the west) Japanese foreigners.[3]

Although Guam and the other Mariana Islands were the first European colony in the Pacific Islands, formally claimed by Spain in 1565, the rest of Micronesia was colonized much later in the Age of Empire. Near the end of the nineteenth century, the region underwent a sequence of shifts in colonial control. In 1885, Germany, whose citizens had decades earlier established trading companies in Micronesia, sent warships to claim the Marshall and Caroline islands. Spain disputed German rights to the Carolines and prevailed through papal arbitration. Pohnpei served as Spanish colonial headquarters in the Eastern Carolines, and Yap played that role in the Western Carolines, with Spanish Catholic missionaries now found throughout these islands. Germany remained in the Marshalls, continuing to develop those islands for economic production, especially the burgeoning copra trade, and allowing American Protestant missionary activities. When Spain lost its Pacific colonies at the end of the Spanish-American War in 1899, Germany extended its program for economic development to the Carolines and the Northern Marianas. The United States, which had earlier maintained a relatively minor presence with Protestant missionaries, whalers, and traders throughout the region, now claimed Guam, close to its colony in the Philippines, primarily for strategic reasons.[4]

Fifteen years later, at the outbreak of World War I in 1914, Japan occupied Germany's Micronesian colonies with little resistance, an act sanctioned at the 1920 Paris Peace Conference when the League of Nations awarded Japan control over the islands as a Class C mandate. Like the Germans, the Japanese wished to promote economic development in their Micronesian territory, and Japanese businessmen had long been active in the region. In addition, they wanted to resettle their burgeoning population in these islands and to integrate the islands into the expanding Japanese Empire.[5]

The islands of Kiribati and Nauru experienced different colonial trajectories. Kiribati (earlier known as the Gilbert Islands) had become a British protectorate (along with the nearby Tuvalu [earlier known as the Ellice Islands]) in 1892; in 1916 it became a British colony. Nauru had been annexed by the Germans in the late nineteenth century. After World War I, it became a mandated territory of Australia, New Zealand, and the United Kingdom.

We use the general Western label "Micronesia" as a convenient form of reference throughout this book. Furthermore, we use it to refer, in particular, to those islands that constituted the Japanese Mandate. However, the reader is cautioned to keep these variations—in geography, culture, history, and World War II experiences—in mind.

SOME SIMILARITIES IN MICRONESIAN CULTURES AND HISTORIES

This portrait of diversity within Micronesia is only part of the picture. Micronesians also share important similarities in culture and historical experience, what some scholars have called "partial connections,"[6] linking Micronesians with each other and with Pacific Islanders in other regions.

Micronesian cultures are based in a past economy of fishing and horticulture that depended on root and tree crops common across the Pacific, including taro, yams, coconuts, breadfruit, bananas, pandanus, and betel nut or kava, and on domesticated fowl, pigs, and dogs. Prehistoric Micronesian material culture (such as pottery, stone and shell tools and utensils, design motifs, meetinghouse construction, canoes, and fishing technology) also displayed broad similarities. Transportation was provided by single outrigger canoes and detailed navigational knowledge, both honed to an impressive degree, especially on the far-flung atolls.

All habitable islands were settled, and population levels were generally high in the precontact period. Horticulture and fishing produced a surplus that supported chiefly hierarchies, though the nature and extent of Micronesian chiefdoms varied. On the productive high islands of Kosrae and Pohnpei, chiefs governed through stratified polities; Chuuk's political order was less elaborate. In the atolls of the Marshalls and Kiribati, chiefdoms often comprised a network of islands. Atolls near Yap were linked to chiefs on the high island. The nature and extent of Micronesian chiefdoms also changed throughout the prehistoric period; but they all contained, to varying degrees, an emphasis on social stratification and on formal respect customs and were concerned with the control of land and its resources. Chiefs served as titular heads of the land and were offered goods and service as tribute by those who held land-use rights. The chiefs, in turn, held the responsibility of local and regional governance.[7]

In addition to this substratum of precontact subsistence, material culture, and social order, Micronesians share broad similarities in their experiences and responses to the various colonial regimes experienced over the past few hundred years. Despite the new sorts of diversity introduced by these regimes, the experience of a colonial bureaucracy had a certain uniformity.

Micronesians were no strangers to Western society when they first experienced European colonial rule. They cannot be characterized simply as victims, given the evidence of armed rebellion, passive resistance, and more subtle political maneuvering that enabled most communities to maintain a good amount of cultural autonomy through several colonial regimes. But the economic, religious, and empire-building strategies of colonial powers significantly altered indigenous control of land, internal politics, and the local economic order. Micronesians under foreign rule came to be, as historian Fran Hezel calls them, "strangers in their own land,"[8] as foreigners exercised military, political, and economic control.

The strength of acculturative forces as well as the loss of autonomy was a complex, gradual, cumulative process under the three colonial regimes. The experience of World War II came after the longest period during which most of the region was administered under a single colonial power—Japan.

JAPANESE ADMINISTRATION OF MICRONESIA

For nearly three decades before the war, Japan ruled the Northern Mariana, Caroline, and Marshall islands. Japanese colonialism was both more extensive and more centralized than that of Spain or Germany; Japan ruled the colony with a stricter and more personal grip. Nevertheless, like Spanish and German colonialism, Japanese colonialism varied significantly across the region, focusing its efforts on some geographic centers and elements of Micronesian life while largely ignoring others.

Japan's dual goal in Micronesia was to integrate the region as an economically useful part of the empire and to demonstrate that Japan, like the European powers, could serve as a civilizing ruler of colonial peoples. Aided by Japanese entrepreneurs already living in the islands, the Japanese Navy (1914–1922), followed by the civilian South Seas Government (Nan'yō-chō), headquartered in Palau, followed an active program of public works, education, police, and hygiene. The well-organized bureaucracy developed fisheries, factories, and agricultural plantations. The areas of greatest economic development included Palau, the Northern Marianas, and Pohnpei, which were judged most likely to return a profit. Although Micronesia was of minor importance within the Japanese Empire, it was gradually transformed into a productive component of it.[9]

Japanese, Okinawan, and Korean immigrants were encouraged to take up residence; in some places, especially on the most developed islands, they outnumbered Micronesians. Immigrants sometimes purchased their own farmsteads, and some men married local women. At the same time, Micronesian elites were encouraged to identify with Japan, and all Islanders were introduced to Japanese language, culture, and work discipline. The peoples sharing Japan's Micronesian territory held ranks in an ethnic hierarchy, with Japanese at the top, followed by Okinawans and Koreans. Micronesians held third-class status, referred to as *tōmin*. They remained socially and in places even geographically segregated. They were subjected to a variety of restrictions on their social and political life and to the strict discipline and harsh punishment of Japanese law. However, Micronesians appreciated the stability and efficiency of this colonial administration. They also enjoyed increased access to wage labor, markets, imported goods, schooling, and health care, as well as links to a system with regional and global connections.[10]

Japanese development on Jaluij. By 1916 Jaluij had a store that was the equal of any in Micronesia. (Micronesian Seminar: *The Japanese Flag Unfurled,* website album <www.micsem.org>)

For decades before the war, then, the Japanese had been a significant presence in Micronesia and had undertaken numerous efforts to shape Islander attitudes. They had achieved some success in their attempts to give Islanders a Japanese sensibility, a preference for things and ways Japanese, loyalty to the emperor, and obedience to authority. Although ambivalent toward the Japanese administration (and with some small amount of organized resistance on

Marshallese girl wearing a Japanese kimono. (Mitchell Library, State Library of New South Wales, and Micronesian Seminar: *The Japanese Flag Unfurled,* website album <www.micsem.org>)

Palau and perhaps Pohnpei and Yap), most Micronesians nevertheless saw themselves as low-ranked but integral members of this expanding Japanese empire.[11]

In the decade before the war, Micronesians found themselves surrounded by an economic boom spurred by the Japanese government's policy of immigration and economic development aimed at economic self-sufficiency for the region. While many Micronesians benefited from increased educational and economic opportunities, the program also created widespread land expropriation, demand for Islanders' contract labor, and relocation of some Micronesian communities. By the late 1930s, even the smallest and most isolated islands had been integrated into Japan's colonial order.[12] In hindsight, elderly Micronesians remember these years as a time of prosperity and pleasure.

Historians debate the extent to which Japan fortified Micronesia before the bombing of Pearl Harbor. The question is difficult to answer because of Japan's strict prewar control of the region and the wartime loss of documents. It now seems that Japan made few or no explicit advance military preparations in Micronesia. Yet as war approached late in the 1930s, aspects of the intensifying prewar economy segued into war preparations. The final years of the decade saw the construction of offensive air bases and support facilities, with deployment of naval units and aircraft in 1940–1941.[13] Bases supporting Japan's eastern and southern front in the Marshall Islands were built at Kwajalein, Mili, Wotje, Maloelap, and Jaluij (Enewetak was fortified later), with lesser development at Chuuk; Saipan, Tinian, and Palau in the west played a support role for the Southwest Pacific advance.

THE WAR IN MICRONESIA

The Japanese attacks of December 7/8, 1941,[14] simultaneously brought the Asian conflict into the Pacific Islands and drew the United States into the global war. The Japanese quickly expanded their "Greater East Asia Co-Prosperity Sphere" (envisioned as a bloc of self-sufficient nations—freed from Western influence, led by Japan) by capturing Allied colonies in Micronesia (Guam, Kiribati, and Nauru) as well as those in parts of the southwestern Pacific and Southeast Asia.

The first months of the war saw a string of Japanese victories. While several Japanese bases in the Marshalls that had been involved in the attack on Pearl Harbor suffered brief retaliatory strikes in early 1942, Allied efforts at first were focused on the Southwest Pacific. But only six months later, in the summer of 1942, the defeat of the Japanese at the battle of Midway, along with Japanese losses in the Southwest Pacific and the successful Allied war on shipping, had turned the tide. Allied Pacific strategy was now envisioned as a two-pronged attack, with drives through the Southwest Pacific and Micronesia. By late 1943, the Allies decided to launch a Central Pacific drive—from Kiribati to the Marshalls, through the Carolines, to the Marianas and Palau, where they could establish air bases close to occupied areas in Asia and to Japan itself.

Realizing the need for a defensive posture in their Micronesian territory, Japan poured in reinforcements and hastily bolstered island installations. Existing bases were strengthened and new ones built, extending military control to more islands. Troops and foreign laborers swamped the indigenous population in many areas, sometimes increasing the population tenfold. Work on defensive projects was stepped up, and the demand for Micronesian labor intensified. Large-scale relocations, confiscation of property, labor drafts, shortages of food and goods, and, eventually, military attack brought the war into Micronesian lives.[15]

Existing Marshallese bases were bolstered, with some 13,000 new troops arriving by the end of 1943. Chuuk's naval base was expanded and its air base developed and heavily fortified; the other islands of Chuuk Lagoon were put under military control to produce food for the more than 14,000 official troops in place by April 1944. New air bases were also established on the Carolinean atolls of Satawan (Mortlocks), Puluwat (Chuuk), and Wolei (Yap). Pohnpei and Kosrae, seen primarily as support locales for other garrisons, were intensely cultivated as plantations, though Pohnpei was also fortified for defense (in 1945, it held nearly 8,000 Japanese troops and 14,066 Japanese, Okinawan, and Korean laborers and civilians, far outnumbering the 5,900 Pohnpeians). As the war moved west, Yap, Palau, and the Marianas in turn received heavy troop reinforcements, and Islanders there were drawn into forced labor in agricultural and military projects.[16]

Allied plans had at first called for seizure of all important Japanese bases. However, lessons learned earlier in the Southwest Pacific and then at Tarawa in Kiribati in November 1943 taught the advantage of a leapfrogging campaign, with only select islands invaded for use as forward bases. Allied planners first targeted Kwajalein, Enewetak, and Majuro in the Marshalls. Those American invasions at the beginning of 1944 marked the start of the final phase of the war. The U.S. Navy organized the conquered region, while proceeding with invasions of the western islands of Saipan and Tinian (Northern Marianas), Guam, Ulithi (Yap), and Peleliu (Palau) in July–September. Invaded islands suffered massive destruction, followed by the establishment of U.S. naval military government and an infusion of supplies and health care.

The other Micronesian islands were blockaded, isolated, and neutralized by bombing and bombardment.[17] Over the next year and a half, these bypassed and neutralized islands experienced great hardships. As Allied planes and warships conducted systematic destructive attacks, the Japanese military further intensified its demands for Micronesian land, resources, labor, and loyalty—all in increasingly short supply as the war went on. By the war's end, conditions on many of these islands had become desperate. Japanese defeat, unthinkable at the war's beginning, became a possibility, and then a reality.[18] Conditions of escalating starvation and stress were relieved only after (sometimes months after) the Japanese surrender in August 1945.

POSTWAR MICRONESIA

In the months following Japan's surrender, the U.S. military government gradually extended throughout the former Japanese mandated islands, and Micronesians faced the double challenge of a destroyed economy and a new colonial order.[19] Under initial U.S. Navy rule, the islands were administered following a largely hands-off approach. According to an official policy statement, Micronesians were to be "encouraged and assisted to assume as much as possible the management of their own affairs and the conduct of their government."[20] Although the navy organized a basic plan of health care and education and introduced democratic institutions, this initial hands-off policy would set the tone for American governance of the region for decades to come.

In 1947, the United Nations awarded Micronesia to the United States as a "strategic trust." Under this trusteeship, the United States retained rights to use the islands for defense, in particular, the right of "strategic denial," which severely limited access to the region, especially by other nations. In 1950, the U.S. Congress passed the Organic Act, which granted American citizenship to Guamanians. The navy was instructed to form a civil administration throughout the rest of the region, and control was transferred to the Department of the Interior in 1951. Other than these political shifts, little changed in postwar Micronesia. Faced with dwindling financial support from the U.S. government, subsequent administrations of necessity continued a hands-off policy.[21]

Over this period much of Micronesia, particularly the less strategically situated Caroline Islands, suffered a significant reduction in the standard of living.

The 1960s were a turning point for Micronesia. A visiting United Nations team in 1961 criticized the U.S. administration's neglect of its territory. Micronesians, by that time, had learned the lessons of democracy and were eager to assume their own governance. In 1965, they established a territory-wide Congress of Micronesia and began negotiations for future political statuses. The eventual results were varied. The Northern Marianas opted for a close commonwealth status with the United States, established in 1976. The new Republic of the Marshall Islands and the Federated States of Micronesia were formed by compacts of free association approved in 1986. The Republic of Palau was finally approved in 1994.[22] Compacts of free association granted these three new nations control over their own internal affairs, while external affairs remain largely in the hands of the United States. This is most significant in terms of military use of the area, including continuation of U.S. bases in the Marshall Islands.

Micronesia's present, then, as well as its recent past, has been shaped by wars, the threat of wars, and preparations for wars, and that legacy will carry into the future.

Chapter 2

CULTURAL MEMORIES AND THE PACIFIC WAR

SCHOLARS HAVE WRITTEN volumes on the importance of memory. They point out that our experience of the present is largely based on, or even embedded within, our knowledge of the past. While knowledge of the past is not unchanging, they argue, it nevertheless helps to keep us oriented. But what is a memory? Our commonsense notion of memory is an individual's experience of some thing or event, acquired in the past, stored in the mind, and available for future retrieval. Recent research, however, challenges this "file drawer" model of memory. It seems that there is more to how we remember than the simple storage of lived experience.

MEMORY

For one thing, when we speak of memory as simply an individual's recollection of past events, we are expressing familiar, but culturally limited, assumptions about time. Western thought tends to objectify and quantify time in a linear way. In the Western viewpoint, only the present can be known with certainty; the past lies behind us, and the more distant it is, the less confidently it can be known. This is a reasonable way to organize ideas about time, but it is not the only one.

Cross-cultural research suggests other understandings of time.[1] Pacific Islanders' understandings of time have recently been explored by several indigenous writers. Tongan scholar Epeli Hau'ofa suggests that some Pacific Islands cultures do employ linearity in their notion of time, most commonly

Japanese tank remnants on Pohnpei, with research assistant Antolin Gomez. (Photo by Suzanne Falgout)

in genealogies. Yet their linear notion of time is neither evolutionary nor teleological as is that of the West; rather it is more ecological, sequential, and circular.[2] Some Austronesian languages locate the past in front and ahead, with the future behind and following. Hau'ofa quotes Hawaiian historian Lilikala Kame'eleihiwa:

> It is interesting to note that in Hawaiian, the past is referred to as *Ka wa mamua*, "the time in front or before." Whereas the future, when thought of at all, is *Ka wa mahope*, or the "time which comes after or behind." It is as if the Hawaiian stands firmly in the present, with his back to the future, and his eyes fixed upon the past, seeking historical answers for present-day dilemmas. Such an orientation is to the Hawaiian an eminently practical one, for the future is always unknown, whereas the past is rich in glory and knowledge. It also bestows upon us a natural propensity for the study of history.[3]

Hau'ofa gives additional support for this Austronesian concept of time, which he describes as circular, and for the heightened importance of the past in the Tongan and Fijian languages that he speaks.

> The past then is going ahead of us, leading into the future, which is behind us. Is this then the case of the dog chasing its tail? I believe so. From this perspective we can see the notion of time as circular. This notion fits perfectly with the regular cycles of natural occurrences that punctuated important activities, particularly those of a productive and ritual/religious nature that consumed most of the expanded human energy in the Oceanian past and still do in many parts of our region today. This is ecological time.
>
> That the past is ahead, in front of us, is a conception of time that helps us retain our memories and to be aware of its presence. What is behind us [the future] cannot be seen and is liable to be forgotten readily. What is ahead of us [the past] cannot be forgotten so readily or ignored, for it is in front of our minds' eyes, always reminding us of its presence. The past is alive in us, so in more than a metaphorical sense the dead are alive—we are our history.[4]

This sense of the past as an essential part of the present is also expressed by one of today's leading Pacific Islands authors, Albert Wendt of Samoa, in the prologue to his poem "Inside Us the Dead."[5]

> *Inside us the dead,*
> *like sweet-honeyed tamarind pods*
> *that will burst in tomorrow's sun,*
> *or plankton fossils in coral*
> *alive at full moon dragging*
> *virile tides over coy reefs*
> *into yesterday's lagoons.*

MEMORY AND CULTURE

Another shortcoming of the perception of memory as a mental storage container is that it overlooks the many forms that memory takes. Paul Connerton describes four different kinds of memory: Sensory memory recognizes and responds to the qualities of sensations, when certain smells, sounds, or textures evoke a time when similar sensations were experienced (as in Proust).

Somatic or corporeal memory involves motor patterns and skills that, once learned, can be reactivated throughout life (as we "never forget" how to ride a bicycle). Semantic memory involves the recall and correct use of a language, as in the names of persons, places, things, qualities, or activities. The most complex form of memory, experiential memory, involves re-presenting epi-sodes of a person's life, and it can incorporate all other forms of human mem-ory: various sensations (sensory memory), actions (somatic memory), and remembered conversations (dependent on semantic memory).[6]

Memory is active as well as complex. James Fentress and Chris Wickham describe how it comes into being through three distinct acts: recognition, recall, and reminiscence.[7] When we recognize a person or thing, we identify it by reference to previously acquired knowledge or experience. In the act of recall, the object of memory need not be present in the here and now; rather we re-present it through an act of will. When we reminisce, we communi-cate to others that which we recall. Memory, then, is an act of will, not a pas-sive mental faculty. And being an act of will—an act that involves the whole human self—it partakes of the entire human condition. That is, memory is part of who we are as human beings; it is an essential part of one's individual mind and cultural endowment.

Although we tend to think of memory as an imprint of reality on the mind of an individual, memory always occurs in a cultural context. The initial work on the concept of collective memory is credited to the French sociologist Mau-rice Halbwachs.[8] Memory, Halbwachs pointed out, is culturally constructed and open to change. Memories of the past, he argued, are largely shaped by a culture's present concerns. In this view, memory, like all knowledge, is created and re-created, and subject to the social, political, and personal pressures of life.[9]

We do not refer here to any sort of Jungian inherited "group memory" but to the way our memories as individuals are shaped by our culture's ideas and values. Memories are typically a mixture of the personal and the cultural. Individual memory is always cultural, because the person who remembers is a cultural being. Cultural memory is always personal, inasmuch as it has its basis in the personal memories of individuals. Yet cultural memory involves the cultural work of remembering, in a construction that is both similar to and different from the construction of personal memory.

Certainly we cannot all remember everything that happens to us. Events that are culturally meaningful are more likely to be remembered than more commonplace practices. If someone asks you, "What did you do last week?"

you will not include the everyday habits of eating meals, getting dressed, or going to the bathroom. On the other hand, if you spent last week in a very different place—say, Rome, or Bangkok, or rural Ecuador—you might very well think the exotic food, clothing, or bathroom arrangements were worth recalling. When people remember, they tend to remember what is important—and what is important to remember depends on what is relatively unimportant, familiar, or habitual in their everyday lives.

Memories of dramatic, consequential, traumatic, and also culturally significant events—such as experiences of war—have special qualities. Some studies have indicated that these "flashbulb memories" can leave a strong neurological imprint,[10] leading people to remember the crucial event in minute detail. These vivid memories tend to endure for years, even decades, without noticeably degrading. Other studies challenge the notion of flashbulb memories, pointing out that although they are vivid, the memories and consequences of an experience may be altered or determined at some point after the initial experience. Rather than being accurate visual transcripts of experience, these crucial flashbulb memories might better be understood as benchmarks—memories forged in the link between personal and public history that allow a person to say, "I was there."[11] It is the existence of these memories that matters—the bearing witness to a culturally important event.

As individuals, we may create a "memory household"[12]—photographs, mementos, favorite books, or names inscribed in a cement walkway, which anchor us to a remembered past. So important are these markers that their loss or destruction may produce disorientation or, in extreme cases, undermine the integration of personal identity. Cultural memory depends even more on such deliberate constructions. It is inherently fragile in a way personal memory is not.

Cultural memory persists only if each new generation renews the effort to recall. We are all aware of how quickly family memories are lost. A community's memories are equally fragile. That is why we often hear the phrase "lest we forget" and why we raise markers, observe anniversaries of important events, and engage in other memorial activities. The effort to ensure remembrance may involve large numbers of people performing different kinds of memory work; in some cases, it can take on truly industrial proportions. Think, for example, of the many ways in which the deaths and sufferings of millions of individuals have been transformed into the collective memory of the Holocaust. Historians, filmmakers, publishers, governments, writers, artists, and museums have all have contributed to the construction, which is ultimately based on personal memory.[13]

Cultural memory, then, is always articulated, though personal memory need not be. What we mean by "articulation" is that cultural memory is created by and for a group, through that group's deliberate statement of the past, which can be in the form of language, but can also be through art, landscape, or other symbolic forms. It is through acts of articulation that personal experiences are transformed into cultural memories.

Often, memories are conveyed and sustained by ritual performances or commemorations.[14] The regular, formalized reenactment in these commemorations makes an effective mnemonic device. Monuments, too, can be used to transform personal memory into collective remembering. Debates about the designs of monuments, the naming of buildings or streets, or commemorative displays such as the Smithsonian's *Enola Gay* exhibit or the Vietnam Veterans Memorial (both American examples) are in part disagreements over whose memories should be given public expression, and what personal and cultural memories "should" mean.

Most commonly, individual memories become cultural through intentional "inscribing" activities of speaking and writing.[15] Language constitutes a major mechanism for creating meaningful memories. The conceptual categories of a language focus attention and impose order on the flow of experience to make sense of events and actions and to simplify and schematize remembrances. Putting memories into words triggers this filtering process. Linguistically transformed memories are then available for reminiscence. In recounting personal experience as reminiscence, narrators produce a work of memory that is further conventionalized and simplified through shared language. Once put into words, memories can be translated into images, placed into established (but not unchanging) narrative motifs, organized to conform to a (somewhat) coherent narrative plot, and articulated in various (old and new) genres of stories and songs.

Conceptualizing memories in language and narrative can erase detail and impose culturally and linguistically shaped patterns on them, but it also makes it easier to remember and retell them. The process of developing stories and songs and passing them on, then, helps maintain cultural memories of an event. Of course, established cultural modes of remembrance are themselves open to change, in form as well as content. But the more formal the linguistic product, the more easily it will be reproduced: songs and written memories are more accurately transferred between people or between generations without loss of information.

Reminiscences in story or song reflect not only the experiences of an event but also the personal and cultural identities of their narrators. As George C. Rosenwald and Richard L. Ochberg write in the introduction to their edited work, *Storied Lives,*

> [W]hat they emphasize and omit, their stance as protagonists or victims, the relationship the story establishes between teller and audience—all shape what individuals can claim about their own lives. Personal stories are not merely a way of telling someone (or oneself) about one's life; they are the means by which identities may be fashioned. . . .
>
> All self-understanding is realized within the narrative frames each culture provides its members.[16]

Narrative itself imposes constraints. Topics worth remembering, themes considered important, the forms of stories and songs, and what they reveal about an event and the identity of their narrators are culturally specific. Beyond that, one community may prefer to write its memories; another will prefer to dance it or sing it, carve it, paint it, build it, ritually reenact it, weave it, or embed it into the landscape.

Finally, however people may represent and remember their histories, an important element of the process is cultural politics. Power differences within a culture, and those between different cultures, affect the significance attributed to events of the past. Representations offered by those in power are often given wider circulation and may be granted more credibility. In addition, persons of different statuses, roles, genders, generations, or communities often have different or competing stakes in how the past should be remembered. Past and current politics also influence what people choose to remember and how they represent themselves to others. This remembrance, in turn, influences how they live their lives, and thus affects political relations within and between groups in the present.[17]

MICRONESIAN FORMS OF REMEMBRANCE

As researchers on cultural memory remind us, ways of remembering have long cultural histories.[18] According to Connerton, it is not simply "because thoughts are similar that we can evoke them; it is rather because the same group is interested in those memories, and is able to evoke them, that they are assembled together in our minds."[19] These culturally meaningful events, Ruth Finnegan writes, are then formulated into performances that are "socially shaped by the particular devices and values developed in specific societies"[20]—firmly based upon the old performative devices, but also incorporating new ones.

In reflecting on our experiences while gathering Micronesian memories of the war, we wrote about their continued importance and use today:

> The changes [that have occurred in the last half century] form a vital part of Micronesian historical and cultural memories—memories that are another important legacy of the wartime era. The memories are personally powerful, embodying such profound experiences that Micronesians feel they should be valued and remembered for their own sake. Further, these memories serve as a source of knowledge and wisdom for the development of local and national memories and for charting Micronesia's economic, social, and political future.[21]

We found that similar performative and expressive devices and cultural values, as well as some common historical experiences, gave familiar contours to Micronesians' memories of World War II, allowing people to share war stories throughout the region in the postwar period. The most frequent and meaningful reenactments of the war in Micronesia occur in cultural performances, storytelling (narratives, anecdotes, jokes), chants, songs, and dances. Two other modes of remembrance are ritual reenactments in commemorative events and the inscription of history on the landscape. The chapters that follow explore some of these common elements in more detail.

Performative Expressions

The most highly valued narratives in many Micronesian cultures are ancient legends and myths that originate with and are connected to the ancestors. Handed down to the current generation through the teachings of elder relatives or the medium of dreams, these tales speak with voices that are simultaneously of and about the past. Micronesians especially value details in these stories—personal names, specific places, explicitly stated facts or other subtle references that allow for intertextual reference, or knowledge of special processes, or of events that had extraordinary outcomes. These are the elements most treasured, and most likely to be hidden from others.[22] Important legends are highly prized, known in detail to only a few, and very selectively passed on. They are considered personal possessions; only certain persons have the right to possess and use them. Different versions are known to exist and are considered valid; yet no one should tell, sing, chant, or dance another's story. Narrating important legends is usually reserved for private contexts of transmission, conditions that permit the restriction of the valuable information they contain and thus the power they possess. When they are told in public, they are only partially revealed and used as important illustrations or parables in formal speeches. Used in these ways, their inclusion adds power, value, weight, and drama to the messages conveyed.[23]

In contrast, stories, songs, and dances relating to World War II are more widely known and are not surrounded by the constraints of who may tell and hear the accounts. In fact, they are often openly expressed with great emotion and in great detail. Nevertheless, war recollections, like all history, are edited and arranged to make a particular point.[24] Like references to ancient legends, wartime experiences can be incorporated into speeches given on special occasions at a meeting or church service. In Pohnpei, telling war stories has often been an element in evening kava sessions, where an elder may share a personal account or relate an anecdote or joke that serves as a summary statement of a common war theme. Occasionally, stories are accompanied by performance of a song or dance from the war era. But more typically, they are informally told by grandparents or parents to members of their extended families, or to others, often as a part of a wider discussion that relates current events to times past.

Micronesians have long used chants and songs as mnemonic devices and as entertainment. Memories of war readily fit into these familiar forms of expressive art. Songs tell of the new people and new things that arrived on their islands during the war years. They mourn forced relocations or laud valorous deeds, describe work on a wartime project, or recount a personal experience. Some songs lament the misery of war; others are teasing, self-deprecating, or bawdy, and serve to inject a moment of hilarity into a more serious discussion. They often include the names of actors and places; thus heroes are made and events transformed into collective memory. The formal structure of a song, furthermore, serves to codify, preserve, and authenticate this history. Micronesians compose and sing about the war in a variety of genres. Songs composed in the style of formal memorial songs are known and sung by many; these are very serious songs, often recounting the misery of war. Others are more informal and personal, known and sung by only a few. Wartime songs were composed in indigenous languages or Japanese, often a combination of both. They are sung in Micronesian singing styles, or in missionary-inspired hymns, or tunes borrowed from the Japanese. Because they contain specific historical detail, songs help codify and preserve this information for the future.[25]

Dance and song are often linked in Micronesia, and some songs were composed to be danced in formal presentations, in competition, or in informal entertainment. Some war era dances are still performed, including movements and gestures that were in vogue during the war. Their continued performance allows dancers and audiences to remember that period through an embodiment of war era experiences. For example, in a Yapese women's dance,

> the forces of the United States and Japan are symbolized by dance movements, as huge whales at sea and immense eagles in the sky. Bombs are characterized as exploding coconuts. The harsh years of Japanese occupation are recorded in the dance, as is the defeat of the Imperial Japanese occupation troops by the American marines.[26]

Although the war years entailed hardship and deprivation, they were also a period of creative energy. While Christian missionaries had discouraged Micronesian dance, some Japanese officials encouraged it. Dances of the colonial era often reflect Japanese influence; expressive art of the war years is often more complex in origin. The movement of people and ideas resulting from wartime relocation and labor drafts offered opportunities for creative exchange, as Micronesians came into close contact with Islanders from other regions, as well as with Japanese, Okinawan, and Korean workers and soldiers.

Rituals and Commemorations

Next to performances, the most important Micronesian means of remembering the war depends on rituals and reenactments. Annual commemorations may mark the local "Liberation Day," usually the anniversary of the end of the war in that locale—when American forces stepped ashore, the Japanese formally surrendered, or Micronesians were released from their wartime suffering. (We do not mean to give the impression that the initial arrival of American forces was regarded by all Micronesians as "liberation"—this was the term used by the Americans at that time, based on their own perspective of the war. Nevertheless, the term "liberation" has come to be used by Micronesians today, especially in referring to their wartime commemorations and occasionally in other contexts.)

Some communities began to mark Liberation Day immediately after the war and to use these ceremonial holidays to cultivate historical knowledge in new generations and keep wartime memories alive. Common international markers of commemoration days (such as closing schools and government offices) accompany local modes of marking holidays, including holding sports and canoe-racing events, dances, church services, and performances of hymns. But not every island holds such commemorations, and in some places where they were held after the war, they have faded away. On other islands, the day is a holiday, but not a means of maintaining a detailed cultural memory.

Guam's July 21 Liberation Day parade (marking the day U.S. Marines began the invasion of Japanese-occupied Guam) has entered its second half century, attracting more than twenty thousand people. Guam's parade, speeches, memorials, cemetery commemorations, and special church services are approaches to public memory making familiar to mainland American communities. Saipan also follows American models of commemorative holidays, with a week-long celebration ending with a parade on July 4. While Guam's Liberation Day memorializes the return of the island to American control after the Japanese occupation, Saipan describes its Liberation Day as marking the anniversary of its release from American civilian internment camps and freedom from colonial occupation in general.

One writer describes the annual commemoration of the arrival of the U.S. occupation force on Kosrae (September 8, 1945) as a holiday "second only to Christmas in importance." [27] Liberation Day is held in each of the four villages of Kosrae from September 6 to 10, recalling the arrival of American destroyers in Lelu Bay and the end of Japanese rule. This four-day commemoration includes a church ceremony with testimonials by elders who experienced the war years. The service also includes hymns, competitively offered by each of the four *kumi* (Japanese voluntary associations, now Kosraean social and religious clubs), as well as songs sung by the entire congregation. It also includes competitive fishing, canoe events, and field games that reflect activities developed during the period of Japanese colonialism. These events are accompanied by older Kosraean traditions such as chanting and dancing, coconut husking, weaving, thatch making, and outrigger-canoe racing. Within these competitive events, however, Kosraean solidarity is emphasized. Everyone may participate—male and female, old and young—and winners and losers are not publicly identified.[28]

Pohnpei's Liberation Day is celebrated on September 9 and 10, marking the arrival of American forces on the island. This celebration was initiated in the later postwar period by the Etcheit family, an expatriate Belgian family of traders who had long resided on the island and who were imprisoned there by the Japanese during the war (see the interview with Yvette Etcheit in chapter 4). As in other Micronesian locations, the Liberation Day commemoration includes church services and speeches that recall the events of war, "liberation," and the importance of freedom. In Pohnpei, the primary focus of Liberation Day activities is on the shore and field athletic competitions.

For the people of Enewetak Atoll in the Marshall Islands, the anniversary is the second Sunday of March. *Raan in Kamolol,* "The Day to Be Thankful," commemorates the end of the battle of Enewetak in 1945, the day the Islanders "came out of the holes," where they had huddled during the battle in which almost 15 percent of their population was lost.[29] *Raan in Kamolol* on Enewetak begins with a speech asserting the apocalyptic nature of the war, its importance, and gratitude for its end. The ceremony is held at the church, where a deacon or church elder recounts the battle scene and survivors shed tears for dead kin and in memory of the terror they experienced. The community divides into four groups—one for each of the three islets that experienced the battle of Enewetak and another for those who were students on Pohnpei during the war—to present hymns of thanksgiving. Everyone participates in the singing; those born after the battle join a group of their choice, often that of their parents or another elderly relative. After the service, each group prepares food for a community-wide feast. The rest of the day is spent visiting and sharing memories of the past with neighbors and kin. Here, too, the commemoration has been elaborated to include competitions and field games, not unlike those on Kosrae.

Elsewhere in Micronesia, commemorations are less elaborate. The Marshallese atoll of Maloelap celebrates January 13 as Liberation Day (the date does not mark a historical event but was chosen by a local chief). The day begins with a flag raising and prayers and includes field games and a general celebration, but there is no reenactment of the war through speeches or sharing war memories. In some cases, the memories commemorated are peaceful, because the act of the United States taking possession did not require military invasion. Examples of this are Arno Atoll in the Marshall Islands on February 16[30] and Yap.[31] Chuuk celebrates Liberation Day on September 23; its modern public commemoration is minimal compared to those of Kosrae or Pohnpei, though government offices are closed in remembrance of the war and its end.

Landscape and Memory

Micronesians, like other Pacific Islanders,[32] value cultural shaping of land, the forms and features of the landscape that reflect the past. Many land parcels or seascapes are tinged with the sacred, regarded as potent and powerful, and treated as taboo. Approach to these important features of the indigenous landscape is often hedged with restrictions, subject to elaborate forms of respect behavior, and sometimes accompanied by the use of protective herbal magic or spells. These features of the landscape are valued because of their connections to important people and events, to the lives and deaths of revered ancestors, and to ancient spirits—especially to those of high status within the chiefdom or those who accomplished unusual, dramatic, heroic, or supernatural feats.[33]

These physical traces play a crucial role in Micronesian cultural memory. They act as tangible proof of the oral historical traditions that tell Micronesians how the world came into being. As discussed above, these traditions are considered a form of secret sacred knowledge that originates with the divine ancestors. Listening to a tale that mentions a particular construction technique used by an ancient builder, the hearer expects to see that technique at the site named in the tale. Such physical evidence confirms the truth and accuracy of the rest of the tale. And confirmation of one oral tradition helps affirm the credibility of the entire body of oral tradition.[34]

Given this generally high valuation of physical remains associated with people and events of the past, it is significant that local people, across most of Micronesia, tend to regard Pacific War relics as having little historical value. Certainly, the remains of war are visible throughout the islands. Denfeld's report of a survey of World War II sites in Micronesia estimated that there are more war relics in this area than in all of Europe.[35] From our observation,

> many remain as they were left: bomb shelters, barracks, mess kitchens, coastal defense guns standing vigil on ammunition-littered beaches. They decay under the tropical sun, reclaimed by the surrounding vegetation or,

rarely, are removed and displayed for tourists. Physical changes wrought by the war remain etched in the landscape—deforested hills, lines of basalt rocks cleared for the Japanese army's sweet potato fields, bomb craters now serving as taro gardens or water catchments.[36]

Yet war relics have a relatively weak connection to Micronesian memories of World War II. Although American and Japanese veterans and their descendants have erected monuments and held memorials at key sites, most Micronesians rarely use wartime remains or locales for cultural memory work about the war. These wartime landscapes can and occasionally do serve as time or event markers, as "time materialized." [37] Yet the abandoned runways, bunkers, antiaircraft guns, or other structures have become a fact of everyday life and subject to creative reuse as housing or as playgrounds for children, or they are simply ignored or worked around as annoying debris.[38]

Why do these war relics—which Japanese and Americans find evocative and historically valuable—hold such a different meaning for Micronesians? As we will see, this is largely because the Islanders regard World War II as a war begun and fought by foreigners. Although Islanders did military work and were greatly affected by the war, their involvement in it was largely an accident of geography and history. In a sense, the war, its technology, and features of the landscape created by the conflict belong to other people's history in their islands. Micronesians do value, however, their experiences of that time, recollected in verbal performances, dances, and ritual commemorations. And just as the landscape confirms the truth of sacred legends, the physical traces of war—the ruins, bomb craters, filled-in taro swamps, denuded forests, and impermeable surfaces of abandoned runways—remain as potent reminders of the war's reality.

Guam, Saipan, and a few places in the Marshall Islands are exceptions to this generalization about Micronesians' relative lack of interest in the war's physical remains. Guam, long a U.S. territory and a base for U.S. Navy forces, shares American modes of public memory more than other islands. Commemorations of the war on Guam are of a sort and scale familiar to mainland Americans, with written memoirs, anniversary publications, and physical memorials, such as the Memorial Wall at the War in the Pacific National Historical Park,[39] as well as commemorative events (see above). World War II sites on Guam were given historical markers and monuments by 1952.[40] The U.S. National Park Service recently built a new World War II museum at the American Memorial Park in Saipan; the emperor of Japan visited it in the summer of 2005. Various American and Japanese memorials have also been erected at landing beaches and other important wartime sites.

THE CULTURAL POLITICS OF MICRONESIAN WAR MEMORIES

Recollections of World War II by elderly Micronesians today, more than sixty years after the war's end, depend not only on what people experienced during the conflict, but on other social and political factors—past and present—that shape remembrance.

There is a "golden age" element to some Micronesian wartime stories. Many elderly informants recall the prewar years with pleasure, despite the fact that, as historians see it, things were going quite badly for the Islanders under an increasingly aggressive economic development and immigration policy in the late Japanese colonial period. From a critical modern point of view, those were years of colonial exploitation, racism, and aggressive acculturation. But when our Micronesian informants recall this era, they are also recalling their own youth, when romance, adventure, art, and other passions were powerful; this recollection affects their sentiments about the era and suggests why certain aspects of life stand out in strong relief in memories of that period.

The "escalator effect," in which each generation imagines that the "golden age" lies in the recent past, is also operating.[41] Of course, the horrors of the war helped give a retrospective glow to the memory of peaceful years before it. But for many elders, the Japanese colonial era also looked good compared to peaceful postwar American times, when much of the region slipped into relative poverty.

For the aging Micronesians we interviewed, stories of the war are often told as morality tales, meant to teach younger generations important lessons learned from working together, overcoming hardship, and living through an era far less marked by materialism and individual freedom and more devoted to community service and honor to chiefs than the current day. In other words, while these stories are ostensibly about the past, for those who tell them they also bear direct relevance to the current day, and particularly to new directions regarded as unsuitable by the elders who learned valuable lessons from the World War II era.

The timing of our oral history project was also significant. In the decades and years just prior to our research, the islands had been negotiating new political statuses with the United States. Some gained control of their domestic affairs for the first time in over a century, or even more. Nevertheless, the United States retains strategic rights in the area (and in the Marshalls, the continued presence of a U.S. military base for missile tracking and testing), and external affairs remain largely in American hands. Our project coincided with the first Gulf War, and consultants worried whether their nation's close ties to the United States might bring war to them once again. Thus, while the moral messages of wartime stories were directed toward younger generations of Islanders, they were also directed toward us, the somewhat younger American researchers who queried and listened as elders pointed out the ways in which Japanese oversight of this region in some ways may have been more beneficial than the subsequent American policy, and instructed us to pay closer attention to our country's actions.

At times, our identity as Americans or the link of our Micronesian assistants to an American research project undoubtedly affected what people told us. We believe it affected some of the topics chosen, the force of the ensuing discussion, and their evaluations of wartime and postwar circumstances. Micronesians are generally polite people. Some, especially those who did not know us personally from our earlier work in the area, retained a measure of polite caution, especially regarding the wartime actions of Americans, in the stories they told.

How we conducted interviews also influenced remembrance. Though largely open-ended, our chronologically organized interview format gave a linear "narrative shape, and with that a pattern of remembering, that is alien to that material," as Connerton warns.[42] While interviews were conducted locally, usually in the narrator's own home, they did not reflect the usual context of storytelling. We believe that in a more natural setting, the narratives would be more contextualized and would follow a more episodic, thematic sequencing, as do other narratives told by Pacific Islanders.[43] Indeed, that is the form Micronesian narratives often took in our earlier fieldwork experiences. The very fact of our focusing on "wartime memories" in themselves, asking informants to provide them "on demand," to recount their experiences to us and on tape recorders, all set up recontextualized situations in which war stories became further reified.

Thus, personal circumstances, modern political realities, and the conduct of our research all shaped the memories of war contained in this book. In the chapters that follow, we will also see that individuals in different indigenous

social statuses, positions within the Japanese colonial administration, strategic locations in wartime Micronesia, and other social groupings not only have
different perspectives, but may even have opposed interests in how the past
should be remembered. Furthermore, personal interaction, negotiation, and
contestation are part of the storytelling process. What is chosen for remembrance, as well as how people represent the past to themselves and others,
influences how they continue to live their lives. On a larger scale, wartime history continues to affect political relations within and between Micronesian
societies.[44]

PART II

Micronesian Understandings of the Pacific War

THE BRIEF REVIEW of the events of the Pacific War in Micronesia contained in chapter 1 represents a standard narrative of the conflict from the viewpoint of military historians. It also displays the power of the historical narratives of the two major combatant powers, the United States and Japan, to define those events. In actuality, no single overarching narrative of "the war" can represent it objectively or in its totality. Military veterans recognize this when they speak in terms of "my war": each locale and each civilian or military group has its own tale to tell. As a result, there are many "wars." The differences in these stories of war also reflect each group's preexisting cultural ideas and values.

In considering Micronesians' thinking about twentieth-century global war against the backdrop of their cultural memory of precolonial and colonial war, we must be careful not to obscure or, on the other hand, to overemphasize the contrast. The particular foreignness of World War II in Micronesia—its unexpected arrival, the overwhelming potency of its technology, the unfamiliar strategies employed, and how it was experienced by local people—was vastly different from Islanders' warfare traditions. Yet in their attempts to come to grips with World War II, Micronesians refer to their own historical practices and use their own ideas about what causes wars and motivates warriors.

Chapter 3

THE MEANING OF WAR

MICRONESIAN SOCIETIES maintain highly valued warrior traditions, pasts in which chiefs and military action hold central significance. In stories of ancient times, warriors waged important battles both at home and against other islands. The actions and events of these battles hold value in the present (just as Americans refer to past military victories for modern inspiration), and well-known martial figures rank as important cultural heroes. Heroic accounts of ancient times constitute some of the most important of all oral traditions.

WARFARE IN MICRONESIA'S PAST

Like modern war, ancient Micronesian warfare changed the lives of those involved. When they reflect on ancient battles, however, Micronesians contend that motives for war did not focus on territorial conquest per se, but revolved around typical Micronesian concerns for status and hierarchy, or in some cases for group expansion and political suzerainty. A war might reorder the ranking of the land and its peoples, transfer sovereignty from one chief to another, change a chiefdom's ruling lineage, perhaps even result in the massacre of a clan or the expulsion of people from their homeland. Fighting in hand-to-hand combat, individuals are said to have asserted their manhood and their loyalty to the chiefdom. Victory was a means of confirming or elevating the status of victors—the individuals, their clans, their chiefdoms, and their lands.

Warfare continued into the era of exploration, trade, and missionization. Its overt forms were suppressed with the establishment of effective colonial governments. Pacification was not simple, however, with European efforts to make Micronesia safe for merchants and missionaries extending over a cen-

A young Chuukese warrior, Weno, 1899. (Micronesian Seminar: *Life 100 Years Ago,* website album <www.micsem.org>)

tury. In the mid-1800s, the Marshall Islanders "had a reputation for hostility toward visitors that was unequalled in the area,"[1] and Chuuk's reputation for violence extended into the final decades of that century. Pohnpeians repeatedly fought the Spanish in the late nineteenth century, eventually forcing them to sequester themselves in their fort, then abandon the island. Opposition to German colonial rule on Pohnpei erupted into the armed revolt of the Sokehs Rebellion in 1908. Micronesians take pride in the numerous fights they waged, and sometimes won, against outsiders throughout the period of historical contact and colonization. Islanders gained allies and enemies, new weapons, and new sources of conflict, yet they describe this as a time when the ancient concerns and consequences of war remained strong.

THE MEANING OF THE PACIFIC WAR

So the concept of war, even major war between two well-prepared enemies, was familiar to Micronesians from their own past, and they brought this understanding to bear in making sense of their Pacific War experiences. Many Micronesian stories cast this war as an extension of the familiar Micronesian story of chiefly competition, seeing it as a contest between the Japanese and Americans to decide the right to rule over local lands and peoples.[2]

What did Micronesians think about the wider meaning of World War II? It is curious that, although Micronesia in the 1930s had phone lines, radios, newspapers, and telegraphs that provided contact with the rest of the world, and many (but not most) Micronesians spoke Japanese, still, many of the Islanders who lived through the war had no clear idea of what precipitated it. This remains true for that generation today, and it is even true for their children and grandchildren, many of whom have high school and college educations.

To Americans, whose cultural training in World War II narratives begins in childhood, this seems surprising. When asked "What was the Pacific War about?" an American high school student will offer an answer that is similar to, though less detailed than, that of a World War II American veteran. It will emphasize matters of national fortune: it was about Japan's refusal to adhere to the capital ship treaty, or the U.S. desire to contain other powers, or the British response to Japanese pressure in Southeast Asia, or Japan's attack on American or British island possessions, or support for the European fight against Hitler. American cultural memories of World War II—shaped by public history in the form of written, film, or photographic representations—outline the significance of the nation's past.

Written sources, especially those that form part of official military history, concentrate on strategic concerns: operational plans, targets, dates of attack, weaponry, casualties sustained on both sides. Indeed, much military effort was dedicated to, and dependent upon, the determination of these facts. After the war, official and unofficial histories and fictions were written for a home audience that wanted to know in more detail about how the Allies had won that war. These presentations are stories about how and why the war was fought, by the Allies who see their nations' experiences as part of the great sweep of global history.

"Great events" of the past typically become part of widely acknowledged "world history" when they are recognized as significant by the groups that currently hold the greatest power. Takashi Fujitani, Geoffrey White, and Lisa Yoneyama refer to "the hegemony of the Allied war epic." They write that these "dominant narratives have tended to nationalize memories of the war."[3]

Of course, history is generally written not only by the victors, but also by the losers. For the Japanese, however, wartime memories have remained somewhat detached from their everyday lives—an uncomfortable and rather unfocused topic of discussion, labeled only vaguely as "that previous war."[4] World War II is not typically taught in high school classrooms, and many young Japanese today obtain their knowledge of the war primarily through the popular media. One of the dominant themes in Japanese recollections of the war, however, is to regard it as a natural disaster—its emperor and its peoples the victims of Japan's military elite.

Winner or loser, the history of World War II is certainly written by the combatants, not by local people who have no strategic role or position of power in the conflict. The Micronesian "veteran's" answer to "What was the Pacific War about?" will be very different from that of an American or Japanese citizen. For Micronesians, their war—the war as they experienced it—was not about matters of global strategy or national fortune. Micronesians—whose national interests did not generate the conflict, though they certainly were, in the long run, shaped by it—have a very different view of the meaning of the war. We do not mean simply that they lack book-knowledge of the political trajectories that brought the two nations into conflict, though that is true for many people. Rather, we are making a larger statement: that while, for Americans and Japanese, the meaning of the war lies in political and strategic and national-history concerns (however they may disagree about them), its meaning for Micronesians lies in a very different direction.

Putting ourselves, insofar as we can, in the place of an elderly Islander remembering the 1930s and 1940s, let us ask what it seemed to them that the war was about. From that perspective, it didn't seem to be "about" anything. There was no reason on earth that a major war should show up on these islands. The conflict was not about Micronesians; they had little stake in it; they certainly had no role in bringing it about. The war was between the Japanese and the Americans. Micronesians were affected only because they happened to live on the battlefield—or, more accurately, because the Japanese happened to be in political possession of Micronesia and decided to fortify it, and the Americans decided to attack Japan in part through these islands. So from that point of view, the war wasn't about anything—it had no local or moral purpose, as far as Micronesians were concerned.

Yet as an intensely experienced period of life, with tragedy, fear, shock, drama, a heightened sense of reality—all the sharpenings of experience characteristic of times of crisis—the war was certainly significant. Elderly Micronesians do consider the Pacific War to be a "great event," in fact "the greatest hardship" of their lives and communities. The memories rank among the most vivid and powerful of their lives. As they look back on it, what were those memories about? What was their war—the war they experienced—about, for them?

We approach this question by looking not at the place of Micronesia in military strategy, but at the themes that run through the spoken memories of those years. Micronesian stories of World War II are personal, subjective, emotional, and concerned with the everyday. Micronesian narratives are about how the war was experienced. They are told primarily to a Micronesian audience, typically in a private or domestic context. Although they are also occasionally told in more public, formal contexts on some islands—as part of Liberation Day ceremonies, church services, or kava sessions—these stories have not been nationalized, especially not to the extent that they have been for the Allies. As we will see, the focus is on how Micronesians survived.

Throughout the region, we find a striking consistency in the events people want to remember and the topics they emphasize, with certain themes recurring: the surprise, or even shock, of war suddenly erupting or falling upon them; the hardships and suffering they endured; and their constant, overwhelming fear during bombardment and invasion. Chapters 4, 5, and 6 examine each of these themes as expressed through narratives and songs.

Chapter 4

THE SHOCK OF WAR

WHEN ASKED TO RECALL the start of the war, many, perhaps most, Micronesians describe it as a surprise, a shock. People recalled that in the late 1930s the Islands were prosperous, with plentiful opportunities for wage labor, with young people, especially, busy making money, traveling, enjoying imported goods, learning the Japanese language and customs. The work and bustle simply seemed part of the economic development that peaked during the prewar decade. Islanders do not recall that the increase in construction projects held any threat at the time. Where Japanese air bases were hastily built, some locales were transformed overnight; but in other areas, prewar preparations went largely unnoticed by local populations. Docks and lighthouses were built, communication facilities updated, and roads improved; yet in seeing and even working on such projects, most Micronesians say that they did not interpret the improvements as danger signals.

Some Islanders were more aware of the world situation. Elites who had greater contact with Japanese colonial officials or who had received advanced education, worked for the Japanese, or lived in town knew about the war in Asia. Urban dwellers recall local celebrations of Japanese victories in China. A few observed or even worked for the military in preparation for the December 1941 offensive, and Marshall Islanders in 1942 experienced brief Allied retaliatory bombings. But most Micronesians—especially those who lived in more remote areas, had less education, or few Japanese connections—do not remember having been warned about the possibility of war. Even if they did hear something about war in China, or the suggestion that Japan's military actions might affect them, how could they have imagined what modern

Toloas, Chuuk, after the U.S. attack of April 30, 1944. (U.S. Navy photo, National Archives photo no. 80-G-227331)

war meant? The overall sense of recollections of the start of the war is that its sudden onset was unexpected; certainly its ferocity, its physical reality, was unanticipated.

Identifying the "start" of the war, though, is a somewhat artificial exercise. In writing a chronological study of Micronesians' war experiences, we learned that the war did not start everywhere, for everyone, on December 7/8, 1941. Instead, we must date the war locally. In one place, people might speak of "the war starting" at Japanese celebrations marking the attacks on Pearl Harbor, Guam, and the other initial targets. Elsewhere, people speak of "the war starting" months or years earlier, when their lands were confiscated for military construction. In the Central Carolines, "the war started" when the Japanese Army arrived in great numbers in late 1943. And some Micronesians speak of the war as "starting" only when American planes flew overhead and bombs began to fall.

MICRONESIA'S ELITES AND THE GLOBAL COMMENCEMENT OF WAR

Sachuo Siwi's recollections of the war's beginnings describe the experiences of a high-status Micronesian. Mr. Siwi's father was chief of Toloas, the headquarters island for the Japanese in Chuuk. With a good education in Japanese schools and connections with Japanese officials, Mr. Siwi was positioned to hear news about Japan's war in China and to observe the changes in Chuuk that accompanied preparations for the start of war:

I will only talk about what I can remember from the time I got out of school, until the time I grew up, until the war, until the time the war was over. . . .

After I graduated [from Japanese basic schooling], for six months I just helped my father, working on our lands. My father was the chief of Toloas. His name was Nachuo. After that six months, the main office called me to work for them. I spent two years working for them on this mountain. . . . [Two years later, Governor Yamomoto] initiated the idea of having meetings at night. They were teaching the tactics which the soldiers learn for war. Men and women—Yamomoto told my father to gather men and women so he could talk to them. There was a big house over there, that's where we had the meeting, at the government meeting house. That was when we started to learn what those soldiers taught us. We made sticks and learned to march with the sticks as though we were marching with long rifles. We learned a lot of things from the soldiers. I never thought about anything else at that time. In fact, I kind of liked the idea—I sometimes joined the local people to learn those things.

After a while—it had been two or three years that Governor Yamomoto had been working in Toloas—at this time, there was a rumor that there was going to be a war between the Japanese and Chinese. They started a tinfoil drive. We were to collect tinfoil and give it to the Japanese. They said they were going to send it to Japan and recycle it into coins. They said they were going to make silver coins to replace gold. But the problem was that, when we collected tinfoil for the Japanese, we thought they were going to pay us for it. But they didn't pay us.

After a while, maybe in Yamomoto's fourth or fifth year, he was replaced by [the new governor] Yorimichu. He was a short man who liked sports a lot. He was the one who first introduced sports to us, like baseball, track and field, tennis. He introduced these things, and his kindness to us was such that he told us to be ready, because there was going to be trouble later on coming to us. After a while, the trouble began to emerge. . . .

Later on, before Yorimichu left, he asked my father to gather all the chiefs in Chuuk so he could speak to them before he left. In that meeting, he told the chiefs to be ready because the war was about to begin in these islands. I'll talk about the war because my father was chief, and none of those chiefs or even the people knew what war is like. Would it be like the excitement of a track and field meet, or a baseball game, or what? That's right; the chiefs went home and told their people to get ready for war, but the people didn't know what war was like. I'll speak for myself, because I didn't know what war was like. I had only seen it in movies, but it was exciting in a movie. I didn't know . . . that it would be miserable.

So Governor Yorimichu left, and another one came. His name was Taka-saka. It was three months after Takasaka arrived when the kumpu *[quasi-military construction workers] came into Chuuk. These* kumpu, *maybe we can say they're like these Seabees, because they fixed roads and built barracks for the soldiers. When Governor Takasaka arrived with the* kumpu, *that was when everything got worse. We asked them why they were building all these things, and some of the* kumpu *told us that Chuuk was going to improve. They said they were building the road because big businesses from Japan were coming to Chuuk. They also said big, big buildings ten stories high that we had never seen were going to be built for the Japanese businesses that were going to come to Chuuk. But that wasn't it. They were preparing for the war. They built bunkers and bomb shelters, and then they started putting the big guns in the mountains. Everywhere, they put their guns to shoot at ships. The* kumpu *did all this. After that, the news got around that there was going to be a war between America and Japan.*

Then, just before the war began, a new governor came. He was appointed from the military section. His name was Aipara. When he came, he became the overall administrator in Chuuk. He was even higher than the previous official, Governor Takasaka. [Aipara was governor when the first Allied photo recon-naissance plane approached Chuuk.]

We were surprised because they had put another siren, a new one, by the office. We were surprised because we were working when the siren sounded, maybe it was twelve noon or a little after. [When] the siren sounded, we were wandering around; those soldiers told us to run to this cave—here on this moun-tain [speaker points]. So we ran into the cave. I didn't understand why we were running. They said it was American airplanes that sneaked into Chuuk and took pictures of the islands. So I thought that was correct, they were taking pictures, because they came in so close to the ground, they came in like this [speaker shows with his hand]. They flew low along this mountain, and when they got to that high top, they flew straight up in the sky, higher and higher than they had earlier. I personally saw the airplane.

After we came out of the cave, the airplane had left. I asked a leader of the soldiers, called Kifuchi, what that was all about, and he said that the war had just begun. And that we were going to be troubled because the war was going to be about our islands. I had never thought of that—that we would one day be in trouble, that anguish would come to us.

After that, some big [Japanese] ships began to arrive. They were large battle-ships—I had never seen them before in my whole life. . . . That was the first time I'd seen them; they were very big ships. Even aircraft carriers. The next morning, when we went downtown, the people were all in white uniforms. They were everywhere. They were sailors who came with those ships. At this time, we lived together on Toloas: the soldiers, the [Japanese] civilians, and the local people. At that time, the downtown was very pretty.

Then, I think it was February seventeenth when the first air raid came. That was when trouble was very big. Because the air raid just came and dropped a single round of bombs on the town, and it was down. People died; also some soldiers died; some got hurt.

It's correct that some of us didn't understand what was going on. Some of us. I myself didn't know that there would be trouble, that people would suffer after that. In the evening, when the planes had left, I went to my office and I learned that a lot of people had died in the air raid. The downtown had been burned down by bombs, everything else was still burning. That was when I realized that we were going to suffer.

The third day after the air raid bombed this place, what could I say? I can't say anything that would really describe the scene at that time. Everywhere I went, I saw dead people just lying around everywhere. Sometimes I'd find an arm or a leg or even a head separated from the body—people were dying out in the open, a messy death. There were no more clusters of buildings, even the offices weren't there anymore. The school building wasn't damaged, but the teachers said that school should be closed at that time.

So that was it for the first air raid. People were very pitiful. That's what it was like. The Japanese were to be pitied. The soldiers and civilians had no places to stay—their homes were gone. They had some trucks, so they hauled the Japanese to that village and spread them around under the breadfruit trees. They were everywhere, under the bushes, under big trees, wherever they could make a home, for they had no more homes. That was when my father told the local people to take care of themselves. He also begged the Japanese to get out of here—that could never happen, because those were soldiers and [they] just made up their own rules to take over our lands. This is one part of what happened at that time—from the time I was born, to the time the war started. . . .

At that time, I remember—ooh, so this is what war is like. I enjoyed all those times when I was happy, when I was only having fun. Now that war has come, war kills people—I just realized what war is all about—what its consequences were—this was the time I started to suffer. I started to worry. I was really troubled. This was also the time my father went to those Japanese and asked them to leave Chuuk because people were dying from the bombs. My father had seen that the people would soon die if the Japanese didn't get out. Because during the first air raid, not only Japanese died. Chuukese people also died. That's why my father asked them to leave, because he said his people were dying from the war, which wasn't their war. But the Japanese wouldn't leave, because the soldiers had their own law.

In the next account, Yvette Etcheit, part of the Belgian commercial family that had lived on Pohnpei since the turn of the century, describes how they experienced the first years of war. As wealthy nonnatives who resided in the town of Kolonia—closely linked to the Japanese before the war—the Etcheits had an early and unusually well-informed perspective on the start of the war. Then, abruptly labeled as enemy aliens within weeks after the bombing of Pearl Harbor, their perspective became severely limited by the conditions of their imprisonment.

Before the war, Kolonia was a pretty Japanese town. The first few Japanese families started to come in 1924. They really started coming in 1935–1936; they started schools, brought their families, established many little shops. They had almost everything—restaurants, ice shops, shoemakers, bicycles, bicycle repair shops—all along the road. Here [where her store is today] was a drugstore; they sold everything, even popsicles. Across the road, where KCCA is located today, they raised pigeons. By 1939–1940 there were even geisha houses; one was located where Federation is today, and women dressed up in silk kimonos. It was a very happy town. On New Year's, everyone dressed up.

In 1937–1938, when the war started in Europe, there were about ten thousand Japanese here, mostly in Kolonia. There were very few Pohnpeians here *[in the town]. They [Japanese] lived in small Japanese-style houses with sliding doors. Then, in 1937, the military slowly began to come in. First it was the navy, a small group of only thirteen or fourteen. We started to see the change when more military arrived. We heard about the war on the radio, on broadcasts from the United States, Australia, Japan. There were also newspapers, but these were three months old by the time they reached us. We were quite up to date. Father listened to the radio every night. So did we kids.*

Our relations with the Japanese were very friendly. As kids we had plenty of Japanese friends. . . . In 1939 Father wanted to send me to boarding school in Japan. He had arranged with the Catholic mission to send me to high school and college in Kobe. He had made all of the arrangements and had to get a permit for me to leave. He couldn't get it. They kept making excuses—no space on the ship, et cetera. We started to suspect what was going on; there were also some troops here by then. Then there were some Japanese rumors that Japan would go to war, but they didn't say with whom or where. The Japanese also started to get stricter. From 1939 on, we were not allowed to leave; we were like prisoners on the island.

December 8, 1941, was a big event here. The Japanese knew right away. In the morning they blew a loud whistle, which they used for mail call. Everyone woke up. Then a car went by, announcing America had declared war on Japan and everyone had to go to the shrine. . . . There was a hill with a shrine; it was like a lovely park with flowers and trees, a Japanese-style garden. Everyone ran there and it was announced that Japan was at war with the United States. We all had to pray so that Japan could win the war. The whole town was there. A Japanese Buddhist priest said a prayer. They explained that the war was on and asked everyone for their help. We prayed, clapped hands. Then we bowed for a minute in silence and prayed that Japan would win the war. That week, school changed the curriculum to include more exercise, more training, more farming. For us, it was more fun! The day of the announcement, there was no school. Afterwards, there was a parade of flags, marching, and singing of Japanese military songs. That night, the same, but with the addition of Japanese paper lanterns. It was fun! This went on for three or four days.

Then on the twenty-second of December, after school we students used to go to the nuns' to have classes in entertainment, art, music, et cetera from two p.m. on. I was there when our maid came running in and said Father wanted us home right away. My sister was very excited; my mother had been very ill. When we reached home, we saw some Japanese policemen in the house. Father calmed us and explained that the Japanese police had come to say that Belgium had broken relations with Japan. They had orders to put us in jail.

We were told to pack our suitcases and go to prison. We got ready, while Father, [Uncle] Leo [Etcheit], and the policemen went on. Father wanted Mother to stay behind; she had dengue fever. The Japanese doctor testified that this was true. Father also asked me to take care of her. So we stayed behind, but could not leave the house. The rest of the family went to prison, located where the current weather bureau is. The next day the Japanese carpenters built a big fence, twelve feet high, and stationed policemen there. They said when the fence was built and they had put the gate in place, they would bring the rest of the family back. This happened on December thirty-first. We had four houses there with a large [field] in the middle; it made a small compound. We kids could play there under the trees.

We were there one and one-half years, until February 22, 1943, when the bombing began. Actually, there was some earlier bombing in January. It was the dry season, and Kolonia burned down. The houses were made of wood and paper, and the wind carried the flames. Also, the night before, a [Japanese] ship had come with a lot of ammunition. They unloaded the shipment in front of our house, but they couldn't move it far at night. At daylight, the Japanese came and moved it. They hid it underneath the houses—they didn't expect the Americans would come! Everyone's houses burned, except our house and one cement building. It was a miracle that our house survived! We didn't know what was happening; all we could see was the fireworks all around us.

Then we left. It was thought the Americans would be landing there, since we were located in front of the dock, a very strategic place. At three p.m. a policeman came with orders to take us. Fortunately, Father had been in World War I. He had gotten us ready with backpacks and survival kits. He had cut up old tires to make sandals. We had this, a suitcase, food. We never saw our house again after this [until the end of the war].

The policeman marched us to Dau Sokelei bridge. Father had a wooden leg, and it broke. It was dark, so they let us sleep in one of the navy houses. Our maid invited us into her house. The next morning we walked to the new prison camp. There were Japanese, Koreans, Pohnpeians, Marshallese, Chuukese there, about fifty to sixty men—murderers, thieves, et cetera. And there was one Pohnpeian girl, who was really glad to see us. Father couldn't stand up. He stayed behind to fix his wooden leg. The new prison camp was located by the current Nahnmwarki of Net's residence, about one and a half miles up the mountain. They had set up a thatched-roof meetinghouse for us there. The Japanese policeman had known us a long time and said he didn't want the women and children there, so he sent us back to the native house and told us to come back there in the morning. The next morning we had permission to build a shed next to the meetinghouse to sleep in. We had to build it. So we kids and Uncle Leo used a machete to cut down small trees; we used coconut fronds for the wall. We were able to stay there. A few days later we found some old roofing; we tried to use this to make the roof and some walls. We had no nails! This small house measured approximately nine by eighteen feet; we divided it into two, for the two families. We were there approximately one year, until December 1944.

Then the police told us they had orders to move the prisoners to Madolen-ihmw to help work in the fields. Times had gotten tough by then and they needed the manpower. . . . The police wouldn't take us there. Instead, they built another, smaller, private camp with a twelve-foot fence, roofing, with a small bed inside. They didn't want us to see where we were going. By this time the Japanese had become harder and meaner; their hate was coming out. They ordered us around. They walked us at night in the bushes. This prison was located near the compound for the police, because they couldn't spare forces to guard us. We didn't know where we were going.

Our old maid brought us a couple of buckets of water every day. We weren't supposed to talk to her, but once in awhile we could say a word or two. She told us that we were in Net, half way up the triangular mountain. We had two very faithful old maids; they moved close to us and watched over us and helped us out. We stayed there until September 11, 1945. We were living in a shack, with just a floor and a roof. If we were lucky, there was something to put on the walls. The Japanese didn't feed us at all, and we couldn't get out of the compound. We were totally reliant on our maids. At the last camp, we lived only on sweet potatoes and their leaves. Other foods had been confiscated for the military. . . . Through-out this time, we were very frightened.

THE JAPANESE CONFISCATION OF LAND AND CONSTRUCTION OF MILITARY BASES

For Micronesians who lacked access to global news, the imminence of war did not become evident until military preparations began. Construction of air bases on Jaluij, Maloelap, Kwajalein, and Wotje (Marshall Islands) began in late 1939; these were operational by the end of 1941 and were further strengthened in the first year of war. Building the air bases meant taking over Marshallese lands—entire islets—displacing residents and drawing in thousands of construction workers, including Marshallese as well as Japanese and Korean laborers. Anko Billy describes how he did not recognize the military implications of these early developments on Jaluij:

From 1933 until 1935, many Japanese came here to survey the land and inventory all types of construction. This is what indicated there would be a change, because when the surveyors arrived, they came and measured all of the locales, but we did not yet know what they were preparing for. They measured Imiej and Jabwor, and then they did other work to prepare for the arrival of the Koreans [laborers]. Then, when the Koreans arrived, they changed to working a bit with BK [Nanyo Boeki Kaisha, South Seas Trading Company, a commercial firm]. Before that, they sent fishing boats and they said they were working for the soldiers. They took money, a type of grant that Japan was giving to certain men who were taking out loans and then working at, let us say, to prepare for war. This money was being used to develop Japan during the movement that they were thinking about in their hearts [literally, "in their throats"].

After these fishing boats came, then the Koreans arrived to work on the end of the pier with people from these atolls. Then the surveyors arrived. They worked at various locations. There was a tank they built at the place called Aktanko, the name of the contract [carried out by the Japanese government]. During this time I was a boy, and it was as if I could not get very excited about these things; but now I am thinking back on them today. I am just becoming aware of the sort of activities they were engaged in, in readying themselves for the battle—but I did not know it was a battle; I thought this thing was a type of development activity. But it was not, for they were readying themselves for a certain type of thing [i.e., war].

While Jaluij had already been a Japanese civilian center, with land set aside for government use, the construction of bases at Maloelap, Kwajalein, and Wotje was more disruptive. Nathan Tartios describes the early, yet sudden, decision to transform Taroa islet in Maloelap into a Japanese military base:

A ship came from Jabwor to take the chiefs, such as Tomeing, Laninmoej—these two were brothers—and Moses. It took them aboard and sailed for Jabwor. They got there and stayed and spoke and spoke, and when they returned, they brought

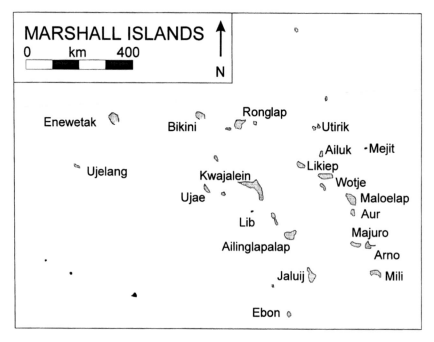

The Marshall Islands

some builders. They arranged to have a meeting of all of the people of Taroa. Now everyone got together and had a meeting, and they said to them, "Well, this islet, Japan is going to take it as a place to do battle." All the old people cried. [Q: What did they say to them? "You are going to have to move?"] "You are going to have to move, because Japan needs to use this place for a naval [air] base for the Japanese. . . ."

Now we left those places on Taroa and stayed on the islets near Taroa. The soldiers began work on that place, to clear it, and began to build the airport. Then they began building the places from which to do battle. Many Marshallese worked with them: Maloelap people, also people from Aur, also Majuro people. A ship brought people from Aur and Majuro to work there. [Koreans were also brought to work.]

I worked on Taroa with the Japanese. I worked with rocks; gathered rocks and separated them from the sand. It was a lot of work. . . . They gave us food, the sun had not yet risen but you ate; there was only a little bit of night, but they would get you up to eat. And then when the hour came, you would line up for roll call: "Hey!" "Hey!" "Hey!" "Hey!" Afterwards, you wanted to say, "Go to hell!" If you did not work, because you were ill, they would really watch you, and if you lied, they would beat you. . . .

We worked, and worked, and worked. There was a time to eat at twelve o'clock—no food at nine o'clock, food to give you a little strength—and then when it was exactly twelve o'clock, you just ate then. You ate there, at the place where you worked, you did not go to where they cooked the food. The Japanese came and brought food to you . . . they used a pushcart and brought the food to your group. They knew how many people worked in your group. Now they brought food and we ate, and ate, and slept, and then, at one o'clock—work time. [Q: What did they give you to eat?] There was rice, a meat, and then a type of liquid they called wasa; it wasn't sweetened. Perhaps they still use it in Japan now; I think they use it. Then we would work, work, work, and when it was quitting time at night, we went off to our camp. Showered for awhile and rested. Oh, and we watched movies, but the movies of the Japanese [kabuki] were humorous. . . . Go back and sleep and then eat first thing in the very, very early dawn.

Mr. Tartios also recalls a work song from that time that tells of the relentless work required to build the Maloelap base:

Untitled Song
Unknown Composer

Dig, digging, and pulling up things.
[In the] early morning light [of] Taroa,
haul us toward you.[1]

I will bite into the air[2] and dig holes
there by me, as you become
my sole obsession.[3]

Most early Japanese military preparations had focused on the more populous islands, where the civil administration already had a presence. However, a few islands chosen for fortification had had little previous development of any sort. That was the case for Satawan in the Mortlock Islands of Chuuk, where an air base was constructed in 1943. Esperansa Samo describes how local people relied on supernatural assistance to understand the sudden changes and to prepare themselves for the war:

[Q: When did you start to think that war was coming to Micronesia?] We started to notice when the Japanese Navy came in and spread all over in the islands, on every island in Chuuk State. We started to notice, or knew, when our spirit medium spoke. Our spirit told the medium that his name was Nickasio Phiach. He was the grandfather of our [current] lieutenant governor of Chuuk State. He told us to prepare everything that we might need to depend on, sometime very soon. Those people who would move in would put us in a lot of trouble, as to food shortages, and also as to our lands. They would fight with another kind of people sometime soon. He told us to beware of those small people [i.e., Japanese]. They would lead us into trouble. They would ruin our peace, unity, and freedom, and also our ways of worship. . . .

They [Japanese] started to collect all the food and store it in a safe place for navy use. We had to donate the food we lived on for them. And we ended up in hunger and fear.

They called on every young man to move to Satawan Island to do hard work for the war preparations. They felled coconut trees and breadfruit trees for the underground shelters. They worked all night and day, without breaks, worked hard with no food. Everything they did to our men, we knew about it from our spirit medium. Our spirit told him all about it. And that's why we are really thankful to our spirit for helping us so much. We had no radio, or anything except our spirit. We depended greatly on our spirit.

The Japanese built another base in the Western Carolines at Woleai Atoll (local population approximately 350), midway between Palau and Chuuk. A small air base built in 1942 was expanded dramatically in March–April 1944, and Woleai eventually held 7,000 Japanese troops. Local people were moved to the shores of Falalap, the main islet, and finally to other islets in the lagoon. Michael Faraguy had just returned home from a contract labor stint in 1942 to find that military construction had started, to the surprise of many:

I think this was 1942, when this group of Japanese came to clear the island [Falalap]. When they came, they came in as if they had no regard for or questions about the place. They came in and started right away; they did not ask the chiefs, they did not explain to the people what they wanted to do. We were very confused about what was going on, and there were many of them. They came in and cleared the houses, cutting down coconut trees to make way for their houses, and did other work. They surveyed and cleared the place for the airstrip. As

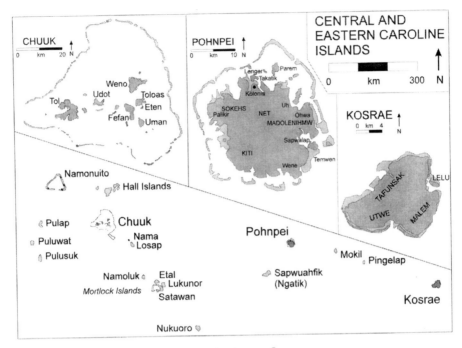

The Central and Eastern Caroline Islands

they worked along, making way for the houses and airport and so forth, we were forced to move. Where we stayed further inland, we had to move close to the shore to make room for them. The way they went about working on the island: if they wanted a place, no questions, no inquiries about properties, including trees and so forth. They told us to just leave our places to make way for them. [Eventually] we thought we were not going to be able to live on the island because we were just living next to the shore. Our houses were all moved to the shoreline. Then a policeman told us to think about going to other islets like Mariyong [part of Woleai Atoll]. At that time there had not been any soldiers, only people clearing the islands. When we had to move to the other islands, the policemen helped organize the local men to assist in the moving. When we were moving to the other islands, the Japanese labor stayed on to finish the airport.

When the airport was finished, the first Japanese group was taken off the island; I don't know where they went. The only people left were those first thirteen Japanese who came in. Then I heard there was going to be a butai [work group] coming in; they said it was going to be Yawema butai. Before this butai came, another group came in, and this was a military group. They came in and started building more bunkers. At that time there was no artillery, just machine guns. Then later on, the boss of the group, when he came, the chiefs went to him and they told him that they would have to leave Woleai. . . .

One day there were some planes leaving Woleai—at that time their airfield was full of planes and some of them left that day. It was becoming a routine for the airfield: on almost a daily basis a plane or group of planes would take off and then come back. And then one day a group of planes left, but only one of them returned, because they met the enemy. When the plane came back, the enemy was very close. Then all the planes took off, they said they were going to Tinian. We were just staying around on Falalap and going to Tegailap islet.

The next morning as we were leaving Tegailap to go back to work on Falalap, it was early in the morning and the sun had not come up yet, I was one of the first ones, we were paddling toward Falalap in our small canoes, we looked north, we saw these planes. They were American planes, but at that time we thought

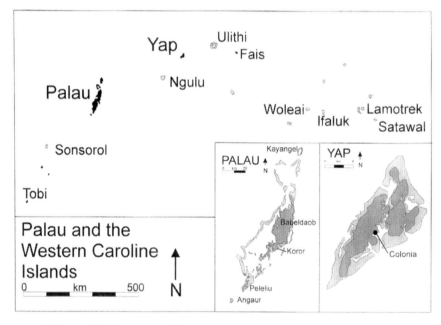

Palau and the Western Caroline Islands

they were Japanese planes. They went and passed Falalap and turned around and were coming toward the airport. They came in; they started dropping bombs on the airfield. That was the start of the actual war for us: they started fighting and bombing more intensely. Maybe two or three days later, in came these big planes [long-range bombers], we heard they were coming from their bases in New Guinea or someplace in the South Pacific. Those planes did more damage to the islands. At the time, none of us remained on Falalap, we had all been moved to other islets in the atoll.

THE INFLUX OF JAPANESE ARMY TROOPS

In the first years of war, while Japan held the offensive position, Micronesians' experiences with the war were limited to a great increase in contract labor and security measures in some key areas. But with the June 1942 defeat at Midway and losses in the Southwest Pacific, Japanese strategy changed to a defensive position, using the Micronesian islands as barriers between the homeland and the advancing enemy. Then, in fall of 1943 and early 1944, some forty army battalions gathered from Japan, Manchuria, and the Philippines were reorganized to bolster the defenses of the Eastern Caroline and Marshall islands.[4]

Micronesians in areas not chosen for initial military construction, who had been relatively insulated from war's effects, found their lives suddenly changed with the influx of thousands of troops. The effective Allied submarine blockade meant that many Japanese troops arrived without supplies, yet somehow housing and food had to be provided. The army immediately began extensive fortification of the islands, confiscating land and conscripting Micronesian labor. These new troops—the Japanese Imperial Army—under pressure and under a different discipline, were perceived as harsher and less predictable than the more familiar Japanese Navy personnel, as you can see from Ichios Eas's recollection from Chuuk:

When the rikugun [Japanese Army] started coming in, they were there, and if they didn't have a place, they would just walk in and move you out of a house. If they wanted to take over your house, they'd just move in today, you'd just move out. Our very own home. My father had a nice house, all glass windows; they just came in and moved us out. . . . [Q: Did you ask, why are you moving us out?] No—we're going to ask the soldiers? We were scared stiff of them. They could just cut your throat. They had swords and guns with them all the time. We saw the guns and swords; that was it! Who was going to answer them back when they were carrying guns?

THE FIRST ALLIED ATTACKS

When thinking about "when the war started," many people identify the first Allied air raids as the key marker. Marshallese actually suffered the first air attack in the region, a small raid on several fortified islands in the Marshalls on February 1, 1942. This attack was intended as a morale builder for the Allies, an isolated effort to strike into Japanese Micronesia well before a sustained offensive could be launched. Joseph Jibōn describes this early attack on Jabwor in Jaluij:

At that time, before Tur was burned [bombed], I was going to school, I was about ten years old. That was on Jabwor, Jaluij, there where I stayed and went to school. . . .

At that time, all the people were sleeping and no one knew a thing about the method that was used to destroy Tur. . . . There were many towns belonging to [various atolls] of Marshall Islanders on Jabwor. There was a town for Arno people . . . Ebon people . . . Kwajalein people, and all of these buildings were full of people. On that morning, the planes flew over us . . . from four a.m. until sunrise. And we Marshallese, when we saw the planes above Jabwor, we said they were Japanese planes staging a practice. At that time, everyone came outdoors and observed the planes as they strafed. That is what they did first, strafe. Then people said, "Oh, the planes from Imiej are also taking off to practice and test their abilities." When the planes were shooting, people were hit, many were hit, but people did not yet believe that these were American planes. They still believed they were Japanese planes. And then when people began falling, they said, "Why is it they are falling? Why is this happening? Don't the army people see that they are hitting them, even though they are dying?" They still did not know that these were American planes flying downwind and upwind over Jabwor and shooting, because of the darkness.

Then, as daybreak arrived—at the time when you could walk around and distinguish which person is which—they began dropping bombs and damaging Jabwor. The first building that was damaged was the Ebon dormitory. That was the first to be hit at the beginning of the bombing. Second, they threw a bomb next to the place where Kwajalein people lived. And all of those buildings where a lot of people were, they died. . . . Many people from all of the various places in the Marshalls were wounded at that time also, but the most damage was done to Ebon people. Now, as it was increasingly light, it was possible to look upward and see that it was American planes with the morning star on them and the American flag.

Well, at that time, everyone began to run off. They just began to understand that the planes were not Japanese planes. When they were running away, the planes damaged almost all of Jabwor and damaged all the ships on the lagoon side. And then, seinen-dan [young men's group] . . . notified people and told them to escape, for people now could not stay there on Jabwor. Some went into the holes [shelters], some went to teinjinjo, the sturdy houses where they could not shoot them, and some ran off to a distant islet. Then, after they damaged those locations at that time, the planes departed and did not return to damage Jabwor.

Well, so many people were killed they could not be assessed. And then . . . I was standing there and watching the rescue squad as they brought the dead. They shuttled them and filled a jenpan *[a very large boat] with people, they filled it up until people spilled out over the sides. There were so many, they could never build caskets to bury them. There were also Japanese who died, and they took them and burned them. Because [that was] the way the Japanese did things, they cremated bodies. But as for the Marshallese, they dumped them all in one boat, they filled it and took it to the islet of Jaluij, dug a single grave, and threw all of the people inside the hole.*

John Ezekiel describes the same event:

There was no expectation that they [Americans] would come. No one foresaw this thing, that many people would be hurt. Because . . . there were training exercises. That morning at four a.m. the practice on Imiej would begin: planes from Imiej flew training flights above Jabwor. This is what people were saying. So the planes were flying as expected—that is, doing practice exercises—but then they "practiced" on the ships in the lagoon and they sank! This was an attack—that is, American planes coming at first light.

Our mother was washing rice and she looked up, but she continued to work, and my father pulled her hair and said, "Don't you see that the sky is filled with fire, don't you see that?" She repeated what she'd been told, that it was an exer-

cise. *"But it is not that sort of thing. You hurry up!"* Because of their slowness, they were still seeking shelter as Tur was set afire. But if the two of them had been slower about getting into the shelters, who knows but that they might have been hit with a shell? Because bullets were coming from there [in the distance] to Lojkar. There were bullets everywhere. Many people died.

The actual Allied invasion of Japanese-held Micronesia began with the attack on Tarawa in Kiribati in November 1943, quickly followed by invasion of the Marshalls in early 1944. These victories, in turn, supported the Allied drive across the Central Pacific with the establishment of American air bases to support long-range bombing. As Allied plans developed, only strategic islands were chosen for invasion, while long-range bombers were used to neutralize bypassed islands.

For Micronesians who had been living behind the front lines, as we have seen, the war had already meant military construction, relocation, and increased labor with the arrival of massive numbers of troops and the imposition of military control—yet they had nonetheless been physically safe from attack until this time. As in the case of the earlier raids on the Marshalls, other Micronesians were shocked at the sudden appearance of enemy planes. Marcus Alempia describes the war's arrival on Pohnpei:

One day I overheard my parents and some other elders discussing a rumor my father had heard about a possible war between Japan and the U.S. I did not know where he heard the rumor. Some time later, the Japanese told us that the Americans had already captured lands in other places. We believed them then because ships stopped coming, and imported goods became scarce. That was how we found out that the war had already started in other places and was maybe headed for us. We were thinking then that even if the war did not come to Pohnpei, we would still suffer, because the ships had already stopped coming, and whatever dependency we had on imported goods was going to be cut off. I remember that the Japanese Navy was already here prior to the war. It was just before the war started that many land soldiers arrived. When they came, my father said that the war was about to take place here.

The soldiers then started to prepare and make gun emplacements. They put up big guns on high ground like Pohndohlap, Sokehs, Kupwuriso in Uh, and other places. My father was made to go work at Lenger where they prepared the soldiers' camp and put up another big gun. They also prepared and dug holes, deep ditches, called jenzi, for the soldiers to run through, and so on. Other big caves were dug and made for hiding. Watching all these preparations made us realize that the coming of the war here was inevitable.

There was a big change here as a result of these preparations. Before the war, we had freedom to get around, and the Japanese were good to us. They only punished those, the elders, who drank liquor; but things started to become a little tougher. They made us work more and seemed to ignore our rights and well-being. We then questioned among ourselves if all the preparation was going to save us from whatever evil was coming, if it was going to keep us alive. We had to think these thoughts then. We all became worried about whatever was going to happen, because instinct made us realize that it was not going to be good. For comfort, some of the elders told us that we could at least run into the caves and hide. It was our parents who were very worried about us youngsters, because of the uncertainty of what was coming. When I think of it now, I feel sorry for them because of what they had to endure.

When the war started, I lived at the Catholic mission in Kolonia with my mother because she was ill. One day a plane flew very high over the island. That day an uncle of mine, named Kulian . . . was out deer hunting. He happened to be on Nahnalaud, the highest mountain on Pohnpei, and when he looked up he was able to see the plane clearly. A few days later, he visited us at the mission and told us that the plane was not a Japanese plane but an American [plane], because it had a white star on it. Nobody else told us anything about that plane. In less than a month's time, another one came in flying very low. The sirens gave us no warning. The gun on Pohndohlap commenced firing, but missed. Then the one on Lenger opened up, and the plane turned toward it and dropped the first bomb ever. . . . Everyone knew that the war had started here. The soldiers staying in the Catholic church and the priest's residence dug a long ditch from the church all the way down to Pohnlik by the seashore. By morning it was finished. That same morning, we left the mission and went back home.

Wendolin Gomez, also from Pohnpei, speaks of the widespread shock of the first American bombing—for Japanese and Pohnpeians alike:

The Japanese told us that there would be war between them and the Americans and we believed them, because they started to practice shooting their guns, conducting fire drills, sounding the air-raid sirens, and even practicing taking wounded people to the hospital and so on. Japanese women made trousers to wear when the war started, and the nurses were given red crosses to sew on their uniforms. Bomb shelters were dug and prepared, guns and small tanks were brought in, as well as more soldiers. Soldiers who had left the island were recalled. Big guns were put up on Sokehs Rock, Lenger, Uh, and other places suited for shooting airplanes and ships. The soldiers were sent all over the island, and they dug holes as bomb shelters. They practiced shooting at targets near Lenger. Some of the soldiers were sent to Nanpohnmal, Palikir, Lenger, Kolonia, Nanpil. They even went up the mountains to prepare shelters. They also told the local people to prepare shelters for themselves. Many local people helped, or were made to help, the Japanese prepare these shelters.

When the war started, I was working at the hospital and my wife was at Dolonier near the shore. . . . On the first day of the war, a lone American plane flew over Sokehs. It flew down low and then went over Lenger. At that point the Japanese started firing at it, but they missed it. The plane then dropped a bomb on Lenger and flew away. Maybe it was only patrolling to check things out. Then others came and started dropping bombs at Sokehs, Dolonier, and Kolonia.

I left the hospital to check on my wife. I found her cooking fish. She had got-ten the fish from the seashore: the bombs killed the fish and when they floated close to shore, people picked them up and cooked them.

The people, including most of the Japanese, left Kolonia for Net. But I couldn't go because we were expected to stay and wait for the wounded to arrive. When they came in they were a mess. They had all kinds of body wounds. Some had to have their arms and legs cut off immediately. Others had big chest wounds that needed to be closed up. Those that died were taken away for burial. Others had their guts hanging out. It was a great mess. By that time, most of the Japanese had left and only the head doctor and a man from New Guinea, called Anat, and myself were left to look after things. The other doctors and nurses went to Lehdau in Nanpil to wait for the other wounded soldiers there. They [the Japanese] had a new hospital built there.

While all of this was going on, I had to drive from place to place looking for the wounded and others who needed medical attention. I patched up minor wounds, but took the serious ones to the hospital.

The first major attack on Chuuk was a massive carrier air raid, called Operation Hailstone, February 17/18, 1944. While the warships of the Japa-nese Combined Fleet escaped by moving west a few days before (warned by reconnaissance planes), the raid destroyed much of Chuuk's military infrastructure and shipping—sending vessels to the bottom of the lagoon. The sudden arrival of the American planes and the bombing and destruction over those two days is vividly recalled by survivors.

Piara Esirom, Toloas, Chuuk:

I was sleeping in my house when the siren went off. I woke up and wondered, What was that? I woke up my children and told them, "We're going to run away. We're going to the Japanese priest." So we walked at night. While we were walking, we saw the soldiers. They stopped us and asked us where we were going. We told them that we were running away. When we looked up in the sky, we saw the planes dogfighting. So we ran to the priest's house. Then we heard gunfire . . . [and] we were very afraid. Japanese and American planes went down.

The sun was rising, and we were very hungry. My children and I were starving. One of my boys decided to go back to our house. I said to him, "What if you get hurt?" And he said, "But what can we do? We are hungry, and if we don't at least have something, then we'll die." So he went to our bomb shelter and cooked rice for us, but a soldier came and scolded him. He took the water and poured it on the fire. He didn't want the planes to see the smoke. We didn't have a kerosene stove. The Japanese soldier left.

The planes were having a dogfight. Japanese planes went down, and American planes, too. The ships in the ocean went up in flames; they were just like fires in the ocean. The American planes were dropping bombs on these ships, and all were destroyed.

Night came, and the soldiers told us to go up into the mountains. Everybody—Japanese women, men, and all Chuukese; all except the soldiers. We stayed up in the mountains, and the planes were fighting. We heard the sounds of machine guns. Planes burst into flames in the air. So we just waited for the bullets to hit us.

Then daytime came, and our hunger. We were losing our strength. We couldn't eat or drink. My boys became friends with the Japanese, so they would go with them and ask for rice. They would bring us the rice and I would give a little to everyone so that it might help us, or at least we would have something in our stomachs.

Then the oil tank went up in flames. It was at night, but what could we do? We couldn't hide, because it was like daytime when that oil tank went up in flames.

My husband asked for a boat to take us to one of the other islands, Udot.

Konstantin Enik, Weno, Chuuk:

During that time, I was at Fanu. . . . And every day, early in the morning, we paddled to Tunnuk, to go to work. We had a surprise when we saw planes, but we thought they were just Japanese planes practicing. That was the first time American planes came, but at that time we didn't know it was the beginning of the war, because we really didn't know about the war. We paddled to Tunnuk, and we went straight to the village at the end of the point, called Upween. Then we walked down, we met the soldiers; they were all in their uniforms. Then the officer said, "Did you guys see the teki that came?" But we didn't know what that word teki *[enemy] meant. We didn't know that was the term for American planes.*

So then we discovered that Americans had come, because we saw one of the huge Japanese planes try to leave the airfield, and those American planes chased it and strafed it, and it fell on one of the small reefs, called Tawenap. We saw the plane fall. At that time, they told us to run away to the mountains, because the Americans had come. And when we started to leave, we looked out to sea and saw huge ships, called akungkang *[gunkan, battleship]. They were outside the reef. We saw those ships shooting at each other. At that time we knew that there was war.*

[Q: What did you feel when you saw that?] At that time, we were so worried, because we didn't know about the Americans, whether they were going to kill us. But those American planes, they only shot at Japanese soldiers, not Chuukese people. But those Chuukese who were soldiers, they shot them, because they didn't know they were Chuukese. They thought that they were Japanese soldiers. But those like us, we were hiding behind breadfruit trees—they flew by and saw us, but they didn't bother us, just passed by. Maybe they said, "Oh, those are Chuukese."

Toli Jessy, Weno, Chuuk:

I was at work in Senetiw, Weno, when it started. I was working when I heard the siren. The siren was in the boat pool, Nepukos, where the soldiers were stationed. When I heard the siren, it was kind of different from the usual siren used to call workers to start working. So I told all my coworkers to get ready to run, because the war was coming. Because I was the oldest among all the local people working in Senetiw, I was responsible for them. About thirty minutes after the siren or horn, I told my coworkers to get ready for work; the Japanese hadn't told us to go home because of the warning.

So, early in the morning, I got outside and I heard the airplanes in the sky. When I looked up, I saw that the edges of the wings of the airplanes weren't round like those of the Japanese. I could also see stars on the bellies of the airplanes instead of the usual red and round paint we'd always seen. This was when I told my coworkers to run, because at that time we had also heard the guns on Witipon, Penia, firing at the American airplanes.

I wanted to stay and watch because I was really amazed, but I had no choice; I had to run or I would die. So we ran up the hill behind [the modern] Stop-n-Shop and hid ourselves there. There, we could still see the American airplanes. I had seen the Japanese airplanes in action, and they were nothing compared to those of the Americans. Ooooh, the way they maneuvered around Mount Tonachaw and the small hill of Tunnuk! They'd come down so close to the sea, I thought they were going to crash, but instead they'd come straight back up faster than anything I've ever seen. And "rrrrrrrrr," they were shooting at the cave [holding artillery] on Mount Witipon in Penia. They got that cave on Witipon all right, but boy did they almost get us too! A bomb had landed a couple yards away from where we were. So we ran again and hid ourselves in the bushes where we thought it wouldn't be necessary to bomb. The American airplanes attacked here [Weno], Toloas, Parem, and Eten. I'm not sure where else they attacked, but between the time they flew from here to those islands, we ran around to look for a bomb shelter.

[Q: So when the Americans started bombing, did you leave your work site?] No, after the first round of airplanes flew from Weno to Parem, that was when the Japanese told us to get out of the bush and go to a shelter nearby. While we were there, a Japanese soldier came running. He had bruises on both knees, on both of his palms; he was bleeding. He probably fell down while running around looking for shelter. Because the gravel we're using today is smaller than that used during that time; it was much bigger.

[Q: How long did you stay in the bomb shelter?] Oh, we stayed there until the Americans flew to Parem; I don't know exactly how long they were gone before they came back to bomb Weno again. But it must have been thirty minutes or so, because before the second round of airplanes came back to attack Weno, we had to run back to our work site. When we got there, our bosses told us to go and hide. They told us not to stay with them, because if the Americans bombed them, *they would die together—all Japanese, no Chuukese. So they gave us some food, and we fled.*

We went to the mountain in Nantaku and took the mountain path to Neauo. On the way we met a group of highly ranked Japanese soldiers; they had so many decorations on their uniforms. They were hiding in a cave in Nepukos. They called us to get in the cave and hide, but I said no thanks. We just kept on walking. Not far away from that group we met another Japanese soldier. He was sitting under a breadfruit tree; [he had] only one eye. The other eye had popped out, and his eyeball was hanging down his cheek. We felt sorry for him, but we couldn't do much; we had to keep going. On the mountain of Mwan village we met the amaraw *[literally, "blue"; referring to Japanese prisoner laborers]; they wore blue uniforms. They were yelling "banzai"—from that mountain we could see the Japanese airplanes go down in the ocean. We could see that the American airplanes were just overpowering the Japanese airplanes.*

Anyway, we kept on walking until we got here—Neauo. When we got here, we saw that those buildings on base had burned down. The Americans had bombed them. When we tried to go see, there was a policeman guarding the way. He told us to go look for the local people, because they had fled the village, and we should go hide with them on the mountain in Wichap. So we went up the mountain and we saw that the caves were already full. I could see that people were just sitting around under big trees, behind big rocks. There were old women, pregnant women, women with month-old babies; they had no cave or safe place to go to.

. . . When we came from Senetiw to our homes in Neauo and then on to the mountain in Wichap, we crawled to the very edge of the mountain facing Toloas and watched the airplanes dogfighting between Toloas and Weno. We could also see the Americans shooting at the Japanese ships in Neauo. They dropped many bombs on those ships, and the ships were quickly sunk. Oooh, how I felt compassion about those Japanese boats, and especially for those two buildings that I helped build. It was really exciting because we had never seen any dogfights, but it was also sad because of the people who went down with the ships and airplanes.

The first air attacks on Yap came in support of the Allied invasions in the Western Pacific, with the first strike on March 31, 1944. Leon Gargathog speaks of the war's arrival:

On our island, Yap, the war here was so sudden, we never comprehended it or heard about it, [or] had any idea what the war was like before it came. We never heard of it, so we could not relate to it, saying, "Oh, this is what we've heard people talk about." All of a sudden it came, and we were so shocked. Some people knew what they were doing, but some didn't. There was so much hardship. After a long time, then people began to realize, "Oh, this is what war is all about. We hear that foreigners have war; this is what it is really like."

Martina La'ew, Yap:

The beginning of the war started the third month on the twenty-first [sic; March 31, 1944] at seven o'clock Sunday morning, while I was in school. In the morning there were four airplanes; we heard a noise that sounded like a machine gun; we ran and hid. The planes were coming from the south, all the way up. We thought, "Oh, those are Japanese planes." We saw something that looked like a star [on the planes], and we thought, "Oh, those must be Japanese planes." Four of them came at first; then another group of four, and another four. They made a circle, groups of four circling high up in the sky. When they were circling, they were high up, but then when they dropped their bombs, they dropped down low. Then we knew, "Oh, this is an attack." So we started to run away.

When the planes dropped down to attack, they first bombed the airport, those planes called sentoki *[fighters]. After that, they dropped other bombs on Colonia. They destroyed some houses, and also Ganir bridge. During that time, we heard all those bombs, so we all ran and hid. After that, we came back to school. A bomb had been dropped on the school, a firebomb, and burned it. That's when I realized, "Oh, this is what war is, and it is very, very harsh."*

After the Japanese Combined Fleet moved from Chuuk to Palau for safety in February 1944, Palau was strengthened in expectation of an American invasion, which came in September 1944. Makino Tariu of Palau (in an account collected and translated by Wakako Higuchi, 1986) recalls the first air raids on Palau:

On March 29, 1944, it was announced, "As the enemy is moving close to us, we are not sure when we can complete this construction [the airport Airai]. You should stand by for the fight." On March 30, 1944, about five-thirty a.m., before dawn, some of us were awakened. We heard the sound of planes. "What?" "Oh, that's the sound of our friendly troop's plane." We had no anxiety. We couldn't see those planes because of their height.

At six a.m. we saw thirty planes in a formation coming from the east. From the group four planes came down, and we saw the flashing from the planes' machine guns. Next, four planes came down and strafed. "It's funny. In spite of our friendly troops . . ."

Something dropped to the ground, and it was about five meters from me. It exploded. I saw a star mark on one plane. Approximately ten Koreans and one Palauan were killed by the U.S. attacks. These Koreans didn't escape, even though the siren sounded.

I returned to the dormitory and took my property and escaped to the bush. Halfway there, I met Timalong and shouted, "Let's go into the bush."

Inside the bush, one [old] man from Ngchesar was holding his head in his hand. Blood was flowing. He had been injured by a flying cartridge. I became fearful soon. We entered the river near the airport. The bombs were sounding. We went to Melekeok. Many people took refuge there. I stayed in Timalong's relatives' house.

On March 31, 1944, I went to see my wife. She was crying under the tree, because her father who was working with me in Airai returned prior to me and said he didn't see me. My wife believed I had been attacked and died.

A widespread comment in wartime memories is that the first attacks came as a surprise, a shock. Indeed, "shock and awe," a standard trope of American military reporters in the 2003 Iraq war, is a favored strategy among Micronesian storytellers reporting their own experiences of World War II. All these personal narratives emphasize the suddenness and unexpectedness of war's arrival, whether it came in the form of land confiscation, labor demands, soldiers disembarking, or bombs dropping. More formal genres also encode this sense of suddenness. This well-known hymn expresses the shock of the war's arrival in Chuuk:

December 8

Composed by Michi

*We were running from the sound of the fighter-plane under the clouds,
there's a shaking like my heartbeat when bombs explode right next
    to me.*

Chorus: Oh, bombs and bomb concussions bring us close to a
          horrible death.
          But we are safe only by depending on God.
          Thanks to God, we are safe.

On December eighth, the war started.
War on the sea and on the land
in all the nations of the world.

On January seventeenth,[5] we were not yet awake, early in the
    morning, the bombing fleet has arrived.
We were startled, we didn't know what was going to happen to us.

The air-raid siren blew in the evening, and we heard the sound of
    firecrackers.
We zigzagged, carrying our mats and our possessions bundled up in
    a cloth.

Chapter 5

HARDSHIP AND SUFFERING

AN IMPORTANT FACTOR shaping individual and cultural memories is how people identify events or conditions that contrast with the day-to-day course of life. Elderly people measure their wartime experiences against recollections of peaceful (though not uneventful) times before and after the war years. Just how different those war years were from the ordinary experiences of life varied greatly. In locales that were not garrisoned or fortified, the war years might have passed with little change from the years before and after, except for the absence of imported goods and administrative oversight. On fortified islands, though, the buildup to war, battles, invasion, and occupation had immediate and profound effects, and Islanders' memories depict that time as one of extraordinary hardship, perhaps the single experience that contrasts most radically with the rest of their lives.

Stories of hardships or suffering do more than emphasize the tragedy of war. Just as different cultures have their own understandings of the meaning of war, so each has different views of the whole range of human emotions and behavior. Hardship and suffering are important concepts in Micronesian cultures, part of a tradition in which to accept hardships on behalf of others, and particularly of the larger social group, holds great symbolic significance. Suffering on behalf of one's family, community, clan, or island carries social value and honor. Suffering conveys a sense of social responsibility and caring for others. This behavior is considered especially appropriate for people of rank and power and is also a major avenue for increasing rank and power.

Wartime narratives reveal cultural ideas about the types of hardships that are most significant. The theme of suffering centers on hardships in the most important aspects of Micronesian life—labor, land, family, and especially food (a dominant Micronesian cultural theme, to be considered in chapter 11).

WARTIME LABOR

The demands of wartime labor—excessive, exhausting, and dangerous— form an important theme in Micronesian understandings of suffering. Subsistence work in Micronesian cultures had concentrated on the plentiful coastal, lagoon, and ocean fishing resources and on planting and harvesting tree and root crops; domesticated animals fended largely for themselves. The

Chamorros and Carolineans greet arriving U.S. troops, after the battle for Saipan. One woman is holding a Christian cross. (Micronesian Seminar: *War Comes to the Marianas,* website album <www.micsem.org>)

effort required for subsistence was periodically intense, but ultimately fruitful. Work patterns were also shaped by the social system. Micronesia's chiefly class were, to varying degrees, themselves engaged in subsistence activities, and they accepted the ritual tributes of food and other goods from their subjects. Chiefs, in turn, used the surplus to sponsor important public activities such as warfare, construction projects, ceremonies, or disaster relief. Micronesian chiefs also called for commoners to labor on public works. Perhaps the chiefly class were the main beneficiaries of these activities; however, some benefits did accrue to commoners. And in some Micronesian cultures, a commoner's efforts could be recognized by the chiefs, who could grant land use rights or elevate an individual's status.

Between the older pattern—which included long periods of intense labor, as in ocean fishing, a major construction project for the chiefs, or rebuilding after a typhoon—and the newer colonial idea of wage labor on plantations, on road building projects, or in the phosphate mines of Banaba, Nauru, and in western Micronesia, Islanders were certainly accustomed to hard work. However, the idea of forced, sustained labor for little or no pay, and with the benefits so overwhelmingly going to others, remained a foreign notion. Wartime labor demands went beyond what Islanders considered reasonable. Toward the end of the war, in some places, most able-bodied men, and in some cases also women and children, were forced to work on plantations or at military tasks from sunrise to sundown, seven days a week. Punishment for noncompliance was severe. And, then, the products of their labor were apportioned hierarchically, usually with Micronesians last in line.

This work song, written by a Pohnpeian woman supervisor, complains of the isolation and physical stress working in the tapioca fields in Palikir on Pohnpei. It was usually sung by women workers as they lay at night in their tiny bunks—too small for them to sit upright in, once inside.

Untitled Song
Composed by Lena Dehpit Rikardo

Our temporary quarters make us really lonesome;
it's worse than being in jail.
Because we have assumed the appearance of frogs—
creeping on all fours, gathering,
tearing up, looking straight ahead.

Solomon Lorrin, a man from Mokil living in Sokehs, Pohnpei, described the harsh conditions of work—and the even harsher discipline meted out against those who rebelled:

We helped the Japanese civilians make their airfield in Lenger. This work, I considered it just like killing people. You had no rights. They placed a gun on Sokehs Rock. We started the airfield in Lenger. Men from Pingelap, Mokil, and Kiti were their slaves at that time. It was a hardship. Our Japanese commander was very cruel. My brother, Soulik, was the Mokilese leader, and Dens, the Nahnmwarki of Pingelap, was the leader for the Pingelap men. Each day we lined rocks from the shore to the mountain. We filled up the wheelbarrow with rock, but the Japanese commander would jump in the wheelbarrow. . . .

Then, they took Sengkin and hung him up. They hung him—when they punished people, they liked everybody to see. The Japanese really knew how to punish people. They hung the Pingelapese man, and their plan was to shoot him. The Nahnmwarki of Pingelap came and saw what had happened. He asked all Mokilese men to go with him and help him stop them from shooting Sengkin. . . . The Nahnmwarki of Pingelap wanted Soulik to go with him and apologize for Sengkin, because the water in Sengkin's mouth started to come out. He thought that maybe Sengkin would die if the Japanese did not untie him.

The name of the Nahnmwarki was Dens. He asked his cousins David and Ernist to paddle to Kolonia and get Soulik, because if they didn't get him then Sengkin would die. Soulik knew some of the Japanese soldiers. When Soulik reached there, the Japanese said, "Hello, Soulik, what's up?" Soulik said, "I came to beg pardon for Sengkin." But the Japanese said no, he was very lazy. The Japanese soldier told my brother, "If you hadn't come, we would have shot him. We were prepared to shoot him." My brother told him, "Don't shoot him, because if you shoot him, you will run out of workers."

Work continued despite the danger of bombing or invasion, as in this recollection by Elper Penias of Uh, Pohnpei (also with Minoru Penias and Bernel Nowa):

I was working on the road at Sapwalap when the war came to Pohnpei. . . . We made the road from Sapwalap through the mountain and it went down to Nanpil and then to Nanpohnmal. We worked on the road at Nanpohnmal at night. We started at three o'clock in the morning. We worked without pay. . . .

The road at Nanpohnmal was in the open field. We divided into three groups. We were about five hundred: men from Pohnpei, Mokil, Kosrae, Sapwuahfik. Twenty-four of us were in the open field. We started at three o'clock because we knew that the planes [U.S. bombing raid] would come at eight o'clock in the morning. We finished off our contract within that time, because we were twenty-four in number, and the guards were also twenty-four. Each one of us had a shovel and a crowbar. We worked with no breaks, only a smoke for five minutes. We sweated all day long. If I started with one big tree, I had to move that tree off the road. At that time, Pohnpei people could not do anything wrong, because the Japanese were really forcing people of Pohnpei according to their laws.

At that time, we ate potatoes and tapioca made by machine. It was like preserved breadfruit. We took off the skin and boiled it. It would not get soft, and the water from the food was not good. We ate that food without meat and did not feel strong from that kind of food.

When the planes came, the Japanese alerted the people to let them know the planes had passed over Pakehi and bombs had dropped at Nandaku airfield. Nanawa of Uh was shot there. He was working with a group at Nandaku. When the bomb dropped, it threw me from where I was standing. It was just the concussion of the bomb that threw me. The Americans' bombs were very strong. They came and dropped bombs at Nanpil and Sapwalap. . . . The Americans dropped bombs, the bombs destroyed the road. We were lucky; none of us was killed. The day that the Americans destroyed the road, we went back and made a tapioca farm at Rohi [Uh].

The Japanese saw labor as a service to the empire, and they encouraged Islanders to share this patriotic vision. Julio Vallazon of Kolonia, Pohnpei, told us,

When they installed the big gun on top of Sokehs, there was no road up there. The big gun could only be moved two feet a day, using a [makeshift] winch to help pull it straight up the cliff. There was a picture of the emperor on top of the gun crate. When people saw the picture of that great leader, they worked even harder for the Japanese. They kept trying to get it up and keep the crate from being scratched, because of the importance of the picture of the emperor on top.

Kalifin Kofak from Losap was working at Toloas, the capital of Chuuk Lagoon, as a fishing foreman when an accident gave him some insight into this Japanese patriotic perspective about war work:

I led a fisherman's group. There were men from the islands of Siis and Fefan who worked with me. We fished. We went to Unileng, a small island of Uman, to start our fishing expedition. During the time I was in Chuuk, I had scars all over—my arms, my chest, and my legs—all over. The reason for the injuries was homemade dynamite. We used large bottles [about 1.5 feet long] of home-made dynamite. We were told by the Japanese soldiers to fish with dynamite. They gave us the explosives. The time I was injured, it was myself and a guy from Siis, named Achimai, with three soldiers in the boat. The bomb exploded not in the sea, but right on the surface. The guys on the island knew what had happened, knew there were some injuries, so they came out. When they got there, they saw that our boat was broken up. Our catch of fish was scattered all over the place.

When the boat came, a Japanese boss named Kein called down to me to get on the boat. I called up, "I cannot get up! I'm hurt." He told the soldiers to pick me up. When I got on the boat, Kein said, "Try your best to hang on, because you are a soldier. Even though you work for the soldiers, today you are a soldier. If you die, where the soldiers are buried, you will be buried." They went to the guy from Siis, and they found one arm missing, one leg missing. He was a best friend of mine. When they pulled him out of the sea, he was still alive. We left the channel of the small island and came to another small island. When they reached the small island, I called to the soldiers who were with the guy from Siis [named Achimai] to help raise him up. I told him, "Try your best; in a little while we'll reach the island." Then the man from Siis said, "Yeah, and tell these guys [the soldiers] to lay me down." Half an hour later, the soldiers called me to look at him, because bubbles were coming out of his mouth. I looked at him and said, "He's dead. Let the boss, Kein, let him know that guy is dead." The leader asked, "Which one of them is dead?" They said, "Achimai, the guy from Siis." "Tell the Chuukese, tell this guy [that is, Kalifin Kofak] to keep hanging on."

They took us to Umutaki, in Enin. The leader called four soldiers to take the dead man from Siis and carry him to where they buried the dead soldiers. The leaders said to bury him immediately, and this man asked—there was one other guy from Siis. I asked the leader, "Can this man take the body down to Siis, to the island?" The leader said, "They cannot. If you've died as a soldier, it's not neces-sary for your relatives to know that you're dead. He's going to be buried here." So they took him. And then they took me to a recovery room.

At that time, I learned that fishing with dynamite was illegal. There were two soldiers with me who had also been injured. The two soldiers told me that, if my father came to check on me and asked how I got the injuries, I should say

*that I received it from the bombs from the plane [a plane that had flown by ear-lier]. And I said, "No, I won't. I'll tell the truth. I was injured by the dynamite."
And the soldier said, "If you do that, then we can be beheaded by the Japanese soldiers called* kensei *[skilled swordsmen]." [Fishing with dynamite was forbid-den.] Kensei, those are the guys who did executions. Soldiers or not soldiers, it was the same—they executed them. "So don't tell what we did."*

In the middle of our conversation, my father arrived. He was working in another work group, and he heard the news that I was injured, so he came. He asked me, "What happened?" I said, "I was injured." "Why?" "Because of my explosive." And the soldiers said, "No! Don't say that!" "I was injured because of those apa *[happa, explosives], not the plane." And they were quiet, and they said, "Now we'll be in trouble." My father said to take me home, and they told him, "What about the medicine? Will you be able to bring him back for the treat-ment?" He said, "No. I'll take him and I won't bring him back."*

He took me and he got me a traditional healer from Losap. He knew all kinds of treatment. I got well before the soldiers did. The soldiers were receiving treat-ment in the hospital, and they were slow in recovering; and I was faster. When I was well, I ran away. I ran from my butai *[work group]. I didn't want to go back to the fishing.*

SEPARATION FROM LAND AND FAMILY

Stories of separation from land and family are central to remembrances of the war—not only because, in fact, many people were moved or forced to travel for work during these years, but also because separation and travel are key themes in Micronesian cultures. As we might expect, where land is so scarce and precious, people's commitment to their home territory is profound. And in this seafaring region, many love songs and heroic legends use travel, separa-tion, and movement as important images.

The abrupt cessation of sea travel due to wartime restrictions stranded many people far from home at the start of war. Tupun Louis of Losap in the Mortlock Islands was a student at the Japanese secondary school on Toloas in Chuuk Lagoon when the war began. Being away from home and family heightened his fear:

They did not tell us that there was war coming, so we had no chance to run to our own places. We were going about our schooling—we didn't know anything that went on, because they didn't tell us. One day, our teacher gathered us, all the Outer Islands students, and asked if we had relatives on Toloas. "Those who have relatives on the island, raise your hands." And there were a few of us left, who had no relatives on the island. Two weeks later, we heard the news that war was coming. Before that time, there were no soldiers, only Japanese workers. At that time, we were not afraid, but confused.

Two weeks after that, the soldiers arrived. "The boys without relatives will not be able to go back home, but get all your stuff and get ready," [they said]. We gathered our belongings. We didn't know where we were going. We got on the boat; the boat took us: we went down to Tol, all the Outer Islander boys. We reached Tol; that's when I was scared. We went down there—there were soldiers all around Tol, at that place. They took us up to the school. We were confused— we didn't know what was going on.

We found out that the head teacher on Toloas sent word to the people on Tol in the school we were in now, to sponsor us. So we were going to stay with the people [who would] care for us and protect us. I was homesick, very scared— thinking back to my parents and family, my sisters. When I left Losap, I left my parents and three sisters—I was the only boy.

The teacher said, "You students from Toloas will continue schooling here. During your stay here, go with the local people, and during school time, you come and have school." One teacher was from Tol, Nimwes. Nimwes told me not to go out with a local family, but rather stay on the school premises. When I heard Nimwes say this to me, that I would not go out but stay at the school, I felt more comfortable; my homesickness abated a bit. Nimwes said all the villages of Tol would feed the students at the school. My homesickness was lessened because I felt closer to home because of the teacher, Nimwes, welcoming us warmly.

That's when I really knew that there was a war. Three months later, I and one other guy from Losap planned to leave the island. The fishing boats came down to the dock, and I sneaked away on one. I was caught by the soldiers and put back ashore. [They ordered:] "Halt!" I called to a guy from Losap, Thaddeus, "Tonight, we'll go and steal one of the army's boats, and we'll row to Toloas." The reason to go to Toloas was that we had some distant relatives there. Now, before the war, there was a ban on travel because the American ships were blocking the seaways. We stole the boat, and we left at night. Rowed, rowed, rowed—before daybreak, we reached Fanapenges. We went into the mangroves, hid in the mangroves, searching for food and shelter from the soldiers. At night we started again, rowing. We reached Tatiw. At Tatiw there were some people from Losap. We stayed there for awhile, but we were not really satisfied, because we were homesick. We wanted to find some people closer to us.

We didn't let these people know, but we left. And on the third night [since we had left Tol,] we rowed on our way to Toloas. On our way before daybreak, we headed for Uman. We reached Uman, and rested and slept on Uman. American planes had not yet come, at that time. [The trip was before the first U.S. air raid.] The Japanese were starting to make people suffer. They took land and food from the people.

Night came. We started rowing again. We reached Ichimanto [on Toloas; the entire trip was about thirty miles]. We got to Ichimanto and we were looking, looking, looking around amongst the people walking, for someone we knew. Our fear increased when we reached Toloas. We started working, without pay, without being fed at work. Here's how they recruited workers: they looked around, and when they saw anyone, they said, "Come and work. . . ."

They were very hard on us. No break—whenever we took a break, they beat us. I worked in a butai *[work group]. In that* butai, *I worked in the kitchen as a cook. That's when my fear also went away, because I had enough to eat. I had food, all kinds of food. I was able to eat, because I was in the kitchen. That was the time I felt confident. I was there, cooking, eating, doing all right—and then the war came: December eighth. December eighth. [Although he gives the date of initial hostilities, he refers here to the first major air attack on Chuuk, February 17/18, 1944.] A battle on sea and on land was taking place. They came and attacked the fuel tanks and the airports. That's when I started to feel scared again—it was very hard to cope with the war, with what was going on. I felt extreme fear. I wished at that time that I was able to go straight to my home island. I would feel comfortable if I died with my family. I remember, it was December eighth. I don't know what year, but it was certainly December eighth.*

At night, there was war at sea; and in the daytime, they attacked the land. I saw Japanese soldiers running around, dead bodies all around because of the bombing, the airplanes that fell down, the ships sinking, and I saw the planes attacking the ships in the ocean, the airports, everywhere I saw the action. I was there. The fuel tanks burned for months, and just imagine—here's Losap, and they could see the flame and the light from the fire of the fuel tanks. I thought that the Losap people were dead [i.e., he thought the same thing was happening there].

After the attack, they went away for awhile. Everything was in confusion. Today, you worked here; and tomorrow, on your way to where you worked yesterday, soldiers saw you and they took you to work somewhere else. They just pulled you around [in different directions]. That was the first attack; they called it kidobutai *[mobile carrier striking force], the small planes attacking, which destroyed airplanes, ships, and fuel tanks. That was the only attack we received here. That's all it took. I thought that was the end. After that, the large airplanes, the bombers, came to bomb. We heard in school that those kind of airplanes came from aircraft carriers. We didn't know where they came from, but they came—daytime, nighttime. They were very big.*

We were hiding in caves in a village. . . .They were bombing from morning until night. The bombing was coming nearer and nearer to our cave. Then it stopped, just a few yards from our cave. Maybe he [the American pilot] was out of bombs. Then he flew back, without dropping any bombs. He flew back and reloaded. Before the bombers came, they [the Japanese] would call out "Kuzu! kuzu! [kuushuu, air raid?]." Then we would hesitate to run for cover, until we heard the bombs actually explode—pow!—then we'd start running for caves, for cover.

When the plane went back to reload, Reverend Rupen was one of the leaders. Reverend Rupen called us together and said, "We will pray now, to God. If He's going to take us, He'll show us whether to stay in our cave, or to move from this place." And then he prayed—prayed, prayed, prayed. After he said "Amen," he looked up and told us, "Let's get out and move to another cave."

There were quite a number of us in that cave—old people, children, women, all together. We were running uphill, toward where the previous bombing had been, running for a cave. There were some old people with children, who were running, who were a bit slow. When the bombers came, they resumed [bombing] from where they had stopped, and continued on. And unfortunately, some members of our group died, because they were running with children, falling, slowing their speed.

There was one circumstance in which the war prevented families from separating. As the war progressed, life on the bypassed Japanese military bases on the Marshall Islands of Jaluij, Mili, Maloelap, and Wotje became increasingly difficult. Last-minute military reinforcements left them overpopulated, food was increasingly in short supply, and Japanese commanders feared Marshallese escape to nearby American forces. Elson Ebel of Mili tells of the Japanese use of threats to family to prevent those escapes:

They said that if you ran off, the remainder of your family would be killed.

[Q: Were there people that they killed?] Many, because people ran off, and they killed those who remained. Laninlan and spouse, Leijekar, Luanbo, Teliji—over in the other location—her husband ran off and they killed her as well, they shot her. They shot off her ears first, to make her feel ashamed, that was what the soldiers of that time did. . . . They said, "Do you want to die?" She said, "I am not afraid of dying. If you want to take my life, take it." They sat her down on the sand and shot off her ear—and then shot off the other ear. Then they shot her in the hands [arms]. She was still alive, she did not whine or any such thing. There were ten-some bullets they fired into her before she actually died . . . such was her strength. Then finally, they placed their guns there [near her heart] and fired right through her heart, and that is when she died. This was done because their husbands ran off. Because the Japanese law was, "If you escape, we will kill the remainder of your family."

Micronesian cultures link shared land and shared kinship. Most reckon kinship matrilineally; especially in the past, these kin groups served as land-holding groups. (Individuals also often have certain rights to the lands of their father's kin groups.[1]) Given the close links between land and identity in Micronesia,[2] the loss of land and the relocation of people during the war made for strong memories.

In this recollection, Ato Lañkio describes how Kwajalein in the Marshall Islands was developed as a major Japanese base starting late in 1939. Many Kwajalein people were forced to relocate to Namu, where they lived as "strangers."

It was not very long after that the Japanese came to a decision, and they said that the school located on Kwajalein had to be moved to Namu. The reason was that they were building up Kwajalein and readying it as a location for war. This was a decision that brought a great deal of sadness, and it was also fairly difficult in terms of the life that we Marshallese led and our own customs. This is because Kwajalein was a location that was extremely important to us. But the Japanese, they would take it with their substantial strength. As for Kwajalein, there was no negotiation about it, and no one discussed it with us. No one discussed it with the high chiefs, that is, the chiefs of these Marshall Islands. In the way that [we] now recall it, the Japanese took Kwajalein in terms of their own power. They did not take it with a feeling of goodness. But in line with the strength of Japan, the decision from Tenno Heika [the emperor] selected Kwajalein, to use it and ready it as a location for warfare.

And so they notified us that we would be moving from Kwajalein. And we prepared all of our various belongings, and our possessions were moved from Kwajalein over to Namu. All of the . . . schoolchildren plus the teachers . . . the people I am speaking about; well, they prepared us and spoke to us about when we would be moving to the atoll of Namu. And so we moved to Namu in that year, 1942 . . . if the way I am remembering it is correct. We boarded a ship . . . [named] Tayemaru. In Marshallese it means "kerosene"—the ship that carried kerosene. This was the oil ship of Nanyo Boeki Kaisha [South Seas Trading Company], the copra ship.

And so we went and landed on Namu, and the Namu people came and met us when we disembarked. And that time was fairly difficult, because there was no building readied for us. There was nowhere for us to live. Instead we landed like a "footloose traveler"—that is, like someone who travels around with no place to stay. We landed there . . . and placed our feet on . . . Namu [islet], Namu . . . and they unloaded all of us and our possessions. . . . And then the chiefs met . . . with the land heads of the Marshall Islands, and they came to an agreement. And they contacted the land heads on Namu, and told them that we should go to a house and begin living there, on the land parcel of Mueninep. . . . All of those who were strangers, who were from Kwajalein, went and lived there in that house on Mueninep. And that is where they remained.

On bypassed and neutralized Kosrae, relocation was ordered both to commandeer Kosraean land for military use and to shift people away from areas of likely bombing. Kosrae was turned into a massive plantation; its produce supported the Japanese troops, imported laborers, and I-Kiribati prisoners, and, as long as possible, was shipped to Japanese garrisons in the Marshalls as well. Palikun Andrew of Utwe, Kosrae, describes the many difficulties of the move and the insecurities it held for their continued livelihood:

In 1941, the soldiers started to come and everything stopped, like the copra making, schooling, and all kinds of work. The soldiers went around the island for one *whole day and told the people in Malem to leave their village and go to Inkoeya, and the people in Utwe to move out to Koasr. The two places they forced us to go are both in Tafunsak. At that time, the governor and Isaiah Benjamin went with me to the owner of the place to ask permission before we could enter or live there. The owner had doubts about what we wanted, and told the governor to ask his son. The son said yes. Then we went back to Utwe and told everyone to break apart their houses and to take them to Koasr.*

We started to take down our houses piece by piece, working day and night. We really worked hard to finish the work that month, because the governor told us to finish that month. During the day, we worked on the houses, and at night we transported the supplies in our canoes. The tide was not good, so we had to drop them off along the channel and come back for the rest. During this time, some of the family stayed along the coastal strip for the time being. After we took all the supplies and families to Koasr in Tafunsak, the governor told us that from now on no one was allowed to return to Utwe; even our own property we were not allowed to touch. That was on July first. We stayed in Koasr for one, two, and then a third year. That was the time the bombing or air raids began.

The same year they told us again that everybody should move out to the mountain, and to take what we could take with us. At that time, the people started to live by the mountain from Likinlulem all the way down to Isra. This was in 1943. There was a famine, and we had to plant taro, bananas, and so on for that period and for later on. They found out that it takes several months to harvest these kinds of plants, so the Japanese told us again to plant potatoes and tapioca, which takes three months to harvest. By harvest time—and we were happy to have the food—the Japanese soldiers told us again to stop harvesting from the plants we had planted. That went for coconut, taro, breadfruit, and everything, which we were not allowed to get. At this time we felt hungry again, but they warned us not to steal at night. Everywhere the soldiers were watching us to keep us from climbing [for] coconuts or picking bananas beside our house, until it was time to harvest them and give them to the soldiers.

Relocation did not guarantee safety. Ela Ringlen and a group from Temwen, Madolenihmw, Pohnpei, sang about the war's arrival there on February 10, 1944, the relocation to Kepirohi, and the dangers of living out in an open field and on the ocean during the war.

February 10th [also known as Ni Ngasudoka Medeki
Pa Kumweki]
Composed by Belpet, Arios, and Ainiris
(Sung in Pohnpeian and Japanese)

All families moved far away from this land—
the happy land of Temwen,
that we were forced to leave.
Sakanadori [fish collecting?], we now live in the open field
and on the ocean.
There is no place for us to hide.

We think you are lucky.
Sio [?] and ride;
ride those on the land,
because there are places to hide.

In chapter 4, Michael Faraguy, Matthew Yafimal, and Patrick Hachigelior
began the story of relocation for the people of Woleai. Eventually, they under-
took an ocean voyage in their own canoes to seek refuge on the island of Ifaluk. Fortunately, once there, they were taken in by the chief and some of their
relatives who lived there:

When the American planes came, they [the Woleai people] had to leave again,
to go to the farthest islet in the lagoon [of Woleai]. They approached a high-
ranking Japanese Navy officer and asked if the Japanese could help transport
them to Ifaluk [about four hundred miles]. But they were told, and they thought
it was good advice, that maybe they should use their local canoes, so that the
Americans would not attack them.

[Q: Did everyone do that trip at once?] One canoe went first, to check out Ifa-
luk, to see whether the same situation held there. And when they returned from
Ifaluk, with instructions that there would be more canoes coming from Ifaluk to
help transport everyone, that's when they traveled together. Then later on, there
were a few individual canoes also.

[Q: Did everyone move, or did some men stay to work with Japanese sol-
diers?] Basically all, most of them. There were some left from the islets of Falalap,
and Mariap, Dowailap, and some of the other islets nearby. And there were also

people from the other places further south, like Falalis and Talasin. But there were few people left from those islands most affected. On the way up, during the transportation, a couple of canoes were lost because of a storm, but they eventually showed up a couple of weeks later—one, more than a month—it landed on Bachailap with a loss of six lives. But the others made it back through the storm after some damage, and required some repairs, since the canoes were full of water.

The situation on Ifaluk was very crowded. [Q: Did you stay with family on Ifaluk, or how was it arranged?] We were going in and we were under the traditional chief of Ifaluk, who cared for us; that's the custom. All the people had relatives there. But the situation was so crowded that every family was pitching in to accommodate as many people as they could. . . .

[Q: Did you all hear any news of what the Japanese were doing on Woleai, or about the bombing there?] We heard no news. Seeing the situation here [in Yap], I thought the islands would be dissolved. Being on Ifaluk, and seeing the lightning from the bombs, and hearing the bombs [on Woleai], we thought there was nothing left.

One of the longest exiles occurred when Japanese troops invaded the British colonial possessions of Banaba (Ocean Island) and Nauru at the end of August 1942. Many of these Islanders were deported to Chuuk and Kosrae. This song was written by I-Kiribati who were working on the phosphate works at Banaba at the time of the invasion. The song tells of their longing for home, their fear, and their determination to cope with the hardships brought by war:

Ai Kakubara Te Bong Aei (What a surprising day this is)
Composed by I-Kiribati working in Banaban phosphate works
(Collected and translated by Mary Lisa Lawson Burke, n.d.)

What a surprising day this is,
the day which is unexpected.
We heard the horn blow four times.
Let's go those who stay.

Let's go all of us
to the cave [tunnel].

We were lying [down] like animals.
We did not sleep well.

The soldiers stand ready for battle.
Let our hearts not be frightened,
but let's be happy.

Don't keep remembering your possessions
and your home islands.
For difficulties have arrived
on Banaba.

Chapter 6

COMBAT EXPERIENCES

WHAT COMES IMMEDIATELY to mind when thinking of the many hardships of war is the trauma of combat itself. As we have seen, the danger of battle or air raids forms part of many Micronesians' recollections of World War II.

At the start of the war, most Micronesians had been impressed with Japanese military preparations, and after nearly three decades of acculturation, they supported Japanese predictions of victory and willingly joined in patriotic activities for the emperor. As we will see in chapter 7, Japanese law did not allow Micronesians to enlist in the military (though a few sons of Japanese men did so). Though some men served in quasi-military roles (such as the Palauan Young Men and the Pohnpeian Death Band), most assisted the war effort through their labor and personal sacrifices. Although they saw military preparations surrounding them, and they participated in military drills, the physical violence of war came as a shock. Islanders immediately realized that the war existed on a scale and intensity beyond their comprehension and that the preparations they had made for it were utterly inadequate.

Combat experiences took two forms for Micronesians, depending on whether they lived on invaded islands or on bypassed islands.

ALLIED INVASION

The January–February 1944 Allied invasion of Kwajalein Atoll was one of the most complicated amphibious campaigns in history,[1] with landings on thirty islets, conflict on ten, and lengthy battles on four. While the United States controlled the atoll within a week, casualties were high, and included nearly two hundred Marshallese. Ato Lañkio, who earlier described how his school class was moved from Kwajalein to neighboring Namu Atoll, continues his recollections with a description of the American invasion:

And so it was at this same time, during this same year, when we were attending elementary school on Namu . . . that for the very first time we heard the sounds of the planes. It was at night, and we were sleeping when we heard the sounds of the planes. The sounds were extremely high up. So we went outside the buildings and listened, because the sounds of these particular planes were substantially different from the sounds of Japanese planes. These new sounds had a pitch with greater velocity and a lower sound. And these planes, as they flew above Namu, were flying in an oceanward direction toward the northeast. I do not know where they were flying from, but it was from the American fleet;

U.S. Marine supplies water to Islanders who survived the battle for Enewetak, February 22, 1944. (U.S. Navy photo, National Archives photo no. 217287)

perhaps they had launched them. But these vessels—on account of the fact that it was night and on account of the intensity of their sound—we said, oh, perhaps these are very large planes.

The planes flew toward us and around us and to the northeast, toward Kwajalein. That is what we were thinking: that they were seeking out Kwajalein and were going to start to bomb it that night. But then a plane fell from the sky, a plane that was flying downward. We could hear its particular sound as it came down. At the time it was coming down, it was almost daylight, perhaps, three o'clock something. It was almost daylight as it dropped lower, and lower, and lower. We could hear the sound, a different sort of sound, a whistling. The sound kept speeding up. After that we could hear it as it crashed and stuck there on the lagoon side of Namu.

Namu was shaken to its roots. The atoll was really bashed around. When you looked at Namu and saw its movement, it was extraordinarily frightening. It was louder than thunder. We had never heard anything like it. And so then, at that time, when those things were falling, there was not a single person who thought about escaping. Not a single person had the belief inside of them that this was a dangerous thing, that it was a thing that would cause people to become ignited and that they might be damaged by it. But the way we thought about it was that we were just practicing [learning about] these things, and we had no understanding what would become of them. But when we saw the atoll of Namu trembling, and when we saw the lightning that was emitted from this object, when we saw that everything was illuminated with the lightning, well, we just remained there in the midst of things. And we were extremely amazed. And we remained amazed, those of us who were there. It was a form of amazement that was greater than we were. It was beyond us and beyond our possible understanding. . . . It is true, we may have had the ability to escape, but given all these various things, the people just cried and were extremely filled with fright.

We heard things butting against the houses and at the base of coconut palms and in the crotch between the branches of breadfruit and in all sorts of locations, and these things we did not understand. We came to understand that these were the fragments of bombs that were tossing back and forth toward us and away from us. And these fragments came to cover all of Namu. At the first light of dawn we got up and we saw one another, and we asked questions of one another. One person died during this time. It was an old woman. This old woman, well, there was just a small wound that we could see on her skin. It was an extremely small wound. But the final word of some people who knew about this, they said,

"This is typical of the wounds from bombs; the locations where they enter are quite hidden." This old woman, her body was black and this is why we knew . . . this is why we thought that she died because of the bomb.

During that same time, more ships came toward us. The fleet arrived. The fleet, and there were a great number of ships, and as evening began to approach there were even more than a lot. These Japanese officials there on Namu, well, the Japanese said, "The Americans are now coming to destroy us, so all the people should enter into the shelter, into the holes designed for escape." And so then during that second night, all of us got into the holes. The next morning things were the same. There were a great number of planes, and it was not possible for people to go outside because the planes were constantly flying down low. And as they flew in this direction there was a great deal of noise, as they were flying to the leeward and to the windward over Namu. And so the morning of—that is, the evening of the second day, it began to—we turned around and were amazed, Namu was vibrating. It was vibrating and shaking. And we could see ships there on the ocean side of Namu. Battleships, belonging to the Americans. And the land was beginning to vibrate, because they were beginning to fire their cannons. During the bombardment, the earth there on Namu moved about, and it was like a small bowl that was being shaken about. It was as if—as if the bowl was rocking and could not stop. In our thinking, the entire American fleet had finally arrived there because as we saw it there were a great number of ships, an incredible number of ships. There were a great number of battleships and huge warships and a tremendous number of planes flying overhead that day. When they were firing their cannon on Kwajalein, Namu was greatly affected; it was moving about a great deal. It was alive on account of their fighting, on account of their bombardment. And because all this was taking place right next to Namu, Namu was shaking a great deal and there was no end to the flying of the planes, to windward and to leeward. At that time the planes, as they flew above Namu, they began to fire on the plane that had fallen out of the sky on the lagoon side of Namu. They kept firing with their machine guns at that plane nearly every second and all hours when they were flying toward us. They fired their machine guns, because people were not emerging from the holes. They just stayed inside the holes, and therefore they kept firing at the plane.

And so on the atoll, on this atoll, people remained frightened; every time the planes flew toward us you would be greatly frightened. To the degree that we could understand it, these planes did not fly toward us to damage people, that is, Marshallese people, but they came on account of the war. They traveled about *in these skies and in these salt waters in accord with the rules of war. Well, it was really an entire week that they continued to fire their cannons on Kwajalein—a week something. And we saw that—we saw that there was really nothing that we were able to do. We knew that these ships, in the way that they were doing these things, they were extraordinarily strong. We understood that Kwajalein had to be extremely damaged. You had this certain understanding that Kwajalein was extraordinarily damaged during this period. And then the thing is, we waited to hear, we just waited for our last days, because we did not believe that we would live through this. But we knew that the strength of America was greater yet than great. We could see how their ships traveled about. Plus the American fleet, in the way that it floated downwind and then floated back upwind. And we could see how they set sail, and we could see the length of the fleet and the size of the ships and the enormous loudness of the cannon and the bombs that they were using—we could see that they were stronger than those of the Japanese. This much we came to understand.*

During those times, during the week that they were firing their cannon on Kwajalein, the Japanese policeman on Namu said, "We here on Namu should wait until they sail, and go and check what had happened there on Kwajalein." Because he said they were not firing their cannon on Kwajalein, but that the two fleets [Japanese and American] were firing on one another. The policeman attempted to send people out [to check], but the people were extremely fright-ened, and they could not move. So the policeman said, "If you will not go [as I order], as soon as the battle is over you are going to make a trip to the execution site, and you all are going to die in line with the laws of the Japanese." Nonethe-less, the people of Namu—that is, the young men whom he had sent off—they did not move; instead they stayed put. And this was in line with their own belief that America had reached this area of the Pacific, and the Japanese no longer had any power. The Americans had already begun to dispose of the strength of the Japanese.

Leban Jorju was on Kwajalein itself before, during, and after the American invasion, and he recalled a scene so horrific that "you had to walk on the bod-ies, there were so many"; he fled Kwajalein for Ronglap, where he met more danger:

When I was on this atoll [Kwajalein] it was really bad. It was just at dawn. First, they saw two planes up very high. The Japanese told us that these were Japanese planes, but then they looked closer and said, well there, way off there, they saw two planes and they said those were the American planes, and all of us ran to the shelters. And those planes disappeared, and on and on things went, and then one day, at first light, some planes flew toward us, the planes that were short and black. They kept coming toward us and set that place on fire. The admiral's house was there, and he stayed inside all through the night. At first light, the planes flew toward us, and they dropped bombs and hit the admiral's headquarters, setting it and some of that area around it on fire, as well as a battleship nearby, filled with Japanese men.

The next morning, and three or four days later, the American fleet came by Kwajalein. They were everywhere, in the air as well as on the sea. You could not see the end of the fleet. You could walk on ships from here [Uliga, Majuro] to Laura [a Majuro islet more than twenty miles distant], for there were that many American warships. They came ashore, and when they landed, as for the tanks . . . they came onto the sand and fired on and burned the islet, and you could not see the lagoon side or the ocean side. There were no people on the ocean side or the lagoon side. They ran off. And then, in the morning—no, it was still during that night—I went to see my [Japanese] friend; he also was running away. And then, the Japanese planes were not able to fly—the airport was totally damaged by the American bombs. . . .

We ran off that night . . . on a Japanese boat, and when we arrived at Rong-lap that was when the battle was really raging, and they told us that the Americans had already destroyed Tarawa [Kiribati]. As soon as we landed, they told us that Tarawa was destroyed. And that was when the battle was really in full force. . . . [Q: Did you have any thought that the Japanese might lose?] In our thoughts, the young men, we [initially] thought they could not lose, they were so well prepared, with planes, submarines, and all sorts of things. My thought was that they would never be defeated by the Americans, because everything was ready.

Ken Lebo was on the south end of Meden islet of Enewetak when American tanks began the invasion:

I looked out, and they were coming. And if we had not built our shelters out of wood, well, we would have died. But we had used it in building. So they came, and came, and came, and it [a tank] was there, on top of the hole [shelter]. One of those tanks was there upon us, and it went off, and another one came toward us. Then another tank, and perhaps it would have kept coming, and I called out to the Caroline Islanders, "You guys get out of here, because a vehicle is coming upon us." [He responded,] "I am going to keep shuttling [goods]." Well, so after that, if it had been a second time, we would have been gone. It would have crushed all of us. But I emerged [from the hole] and I called out, "Aahhh!" [This is no good.] Oh, so then they [the others in the shelter] told me to go outside. I yelled out, "Oh, Kanaka [Islanders]!"

[Q: How many tanks were there?] There was one, and there were many others there to the north. It was overfilled with them. And so this tank came up, and told me to come toward it, but there were others to the north, there were many, because there were many Japanese there; they had already shot them [the Japanese]. And so, when we went off along the lagoon side, toward the northward, there were many Americans spilling out.

[Q: And so you got out and said, "Kanaka"?] Yes, "Kanaka," and they told me to come there, toward them. And so I tried hard, and tried hard [limping along on a wounded foot], and I grabbed hold of the vehicle. And they asked, "Are there other Marshallese?" And I said, "Yes, there are some there and some over there." [Q: How many holes were you in?] Well, how many were there? One, two, three, four, five, six; there were six. Yes, there were six holes. And so that fellow told me to go and bring people toward him. And so I called out to that fellow, Ading, Harry's father, "Hey, get out of there and call to the others to come. Gather those there by you, together. Are they alive or not?" Well, there were some who had died—my mother and one of my children, plus the mother and father of my wife. Plus Taniel and that fellow who was his older sibling. They were dead. [Q: All in a single hole?] In a hole that was off there, just a little bit. [Q: And it was the same tank that crushed them?] The same tank. [Q: What were these holes made of?] Well, they were made from tin. They dug them and then brought tin and then put sand on top of it. They were very soft. Yes, soft. Well, if they had been made of cement, it would have been good. But these vehicles [tanks] were very, very heavy.

ALLIED BOMBING OF BYPASSED ISLANDS

Invaded islands suffered the brief, intense blow of attack, after which they came under U.S. Navy control. Although the violence of invasion had been traumatic, Islanders in conquered territory were then quickly relieved of the stresses of food shortages, hard labor, and continual air raids as they came within American lines. But the bypassed and neutralized islands—including heavily garrisoned Japanese installations at Jaluij, Mili, Maloelap, and Wotje in the Marshalls, Chuuk Lagoon, and Palau, and even the lesser garrisoned islands of Pohnpei, Kosrae, and Yap—had a different experience. They were attacked by U.S. bombers from Kiribati and Marshall Islands bases flying almost daily (in some cases, twice daily) runs, and also by occasional naval bombardments. For another year and a half, foreign troops, laborers, and civilians and Micronesians alike endured these attacks, accompanied by fear of imminent invasion, shrinking food supplies producing a growing threat of starvation, and ever more stringent security and disciplinary measures as the Japanese became increasingly distrustful. For each survivor, certain memories of this time stand out. Their recollections, like those of combat veterans, are brightly illuminated, as we can see from these narratives:

During the war, I was very nervous and a little scared. I almost died at the bridge at Doweneu. The planes started dropping bombs there. I was coming from Palikir to see my family. A soldier asked me where I was going. I said, "To Net." He said, "Hurry, the planes are coming." I reached Namiki [in Kolonia] and the siren in the post office went off. Everyone hid. I rushed off toward Net . . . I was standing by a house near the bridge when four huge [bomber] planes approached. I walked under the bridge to hide, and soldiers there saw me there and said, "Hey there, watch those planes; they're going to kill you if they see you." I ducked down, and a man from Net joined me, just as four bombs went off. One bomb was only six feet from the bridge; three others landed in the water. The Americans were trying to blow up the bridge so the Japanese soldiers couldn't walk on it or hide under it. So I told the other man, "Let's run." When we started to run, a Japanese soldier told us to go back and hide under the bridge. We were more afraid of the bombs than of the Japanese soldier, so we just took off. When we were trying to climb up from under the bridge, I was wearing tabi [Japanese-style socks] and I kept slipping back, but the other man was barefooted and climbed out faster. We kept running to a house called pampei, a guard house. I jumped over something I thought was a piece of wood. Then I realized that it was the foot of one of the soldiers. Then I jumped into a ditch, and the bombs kept exploding. I reached the bridge where the office in Net was located. The people there said to stop running, because the bombers had already left. But I kept running anyway. I met other people from Net who were looking for their children in school. School was still going on in Kolonia. I almost died. This is the type of hardship that really scared people. I was lucky. If I hadn't run . . . (Andonio Raidong, Pohnpei)

[During the attack] we ran to different places, like under the rocks, trees, and other places. My husband, me, and our daughter—and also other people—ran beside a stream called Neuwo. But when the bombs fell near where we were, we felt that it was pulling us from the place [they were hiding in a high-elevation place; when a bomb hit below them, they felt a physical pull from the explosion—not a push, but a pull].

One time, my husband and I laid our daughter on the rocks. We tried to put some clothes on top of the rocks to make the child comfortable to sleep. There was a woman named Rosy who lived there; she called us to her house. Finally we went there, but we didn't sleep at all. If you looked at Toloas, all the tanks of oil and gasoline were burning. Especially when the siren blew, even if you were sleeping, you got up and ran to the cave or hid somewhere.

[Q: What did you eat?] While we were running around, we didn't eat. But if you had a little food you had forgotten at home, the husband ran back fearfully and took it. But when the planes came zigzagging down, we lay face down on the ground and tried to hide. This was what I could say about the entapi [starvation]: we were scared of the soldiers and the bombs we were suffering from. The [machine gun] bullets came like falling rain.

One day, when we were staying in a place called Nemwanger, one of my relative's children died. But even though that child had died, I didn't care—I ran for my life. My husband told me to run for my life. On our way to we knew not where—just running—we saw two brothers carrying their father—but we didn't stop until we reached a place called Tonapwok, and then the planes came. My husband told me to lie flat on the ground. When the planes left, we started to go down the stream. As we reached there, Nipwitik was there, hiding under a piece of wood. She is a close relative to me, but we didn't stop. I could say that, at that time, nobody cared for anyone else. (Simako Onuson, Chuuk)

A chief asked me and two other women to get some taro for men who were going to move a house from Wottegai to a small islet they were inhabiting. That morning when we went, the old man told them that when they got to Wottegai, to ask one of the men who worked on the house to accompany us to the taro patches. After we got there, we went to see the men and asked them to accompany us to the taro patches, but they [the men] were upset that we [the women] had come to Wottegai in the first place. They were upset that we had left our hiding place [the islet they had moved to for safety].

So we went by ourselves to the taro patches. We finished putting our taro into the baskets when the air-raid warning [a cannon] started. When we heard the first warning, we tied up our baskets and picked them up to leave. Then we went toward where the men were. On our way, we heard the second warning, and we started running to the men. As we arrived, the men had scattered, looking for a place to hide. We asked them where to hide, but no one answered us. So I got upset, too; I told the two women to come with me, and we went to our canoe. We put our canoe in the water, jumped in it, and started paddling. We only had one paddle and a pole. One used the paddle, and one used the pole. We were not too far from Wottegai when the plane started shooting with the machine gun and bombing, starting from the east, moving toward us. We jumped in the water and swam with the canoe toward the nearest island. When we got to the island, we hid ourselves—and not only from the planes, but from the Japanese who went there to get food. (Ignacio Letalim, Woleai)

Venito Gurtmag recalls the first night raid on Yap:

[He had moved from one assignment to working on an airport in Thol.] We lasted there only two weeks. Then we all had to run away. The reason I can't forget it is that it was the first time that light was used [phosphorus flares?]. It was a night raid. You know, the plane dropped a light, I think a flare, that came down. And then the plane went and turned back, and came again, and then started bombing, and that was the end of us. We all ran away.

That was the first time here on Yap that a flare had dropped, that there was night bombing and a flare was dropped. The plane came first, dropped the flare— all lighted—and yet we were down on the ground. We had removed all the trees so that—wood, trees that we had chopped down [made piles of debris]—so there was one fire here, one fire there, one fire there—all over the place, the cleared place where we had gathered everything together. Then that plane came and dropped a bomb, right—four, four lights.

I always thought of myself as being a slow runner. But I remember four flares—and then there I was, in Toming! And the four flares were dropped, then the plane went, came back, and started bombing. My group was not working; I was asleep. Me and another guy here, by the name of Tifiin, we ran. We ran all the way from there to Tagren, the German channel, across the German channel—and the road now is good, it is not like before. The road then was very bad, and all potholes—not a road like this, all these village roads—but we ran. Then we had to climb mountains, then we came to Edet, and then came out on the lee, then went to the other side, in Fanif, and came from Fanif to here. And when we reached here, the last flash was still visible.

Then I realized that I had never run so fast in my life. I never realized how fast [I could run]—I'd always thought of myself as being a very slow man. [Q: So you ran all the way from Tamil?] And it's not a straight line, it's not a good road, we had to take many detours and diversions; but when we reached here, the last flare was still visible. And we were the first people from this village to reach here. And when we reached here, we were asked by the few people that remained, about one's father, brothers, how are the people? And we said, "We don't know, we're thinking—we're thinking that they're all dead." But we were wrong. No. See, we were the first ones to get here. We got here, and still the last flare was still visible—so. You know how flares are, they come down slowly. But even so, it is still a long way from Tamil to Weloy!

Pilar Soumwei was on the islet of Kuttu in the Mortlock Islands, Chuuk:

First, a ship came from Satawan. Some men were going out in their canoes to meet the ship that was coming down from Satawan to trade coconuts for cigarettes. At that time, I was just giving birth to one of my sons, Louis. While the men were approaching the ship, the Japanese were trying to give them signals to go back to shore, because there was a battle going on. The men were not able to read the signs until they were alongside the ship. At the very last second they knew what was going to happen; the men tried their very best to paddle back to shore as fast as they could. Some of them were leaping off the canoes hoping they would reach the shore first by swimming instead of paddling. As soon as they reached the shore, they shouted, "Women and children, run for the taro patch!" So all of the people ran for the western part of the island. I was carrying my baby, the younger one; I was holding his hand, and the other child was holding one side of my skirt. I was trying my best to go faster, if I could....

As soon as the men urged us to run ... the ship was escaping from Satawan on its way toward Kuttu. And then up in the sky we could hear a plane coming down so low, and its sound was making us more frightened. The plane was bombing the ship, but the ship was whirling and trying its best to move away from the bombs, and it was doing fine for awhile. [Q: Were the American planes dropping bombs on Kuttu?] No, they were only bombing the Japanese and the

Japanese ships. They only fought between them, but we were still afraid. All around Kuttu was very smoky as a result of the bombing.

[Please continue telling about the time when you fled for the western part of Kuttu.] We were fleeing toward the western part of the island . . . and guess where we were going [she laughs]? We were all standing around under a big breadfruit tree, not knowing which direction to go further [i.e., they had come to the end of the islet, and had no place left to run]. [Q: Where were the American planes, then?] The planes were trying their best to bomb the Japanese ships. . . . They were not aiming at the island, but they chased the Japanese ships around. We could see big smoke clouds coming up above Satawan. Yet the people of Kuttu were very afraid of what was going on. Kuttu people, mostly the women, were sobbing for the men staying on Satawan when the big smoke clouds were billowing up above Satawan.

Yes, we really ran for our lives that time, toward the westward end of the island . . . some of the people did not stop to wait around the west. Instead, they walked on the reef all the way to the other uninhabited islets. Some of the men finally returned from Satawan by escaping. My husband was among those returning. So the Americans were bombing hard on the Japanese ships, which were whirling round in circles in the lagoon trying to escape that bombing. There were thousands of fish floating in the sea. We ate what we could, but there were too many.

[Q: How about you, were you on Kuttu, or did you also walk to the other islands?] No, my husband told me to just stay on Kuttu until the battle was over, but I was not sure of that myself. So we went to the other small islands. The women were walking up on the reef, carrying babies, toddlers, and belongings.

A poignant song recording feelings of helplessness and danger was composed by the granddaughter of a lesser chief in Ebon, Marshall Islands. She suffered from Hansen's disease and had been sent to an isolated leper colony in Jaluij before the war arrived.

Untitled Song
Unknown Composer (likely Labo)
(Collected and translated by William Davenport, 1953:235[2])

The morning of the day when I arose,
everything was almost destroyed

from the bomb's thunder on land,
in the sea, and in the air.

The powerful heat of the bombs;
the sound of the machine guns scare me.
The powerful heat of the bombs;
the sound of the machine guns scare me.

On the towers the people,
looking with binoculars,
saw the dipping wings of the airplanes.
Diving down, dipping their wings, way on top of the clouds.
The many droning planes, racing to the target.

Cause the bullet,
but there is no way to escape.
But there is no way to escape.

I am counted with the dead and injured.
Dead before the gun and sword.
The enemy surrounds us.
Now we stand for our lives.

For me, I would like to win the bravery medal for which the
  military compete.
For now, I am between life and death.
For now, I am between life and death.

PART III

Micronesian Vantage Points

NARRATORS TELL THEIR tales from particular vantage points and with particular psychological tones. The nature of the war being waged, the roles of participants, and the variety of individual experiences combine to create distinctive war stories. The experience of war differs—often dramatically—depending on where one is and what is happening at the time. In a world where mere chance can put one in the way of a bullet or grant a miraculous escape, it is impossible not to realize that memories depend on a person's vantage point.

Historical events that come to us in the form of memory once had an objective reality, of course. All the Islanders who ran for half-finished bunkers at the first sign of Operation Hailstone—the overwhelming air raid on Chuuk of February 17/18, 1944—experienced the same reality as the U.S. carrier pilots coming in low to strafe the airfields and the same reality as the Japanese sailors scrambling to get their ships under way to escape from the targeted lagoon. As they remember these events, however, each group speaks in terms of individual experiences shaped by their particular vantage point.

Part 3 asks how Micronesian experiences of war shape narrative form. The way the Pacific War was fought—the facts that Islanders were surprised by a war that started far away and then abruptly entered their lives; were caught up in a foreign war but were marginal to its instigation, prosecution, and resolution; found themselves held in a largely fixed position within a war characterized by great mobility across a global expanse; and struggled to cope with two very different groups of combatants (one familiar, one largely unknown)—helps mold the manner in which wartime narratives are told.

Chapter 7

"IT WAS NOT OUR WAR"

THE JAPANESE BEGAN the Pacific War confidently, with a strong offensive against U.S. and British possessions in the region. For the Allies, the Pacific theater was a secondary front: they decided to defeat Hitler in Europe before focusing their forces against Japan. Once engaged, though, they mounted a two-pronged drive, along with attacks on shipping, to dominate the region and press the war to its conclusion in the Japanese homeland. The first and best-known trajectory of this offensive followed General Douglas MacArthur through the Southwest Pacific; a "second road to Tokyo" followed Admiral Chester W. Nimitz through the islands of Micronesia. By the time combat reached Micronesia in early 1944, Japan was fighting a defensive war, using fortifications on the islands of the Mandate to slow the Allied approach to Japan itself.

These offensive and defensive roles are the familiar ones of military strategy. The indigenous peoples of Micronesia, however, had much less powerful and decidedly different roles than did the major combatants. Although their status in relation to the Japanese had varied throughout the area during the colonial period, they were consistently disadvantaged within the overall power structure. Recall that the empire's ethnic hierarchy ranked Japanese citizens in the highest position, other Asians (Okinawans, Koreans) at the intermediate level, and Islanders in the lowest place. By the mid-1930s, the influx of immigrants, aggressive economic development, and the taking of land for infrastructure improvements had lessened Islanders' hold on their own lands. As war began, tightened security, the influx of troops, and the eventual takeover by the military made most Micronesians nearly powerless in the public arena.

Japanese officers pose on the deck of the battleship *Krama*. (Micronesian Seminar: *The Japanese Flag Unfurled,* website album <www.micsem.org>)

CAUGHT IN THE MIDDLE

Micronesians' stories reflect their position of being caught in the middle of a foreign war—one initiated, designed, and led by others. As some elders say, Japan and America went to war with each other; Micronesians were simply in the way. While no statement can typify the experiences of every resident, in most cases Micronesians saw themselves largely as victims of actions beyond their control. Even accounts that put Micronesia at the center of the war narrative—such as one story claiming that the first atomic bomb was originally aimed at Micronesia—place local residents in positions of relative impotence, powerless to affect the course or outcomes of this war. Micronesians remained largely cast either in the role of supporters of the Japanese cause or as onlookers and bystanders. They had little other choice. (However, in chapter 10 we will see that they did attempt countervailing action, coping with, resisting, and even rebelling against their position in the war.)

Leon Gargathog of Yap offers a clear statement of his understanding that

U.S. aircraft carriers. (Micronesian Seminar: *Campaign in the Marshalls,* website album <www.micsem.org>)

the war took place between foreigners, and was beyond the control of Micronesians:

So the war came here looking for the foreigners, not because of us Yapese. The Americans came looking for the Japanese—they're the ones doing the talking, not us. That's why they were coming here, bombing, strafing. That sort of gave us a little peace of mind [knowing that it wasn't us they were after]. Sometimes the Japanese would ask some people to go work with them, and then they would get injured. Then we'd question: there is something to this, people are being wounded. We said, "The Americans are here looking for the Japanese, and yet we are also hurt. Now what?" So everybody was frightened. But we kept on persevering.

When we asked Kame Rapun of Tol, Chuuk, whether there was a difference between how the Japanese Navy and the Japanese Army treated Chuukese, he responded with a more general statement about Chuukese impotence in the face of military control:

As for the [Japanese] navy, they mostly stayed on Toloas, since they were on the ships most of the time, while the army scattered out in the villages and lived among us. But, generally, I would say it was the same, because they never asked for any permission, made no request of any kind for any kind of [confiscated] property. The army were the ones mostly troubling us. Because they lived among us, they gave us the most unpeaceful moments in life. Even when they did their training, there was never any notice to the public or any warning letting us know not to approach certain areas used for training. They really did not care a bit. So when the training went on, and a soldier aimed for a coconut tree but hit a human being, so what! It did not matter whether the bullet hit a person, a dog, or a coconut trunk.

Islanders described their feelings of powerlessness in poetry as well as prose. In this song, the people of Butaritari, Kiribati, speak of the period when the Japanese occupied their island.

E A Roko Te Bong Ba Ti Na Noko
(The day has arrived that we will go)
Unknown Composer
Butaritari, Kiribati
(Collected and translated by Mary Lisa Lawson Burke, n.d.)

The day has arrived that we will go;
we will follow the excellent wind.
We don't know where we will arrive,
we wish (?) ocean current of our homeland.

The wave flows over us,
we are almost dead.
We are thankful for the decision,
for we have arrived at our homeland.

We are truly the seven old men (elders)—
Bauro, Timau, Kanoua, Leta,
Tem Bauro, Moauata, Nanorinano—
before our questioning decision.

We turn to face the commander,
we are held by guns.
We will consent to the decision of everyone,
of hoping for the things of all.

MICRONESIAN WARTIME ROLES

Islanders' war narratives often reveal an attempt to understand their situation from a perspective of warring chiefly societies. But in the Pacific War, Micronesians did not play a "warrior" role. As noncitizens, they were excluded from the Japanese military and were assigned as laborers in military construction, light manufacturing, and agricultural work. As we shall see, a few groups of Micronesian men were recruited for quasi-military work groups, but for the most part, Micronesians were encouraged to support the emperor through military labor and agriculture. In the words of Raphael Gisog of Yap, their "tools were their guns"; their war work was represented as a type of soldiering.

Yapese were brainwashed to the point of "his tools are his guns." [Q: His tools are his guns?] It's like fighting. So his tools, that he wakes up in the morning and gets and goes, they're using that to fight. And instead of fighting, they're working. For the Japanese. So they should consider that work itself as a fighting. So on an average day—there isn't any such thing as an average day, depending on how you feel. Like, [you might think in an ordinary job] you can either slack today or no, because you're going as a fighter, and you're doing it as a fighter—so on a fighting day, just like on a fighting day, you go, wake up in the morning and start working, and anything that comes in front of you, goes, with your tools.

Aten Niesik, who was assistant chief of Udot in Chuuk, describes how he used such patriotic images of "soldiering" to argue for Micronesian rights:

There was a labor supervisor who was fighting with a Japanese soldier. He was from Udot, [named] Senip. According to the Japanese government rule, Japanese to Japanese, nobody could fight one who was higher in rank. For example, civilians could not talk against a lieutenant. The lieutenant might slap you and slap you, but you must just stand there; you cannot answer him back. It was thought that when a lower-ranked person fought against or answered against the higher rank, the lieutenant, that was as if you were fighting the emperor of Japan.

That's why, during this time, there was trouble between Senip and the soldiers, because Senip answered back to a higher-ranking soldier. Then he fought him. They held a meeting about him, to decide whether they were going to execute him. At that time, I was part of the meeting. Also at that time, we had a word we used to say every morning, called "seishi [oath or pledge]." That's Tenno Heika's [the emperor's] farewell message. The first part said [he recites it in Japanese]; that means, we are Tenno Heika's people. Second, [giving it in Japanese; then,] that means, we are going to give our lives for Tenno Heika. That's why we were in trouble [because of those words]. And that's why we had a meeting. And they said, "Why did that Udot person answer back to the Japanese soldiers?" They asked me to answer the question [as assistant chief of Udot, and the only Udot person at the meeting].

So when I answered, I said back to them, "What about Tenno Heika's message? The one that we say every day, 'We are Tenno Heika's soldiers.' What about us—aren't we Tenno Heika's soldiers? Are only you Japanese people Tenno Heika's soldiers? We are the grip of Tenno Heika's gun, Tenno Heika's people. We are not English soldiers or American soldiers, but Tenno Heika's people. So why is there a separation between soldiers and us? . . . Those people who are in Japan, they are the ones who fix bullets for guns, guns on the ships, and artillery, and planes. If you are at war, and you don't have the grip of the gun, you will be lost. Us, we don't make things like guns and bullets, we just farm, plant potato fields, and grow fruit."

They said, "You're right. We're the same, you and us." So that time I won.

Consider also this song about the relentless work under dangerous conditions by young men from Palau:

Ta-Re-Belau
Unknown Artist
Babeldaob, Palau, 1945
(Sung in Palauan and Japanese, after Japanese song style)
(Collected and translated by Wakako Higuchi, n.d.)

We are a group of young men
from all over Palau.

Our camp is in the middle of savannah.
We are lonely, all of us;
there is nothing to do for fun.

From morn till night,
over the clear surrounding area,
airplanes keep flying over
with the loud sound of their bullets.

We Palauans are
young men from all over.
The enemies are flying over us,
but we have to keep on working.

The bullets are falling
just like we're in the rain.
But with the war approaching its end,
the sound of airplanes is diminishing.

One characteristic Micronesian response to difficult experiences is to mark and control them through art and humor. The following dance song, which Venitu Gurtmag of Yap helped compose as a member of a young men's work group, humorously describes four kinds of wartime work done by Yapese at Japanese headquarters (*sirebu*; or *shireibu*, in Japanese): carpentry, agriculture, fishing, and cooking and serving in military kitchens. It was written near the end of the war, when the daily B-29 bombing raids had become predictable. Unlike the all-male work groups of fishermen and farmers, both men and women worked in the kitchens—hence the flirtatious end of the last stanza:

Work at Sirebu
Composed by "Tiger Group," Yap
(Translated by Andrew Kugfas)

The work at Sirebu will never be forgotten.
Now we're all going to separate and do our carpentry, because it's
    getting late.
The carpenters are striking at the nails,
but the nails aren't being hit because the carpenters are all drunk.
The nails are bent because a man [Japanese soldier] is standing at
    the door watching.

In the morning, the bell rings for roll call, and I'm still sleepy.
We're all going to go to work because it's getting late.
The farm workers use hoes, their furrows are all crooked,
because they are too sleepy, and because the air raid is coming.

Early morning, it's still chilly, all shivering, and I am diving in the
water.
Taking their [Japanese soldiers'] thought into myself:
never mind this cold, because we're going to have fish with our meal.
Light it, throw it [dynamite]—because something is humming!
[B-29 approaching]
"Don't worry—it's one of ours."

Working in the kitchen is very hard.
We're all going to go out now and search for food, because it's
getting late.
Oh, please wait for me, [girl]friend, have mercy on me, let me go
with you—
the other winks and says, "Come! Come!"

SOME MICRONESIAN HEROES

The Japanese used Micronesian labor primarily for agriculture and construc-tion, but several stories and songs acclaim the few men who took on military tasks on the Southwest Pacific front or elsewhere. At the time, Micronesians believed these men had been singled out for their courage and loyalty to the Japanese cause and were embarking on potentially dangerous assignments. If they succeeded in their mission, these individuals, their families, clans, chiefdoms, and lands would merit high status in Micronesian terms. People believed their sacrifice and devotion would bring honor from the Japanese as well. In retrospect, some of our interviewees had other thoughts: that perhaps the men's service and their lives had been exploited (see "Memorial Song of Kosrae" below). Because of military security and restricted communications, relatives seldom heard from those sent on distant service. Only when survivors returned was it learned that they had worked as military laborers—as steve-dores, carriers, and in other manual service—rather than as soldiers. Despite their noncombatant roles, those who returned were greeted as heroes.

Palau, the capital of Japanese Micronesia, was home to many Japanese immigrants, and Palauans experienced heavy Japanese influence. The following two songs about Palauan wartime volunteers reflect the influence of Japanese song styles. In the first, a young man tells about the sixty Palauans who were drafted to work for Nantaku (Nan'yo Takushoku company) in a survey group sent to New Guinea. They were known as the Palauan Young Men, or the Palauan Volunteer Group. This song tells of their departure and of the hardships of starvation, sickness, and loneliness they endured in New Guinea. The song is still performed today, as a group or solo, usually without instrumental accompaniment.

Palauan Volunteer Group

Composed by Emau from Melekeok, Palau, in 1944
(Sung in Palauan and Japanese)
(Collected and translated by Wakako Higuchi, n.d.)

I'm leaving home and
going very far.
We, young Palauans, are on
our way to the South.

There are about sixty of us.
We are Palauans,
but what we do is for Japan.

I just want to let you and everyone know
our work is difficult, it's a
matter of life and death.

The dangers and the snakes
are difficult to describe.
We crossed dangerous rivers and plains.

From inside the forest we stare at the sky.
How I miss my girlfriend back home!
Tell her about this hardship—
I am longing for the good times we had.

I'm in a foreign land, and the dawn is
approaching.

I stand envying the moon—
rising in the East, they might also
see it in Palau.

I depend on her kindness,
and I often dream of her.
But now what is happening?

Mesubed Michael of Ngchesar Village, Palau, also wrote a song about the Palauan Young Men. Its melody is adapted from "Aikoku no Uta" (Patriotic song), popular in Japan during the 1930s. It is largely in Japanese, with the second and third verses in Palauan.

Palau Chosatai No Uta (Song of Palau reconnaissance unit)
Composed by Mesubed Michael, Ngchesar Village, Palau
(Sung in Japanese and Palauan, adapted to a Japanese prewar song)
(Collected and translated by Wakako Higuchi and Moses Ramarui, n.d.)

1.   *Far from our home,*
     Palau youths advanced toward the south,
     some sixty members of a survey group.
     On our shoulders rests the name of Palau.
     The opportunity for us to devote ourselves
     to the emperor's country, Japan, has come.

2.   *Reporting our news to everybody*
     was hard work, which was at the risk of our lives.
     Bandits in the mountains, and snakes, were
     the dangers, which was beyond words—
     conquer steep mountain road and river.

3.   *Evening sky is extensively deep in the mountains.*
     Thinking of my loved ones who are in the city [Koror].
     The image of the gentle lady is
     the very picture of them come to my mind. . . .
     The night wears away in unknown country.

A firsthand account of the experiences of the Palauan Young Men comes from Elibosang Eungel of Airai, Palau (collected and translated by Wakako Higuchi, 1986):

In late 1942, I heard from my friends that Palau-shicho [Palau District Branch] was recruiting Palauan young men to go to New Guinea. More than sixty Palauans were selected as members, and I was one. There was no examination. Former convicts and other persons who had problems were also selected. We were called Palau Seinen [Palauan Young Men], but were members of the chosatai *[survey group]. When we started to leave for New Guinea, one official in the Palau-shicho said, "Please work hard together for the sake of our country."*

We took one goyosen *[government ship; about 10,000 t] which came from Japan. There were two other ships and all three carried many Japanese—scholars, professors, company employees, government officials, civilians. I heard that our work was to survey the natural resources of New Guinea. After three days we arrived in Manokwari. We were divided into small groups, and each one stayed with Indonesian families.*

The next day we were formed into eight groups, and I belonged to Number Four group. The hancho *[leader of a group] was Siakang Kulai from Melekeok. We started to unload food, oil, and gasoline from the ships. Food was placed in storage. Oil and gasoline were transported to the mountains. Our [Number Four group] included Shibayama Taii [lieutenant], Sato Taii [lieutenant], and five people of the naval landing party and others, to total thirty people. Professor Hatakeyama, Kyoto University, was also a member of my group. We went to Momi. Our destination was Angi, where there were two lakes. The Japanese said the climate there was the same as autumn in Japan.*

We were told that there were ruins of Dutch villas at Angi. It took four days to go from the beach in Momi to Angi on foot. The Japanese surveyed everything—insects, grass, trees, temperature, geological features, et cetera. We Palauans measured how many miles we walked and put up posts, each with a number. We didn't need to carry many [pieces of] luggage on our backs, because sixty Papuans were hired as carriers. We returned to Manokwari and helped minseifu *[civil government]. We built housing, made roads, and carried construction materials. We also worked for the Oji Seishi Company [the biggest paper company in 1985] as carriers. We didn't get any salary, but got* gunpyo *[military scrip]. We bought banana fries et cetera in the stores there. I enjoyed New Guinea. Our work was not heavy. However, we were afraid of malaria. Only one Palauan, Belesock, died there.*

We returned to Koror after six months. Everybody welcomed us. At that time, all Palauans had been drafted for the construction of their airport or worked as stevedores at Malakal. They served as choyo-ninpu *[drafted laborers]. I wasn't* drafted for either of these activities, but I was ordered to join Palau teishin-tai [volunteer group], which went to New Guinea after my return. I didn't know the reason why I was selected again. Other members enlisted as volunteers. I was in the same group as Simon Ramarui.

In August 1943, we, twenty-nine Palauans, went to Manokwari after stopping at Angaur because of a typhoon. We joined Kaigun Rikusen-tai [Japanese Marine Corps]. In those days, the war situation had worsened for the Japanese. We moved food and ammunition to storage inside the mountains and dug shelters.

On May 25, 1944, we carried five hundred kilograms of ammunition to Biak island and returned to Manokwari. It was two days before Kaigun Kinen-bi [Naval Memorial Day]. On Kaigun Kinen-bi, May 27, 1944, U.S. mechanized troops occupied Biak, where Taiwanese Hoko [Hokoku-tai?; corps' name] and Japanese Army troops were stationed. We were lucky. But we heard a rumor that the U.S. would invade Manokwari soon. We were ordered, "If the U.S. starts to land here, Palau Seinen [Palauan Young Men] should carry ammunition." However, the U.S. didn't attack Manokwari. We believe the reason the U.S. forces didn't attack was because they thought there was a big military force stationed in Manokwari. The roads there were very wide and had been constructed according to the order of an army commandant.

When the progress of the war turned worse for the Japanese, many Palauans were suffering from malaria. Eight Palauans were transferred to Makassar by ship. We were ordered to rikko [walk overland] to Sorong with a group of Japanese troops. But we refused, saying, "If we shall die finally, we want to die in Manokwari." We knew the U.S. troops had not come to Manokwari, and even if they attacked there, the damage would not be so heavy. We stayed in Manokwari, but a group of Japanese soldiers started to Sorong with food for one month. It was said that almost all of these soldiers died along the way.

There was minseifu [civil government] in Manokwari, whose top person was a civilian attached to the navy. Commander Sato was with us until the end of the war. It seemed obvious that Japan was close to defeat, so our work was to gather food. We Palauans took fish and wild pig. The Taiwanese Hoko-tai [Hokoku-tai] and Japanese soldiers cultivated farms every day. Though U.S. planes dropped bombs on our location, they did little human damage. We sometimes remembered Palau and our relatives, but nothing could be done. I knew Saipan and Peleliu were occupied by the U.S. then.

In August 1945 we gathered in our plaza and heard, "The emperor surren-

dered for the benefit of Yamato-minzoku *[the Yamato race]. The war is over."*
Everybody, including Dutch and Australian POWs, showed up in Manokwari
town. After the war, Papuans registered complaints concerning the wartime
activities of Japanese soldiers to the Papuan police and Allied authorities. The
Papuans claimed that Japanese soldiers had beaten or killed Papuans.

A representative of the Allied Forces, an Indian captain, asked us where we
Palauans wanted to go. All of us answered, "We want to return to Palau." A few
days later, our captain said, "You shall go to Palau by way of Japan." We dis-
cussed this and insisted, "The autumn season is coming to Japan, so that it will
be too cold for us to stay there. We may suffer from illness." Our captain agreed
with our concern. A few days later, our captain of a repatriation ship came and
said to us, "Let's go to Angaur. We can't enter the main Palau harbors because
many ships are sunk there." We said, "We want to go to any place, as long as it
is in Palau."

In September or October 1945 we arrived at Angaur after two years' absence.
The view of Palau from Angaur had changed completely. The islands looked so
white. A Palauan on Angaur who knew me said, "You will find something in
your home when you arrive there." My father had died during my absence.

We took a small ship to Koror. We were so surprised that Koror was so differ-
ent from the prewar days. There were no houses or buildings, and many Ameri-
cans were stationed there. I returned to my home with only one piece of luggage.
All my family welcomed me.

Another well-known Islander volunteer group was recruited from Pohnpei. Called the Pohnpeian Death Band in a Japanese account, because of the
danger of their adventure, this group of about twenty young men recruited on
Pohnpei—from Pohnpei, Yap, and Chuuk—traveled to supervise laborers in
Rabaul (New Britain, Territory of New Guinea) in June 1942. The survivors
returned to Pohnpei in October 1943—not to safety, but to find themselves
working for the Japanese military there as the air attacks on Micronesia began.
This song, recorded for us by Ludwig Alex of Mokil, is sung in Pohnpeian and
Japanese:

Untitled Song
Unknown Composer

News has surfaced that really breaks my heart—
they selected my sweetheart and took him to the land of death.

*Left every family in a hard place, crying, because the country is far
     away.*
All the families are crying, because they only returned for their funeral.
Greetings, my oldest brother, I am going.
Greetings to you all, because I am going.
My oldest brother, sayonara *[goodbye].*

The experiences of another group of Pohnpei men, those drafted for work
on Kosrae in July 1943, are well known in Pohnpei in part because a song
composed by two of them remains current, known and sung by younger generations. The 179 men from the chiefdom of Kiti spent the final period of the
war working on military projects on Kosrae, where they shared the difficult
labor conditions and food shortages of other workers there. The "Memorial
Song of Kosrae" is a formal song of commemoration, a type usually composed
following a significant event, such as the death of a notable person. It is sung in
Pohnpeian and Japanese, to the tune of a Japanese marching song.

Memorial Song of Kosrae
Composed by Linter Hebel and Salpa Martin

*Running there, Kosrae suddenly appears,
with mountains like those of Kiti chiefdom.
I begin to recall our happy chiefdom
that we were forced away from.*

*At one o'clock we reached the open sea of selfishness,
all of us prepared and going forth.
Myself, I believe there is no authority
for throwing my life away.*

*All of us total a hundred seventy-nine.
Four went away from us.
Six died.*

Chorus: *Quietly resting from our servitude.
Free from death.
All of us enjoy singing
praise to our chief,
who is the ruler of the world.*

We no longer believe
we are awaiting death.
There is shocking news.
Maybe we were dreaming.[1]

Chapter 8

THE TYPHOON OF WAR

GIVEN THE REMOTENESS of the islands, the effective Allied blockade, and laws prohibiting travel and the spread of war-related information, it is hardly surprising that most Micronesians knew little about how their experiences compared with those of others in distant locales. And in fact, we have seen that there is little reference to the wider view in wartime narratives. Instead, stories concentrate on personal hardships. The repetitive nature of those hardships lends itself to condensation: that is, a few dramatic incidents stand for the whole of the long period of suffering (for example, the repeated bombings or ongoing food shortages). This style of narrative also employs familiar local elements of myth and storytelling, in part told as habitual narratives in which events happen over and over again. Although stories about the initial arrival of the war are told in dramatic detail, those that follow typically are not. Peaks in the action, or climaxes, are limited, and those that do appear are caused by the actions of others. For these reasons, as well as those noted above, peoples of Micronesia commonly represent themselves as relatively passive victims of a disaster beyond their control.

The amount and sophistication of the war's technology (especially apparent on islands where land battles were fought) and its regular, repetitive, seemingly unrelenting bombardment (especially on the bypassed and neutralized islands) contributed to this sense of powerlessness. If advanced technology was a godsend to Allied forces, it verged on an otherworldly, supernatural force, or at least a strong force of nature, to Micronesians, who had not even known of its existence before they experienced firsthand its destructive force. The war blew across the islands like a violent wind, trailing devastation. Micronesians could do little more than endure its brutal passing. Peter Ianguchel from Yap uses this metaphor, explicitly likening war to a typhoon, in discussing the aftermath of war and the departure of the Japanese:

The chiefs of Yap said that those things left behind by the Japanese became the property of the Yapese on whose land they were located. Historically, war is like a typhoon. After a typhoon, whatever you find on your property becomes yours.

Islanders from many areas, with many different wartime experiences, reflect this sense of impotent waiting while the war raged:

[Q: What were people's ideas about the war?] Our ideas about the war—we just believed that we were going to die. We lacked food, because they [Japanese] con-

Utter desolation on Engebi islet, Enewetak, after U.S. naval shelling and air bombardment, February 19, 1944. (U.S. Navy photo, National Archives photo no. 80-G-216031)

trolled our food from the sea and on land. They controlled our lands, or islands. There was nothing for us to survive on. We were kinrosi [labor service, volunteer or drafted] of the Japanese. There wasn't any sign of life for us to believe we could take it anymore. (Koko Suda, Oneop, Satawan, Mortlock Islands)

I myself did nothing to prepare for the war. I was just awaiting death.

During the war, there was no fishing and no fires were lit. Otherwise, you could get shot. I had to cook in my rock oven at night and take food to my parents in the morning. People could no longer figure out what would happen with their lives because they were afraid, in shock, hungry, and searching for food. Perhaps some people were in shock. Many people had never heard gunfire or planes before. (Robert Gallen, Uh, Pohnpei)

Everyone was unhappy during the war. We were afraid. Every day I said to myself that maybe today was the day that I would die. (Yosko Miguel, Kiti, Pohnpei)

WAR FROM THE SAND SPITS

The way survivors and veterans talk about war is shaped, in part, by their vantage points. Gabrielle Rosenthal[1] compared German oral narratives of World War I and World War II, discovering that these stories are told in very different ways, even by individuals who experienced both wars. World War I, Rosenthal explains, was fought as a "war in the trenches," a vantage point from which experiences were diffuse, chaotic, and repetitive. Personal accounts of this conflict tend to consist of a single image or brief evaluation; they tell the story in condensed form. The especially burdensome nature of these experiences, she believes, is linked to the way veterans' accounts represent war as a natural disaster, where soldiers were victims of a power largely beyond their control. They lived day to day, in a relatively passive endurance of their situation.[2] Rosenthal also found the World War I stories to be more difficult to collect; they tended to emphasize war operations—external dates, places, units, date of conscription, descriptions of places, evaluations of experiences, and so on—rather than sequential narratives. In contrast, World War II was fought as a "war of mobility," with different implications for narrative form.

The Allied war in Micronesia was one of island hopping, with land battles fought in parts of eastern and western Micronesia, and bypassed islands rendered impotent through regular air attack while the main thrust of invasion continued toward Japan. For American and other Allied forces, the experience was largely that of a "war of mobility," to use Rosenthal's formulation. Their stories tend to be linear, sequential, epic narrations, as well as accounts that stress certain themes: death, bravery, or cleverness, for example. But the vision of the war was different for bypassed Japanese garrisons in Micronesia and for Micronesians themselves, who experienced the American island hopping and bombing as isolation and continual siege. In sharp contrast to American military histories, then, the local experience was similar to "war in the trenches"— or, we might say, a "war from the sand spits," with limited mobility and little opportunity to grasp the big picture of the conflict. While American military personnel proceeded along a narrative trajectory of attack, encounter, and conquest, Japanese troops and remaining civilians and Micronesians became increasingly huddled on blockaded islands, restricted in movement and even knowledge about the wider context of the war.

By war's end, U.S. planes and submarines controlled the air and the sea-lanes, severely limiting travel and communication. In describing the final days of ship travel, Klemente Actouka of Pohnpei indicates how the sense of mobility characteristic of the earlier seafaring Micronesian world contracted as "the seas closed" (in a Marshallese phrase) under the threat of Allied submarine and air attack:

Before the war, I was traveling on a ship; the ship that transported goods for the soldiers. Civilians took care of the ship and the soldiers took care of the guns. Before the war, I was on a ship called Nanyopwehki. This ship traveled a lot to the South Pacific before the war. We went to Tinian, Rabaul, Samoa, New Caledonia, Fiji, Tonga, Vanuatu, and the Solomons before the war. This was during the "business times."

Maybe I was twenty years old when the war started. I was in Chuuk. During that time [Admiral] Yamomoto's ship was in Chuuk, too. A plane came to Chuuk at that time, and Yamomoto's ship left by sunset. After three days, we left Chuuk for Pohnpei, and when we got to Pohnpei the bombing of Pohnpei had already begun.

The first plane that went to Chuuk was a lookout plane. We were already in Pohnpei when the bombing of Chuuk started. The day we reached Pohnpei was the same day that the bombing of Chuuk started. I heard that there were forty-three ships sunk in that bombing. They were transport ships carrying goods for the soldiers. We were in Pohnpei for one day and then we left for Kosrae. This was the last ship.

We got to Kosrae, I forget the year, but it was on March twenty-fourth at seven o'clock in the morning when the ship sank. It was destroyed by three American planes. We swam from the ship, and we were lucky because we were on the reef, not outside of it. Six soldiers were killed; two lived. And three passengers died. All of us that lived, including the two soldiers, numbered eighteen. Nine people from the ship were killed. And from then on, I was in Kosrae for one year and six months.

As the military powers joined in conflict, local people were commonly—though not always—forced to the margins. As we have seen, they were removed from their lands to make way for Japanese fortifications; relocated from likely targets to safer, more "rural" areas; and in the latter part of the war and after surrender, relocated when the U.S. military took land for its own bases. Sometimes this marginality was a welcome refuge, as when Chuukese from islands targeted for bombing were evacuated to less-fortified islands in the western part of the lagoon. On the other hand, marginality on bypassed islands was often experienced as a type of class deficit, where locals were expected to sacrifice food and labor to the Japanese military without compensation; their concerns, as noncitizen civilians, were pushed aside in the urgency of prosecuting the war.

Although some able-bodied men and women who labored in war work gained respect, increased their rank, and sometimes developed a wider perspective of the war, most Micronesians experienced social, as well as physical, marginalization. The sense of being entirely "out of the loop" during the war is often a marker of the common person's feelings of disempowerment. In the final months of war, especially on the bypassed islands, unequal access to information was a critical index of the battle for power between the starving Japanese and local people. The Japanese knew they were losing. At the same time, they were almost entirely dependent upon local people for their subsistence. They needed to maintain control over Islanders, which they did in part by restricting the flow of news.

Micronesians remember their ignorance about the progress of the war. News of the turning tide of war after the battle of Midway in 1942, the imminence of the Allied attack on the Marshall Islands at the start of 1944, and the end of the war were restricted by security concerns and propaganda. Islanders who spoke Japanese and worked closely with Japanese civilians or troops were most likely to track such news. Indeed, people's rank undoubtedly could have been measured by their access to privileged information. Geography also mattered, with those living in urban areas, or areas with larger Japanese populations, having more knowledge.

LEARNING THE WAR IS OVER

We usually think of the end of the war as a clear-cut event, but just as Micronesians date "the start of the Pacific War" to different times—depending on their community's particular hardship—so can the war's end be dated to local experiences. In the former Allied colonies of Kiribati and Guam, "the war ended" definitively with Allied victory in battle and the establishment of military government rule. But war's end was experienced quite differently in islands of the former Japanese Mandate. For some, the sense of being out of the loop lasted until the final moments of the war, with Islanders recalling that news of Japan's surrender was kept from them.

Joseph Ernej reflects feeling out of the loop when he describes the arrival of the U.S. Navy invasion fleet for the battle for Enewetak. Based on his own observations, he speculates that the Americans initially offered surrender. (This event was also described by Ken Lebo in chapter 6.)

Perhaps there were a hundred [ships], because the entire lagoon was filled with them. . . . We [Enewetak people] looked out upon it and said, "Oh [watch out]!" but they had not yet landed. They just stayed there. . . . They went everywhere, Enjebi, Biken, that entire lagoon area was filled with ships. But they had not yet fired a shot. It was a thing of amazement. They just went out there and sat around for a while. We said, "What is it that they are doing?" Perhaps they were communicating to the Japanese and saying, "You, admit your error, surrender right away." But the fellow [Japanese officer] on this islet said, "No, we are not going to." And, well, they [the Japanese] did not talk things over on this islet. There was no such thing. They did not surrender. That fellow who was in charge of this islet was evil. He said, "Just keep going until every single person is dead."

Ernej and a companion were commanded to deliver a letter from Meden to Enewetak by sailing canoe, but "this was the time when they [the Americans] thought about placing their foot upon the islet . . . the time that the real battle began." During the invasion of Enewetak, Marshallese hiding in rough underground shelters ("holes") were crushed by invading U.S. tanks; of twenty-five

Enewetak people on the islet of Meden, Ernej says, fourteen were killed. As danger approached, Ernej and the others still had no information about what was happening; his account of the tragedy indicates his awareness of his lack of knowledge:

Well, that was the thing that damaged us, the Meden people. They crossed over the hole [with their tanks] and people died. Perhaps they were coming up on the land and there were so many trees, fallen kiden *[Messerschidia argenta], they did not see us. Do you see the holes where John and Mark were? Well, that is the place where the vehicles came and hurt them. There were many people inside, but the tanks came and . . . and so then, they just died. They did not shoot them, but they traveled over the top of them [crushing them].*

Raphael Gisog describes the gradual and somewhat confusing end of the war on Yap:

I learned that Japan had lost because a ship arrived, an American ship arrived, and they called the commander, along with a Yapese by the name of Mo'otan of Weeloey. He went with Edo and a number of officers to visit that ship. They visited the ship and when they came back they were given things, including Chesterfield cigarettes, and Lucky Strikes, and Camels. The Yapese suspected that something odd was going on; maybe Japan had lost the war. That evening I had finished working, so I went home. The family that I went to in 'Okaaw village— the Yapese man who went with [Commander] Edo came back and stopped at that family and gave cigarettes, those Lucky Strikes and Chesterfields. And in the morning when I went to work, I was given cigarettes by the Japanese—and you must understand that at that time cigarettes were very, very scarce. So when I went to work in the morning, Edo also gave me cigarettes. A few days after the planes came very low, there was a big party at the commander's house, attended by commanders from all over Yap; and I heard also from some of them that the war had ended, not knowing who won before the ship arrived. Maybe they themselves knew, but I didn't know. And there was a party held at Edo's house because he was the commander in chief of Yap.

In this account of the end of the war on Kosrae, Osmund Palikun notes how the Japanese military authorities carefully managed information; the official word that the war had ended was disclosed only one day before actual surrender:

On September 7, 1945, there was a meeting for all the top Japanese officers. Our boss at this time was Fujuhara Aso. He was a master sergeant in the [Japanese] army division and in the navy he was a petty officer. He was there at the meeting that was held in Malem. That is where Kaka lived. After the meeting, he came back to Lelu and told the people that the war had stopped. He didn't mention that the Japanese lost. He just told us, "You are free," and that there was no more war.

But, maybe two weeks before that, there had been a white flag raised on the other side of Lelu, across the harbor. The meaning of that white flag was to show that Kosrae had surrendered, because at other places they had already surrendered on September 2, 1945, but we surrendered on September 8. On the morning of September 8, 1945, two American ships arrived. The names of those two ships were U.S.S. Hyman and U.S.S. Soley. They came to raise the American flag in Kosrae. So we gathered on the other side of the harbor [Sanrik]. On that day, the Japanese came and signed a document that showed that they agreed to surrender. From this time on, everyone was free; no more work.

Ichios Eas was on Tol, Chuuk, at the end of the war. The news was leaked to him by a Japanese soldier, who swore him to secrecy:

At that time, my wife and I were at the department called Yoshta butai [work group]. I was the supervisor for our group, but I was not told, nor was any other Chuukese. We feel that there was a regulation against revealing it to us. Even when the war was over, they [the Japanese] did not let any Chuukese know. But when the war was over, they had a departmental meeting, excluding us. But there was one soldier who came down after the meeting and revealed to us that the war had ended. He also told us not to tell anyone, or they would cut off his head. We did not believe him, until the Americans came to take the Japanese away. That is when it became clear to us that the war was in fact over.

On Fefan in Chuuk, Tarup Ounuwa also recalls that a Japanese soldier secretly told him the news:

The soldiers knew about it [the end of war], but they didn't tell us. One soldier who worked on the mountain came down to their base. He was asked, "What are you going to do here?" [He answered,] "I just came to give you a cigarette, and to tell you that we've lost. You guys don't have to worry, because the war is going to stop." At that time, I was cooking in the cookhouse, and I just heard this from the soldiers who talked to one of the keri *[policemen] inside—he was a Japanese* keri—*and that man said, "Don't talk too much! Because we don't want anybody to hear." They said they were going to surrender, because a big bomb had been dropped on Nagasaki. One of the soldiers told him not to speak loudly because there was a Chuukese present, and they didn't want me to know. He said that if I knew that they'd lost, I'd go out and tell the Chuukese, and they were afraid we might beat them. So they didn't tell us because they were afraid of us. So they just talked in secret, they didn't tell anybody. That's why nobody heard about it.*

Chapter 9

QUESTIONS OF LOYALTY

LAYERED OVER ACCOUNTS depicting Islanders' relative powerlessness, lack of knowledge, and shock are themes speaking to the challenge of coming to terms with two sets of foreigners, the war's major combatants: Who were these warriors? Why were they here? What would be the fate of local people as a result?

We should not underestimate the sophistication of these questions. Micronesians at the time of the war—and perhaps even more today, after additional decades of colonial and postcolonial political experience—were at home with complex social and political interactions. Indeed, stories about both groups are complex and multifaceted, reflecting the long period dealing with civilian Japanese before the war and the even longer postwar history of relationships with Americans after the United States took over governance of the region.

It is revealing that Micronesian stories set during the war are largely focused on the Japanese. And despite their long affiliation with Japan, elders do not represent the Japanese unproblematically in accounts of this era. While an occasional speaker may reveal strong loyalty to the Japanese in the stories he or she tells, by far most interviewees were neither consistently loyal nor, at least in hindsight, supportive of the war. Far fewer stories dating to the actual wartime period elaborate on the Americans; instead, most stories that focus on Americans begin near the war's end, and especially after American occupation (these will be discussed further in chapter 12).

THE JAPANESE AS FRIENDS AND ENEMIES

Recall that Japan had been the colonial power in Micronesia for almost three decades before the war. Though their economic development policies were

Islanders who emerged from cave shelter, on Angaur, Palau. Received December 23, 1944. (U.S. Navy photo, National Archives photo no. 291698)

self-serving, the Japanese had also established well-regarded schools and hospitals. Although their style of punishment was strict and often embarrassing for local people, they had also established a clear-cut set of laws as well as a policing system. While business favored colonizers, Micronesians had many sources of income. Urban areas offered wage labor; outer islands benefitted from small-scale markets for handicrafts and for copra and other raw materials. Beginning in the late 1920s, immigration policies encouraged Japanese and Okinawans to settle in Micronesia. While Islanders say they worried about the risks of too many immigrants, many established friendly relations with the newcomers, even ties of marriage or adoption.

Thus, Micronesians had strong, long-standing links with Japanese institutions and individuals by the time war approached. Their everyday lives were shaped by Japanese laws, expectations, and the example of thousands of immigrants. Especially for elites, and in developed areas, Micronesians were considered, and considered themselves, members of the empire.

As Teruo Marcus (Weno, Chuuk) describes life before the war, note the personal, detailed depiction of individual Japanese and remembered interactions with them:

Before the war, the food sources were abundant and varied. Store items were cheap, and the Japanese distributed food, too [to their employees]. The ones who stayed behind here on Weno prepared local food such as pounded breadfruit, taro, and other things, and delivered them to the ones working on Toloas. The reason people delivered local food to workers on Toloas was that they wanted to eat their share of rice given by their employers [i.e., workers would give rice to those who gave them local foods]. That's how things were, way before the war. The Japanese were very generous.

Let me tell a story of two brothers who came to Weno and established their business venture. There was one time the business was bankrupted, but the elders from Osap [a place in Iras on Weno] lent them their uninhabited lands to grow copra, and the proceeds were to be used to run the business. For this generosity, one of the brothers took one of the local fellows to Japan and paid back the hospitality given to him and his brother, and brought him back here. After the eldest died, I and a guy named Rochon took his place in staying with the brother. During our stay with him, he treated us just like one of the Japanese—he wanted us to eat at the table with them, too. I'm only saying this to show how generous the Japanese were before the war. . . . The only problem was that local people were not allowed to conduct or to have a business. They didn't educate the Chuukese on what was beneficial and essential for the development of a society economically.

As we see from his comments, Micronesians understand that the Japanese colonial order was organized for the benefit of colonists, not Islanders. Yet they also recall good feelings and benefits from those times, as in this description by Esperansa Samo:

Before the war, on our islands, Moch Island in the Mortlocks, we [Mortlockese and Japanese] really lived in peace. We worked together, helped each other, loved each other, and shared our foods together. As far as our chief, he was happy and treated us well. He loved his people very much. Our churches were well organized. . . . Our relationship with the first Japanese newcomers was peaceful. The Japanese newcomers were mainly businessmen. They were nice to us, and friends. They sold many things at cheap prices. We lived together harmoniously.

Islanders who lived in immigrant-populated areas agreed that when the war began to transform the islands, relations with the Japanese became complicated. People recall that in a very short time the Japanese ethos had changed, and the taken-for-granted patterns of daily life were turned upside down. Hierarchical relations between the Japanese and the second- and third-class peoples hardened. Changes were not all negative, however; many story-tellers who were young at the time remember the excitement and the increased economic and social activity that accompanied the move toward war, and in some cases shared military preparations and training brought local people and Japanese closer together.

Istor Billimont lived on Siis Island in Chuuk Lagoon, where he met many immigrants and officials. He began a conversation about the prewar era by noting that some Japanese were good to Chuukese, while others used force or threats and "did not want any local people to eat with them, nor did they allow them to walk outside their houses." Then he describes a friendship with a Japanese boy that continued for nearly fifty years, to well after the end of the war:

I had a friend named Saito. We worked together, and it was like we had the same mother. We loved and cared about each other. . . . We worked together in the village called Sapuun, Toloas. At that time we used to transport gasoline to Eten Island and transport back the empty drums to Sapuun. At that time we were friends, because he was the only one among the Japanese who was very nice to the Chuukese. When he came back from Japan to visit me, he told me that all the Japanese were dead because they were bad during the war. [Q: When was the last time he came to Chuuk to visit you? What year?] 1990—either in September or February. [He visited] four times. The first time he came out here, he had trouble finding me. He asked a man named Osien at Christopher Inn about me. When we met, we did not recognize each other. I recognized him after he mentioned some of the names of Chuukese we used to work with. . . .

[Q: How did the friendship between you and your friend Saito begin?] We worked together [at a gasoline depot], and we liked each other because at that time we were the young ones among the workers. Sometimes he would invite me to drink his tea with him.

Recurrent themes in war stories indicate turning points in Micronesians' reassessment of their relationship with the Japanese. These mark moments when Micronesians recognized that the ground had shifted, and the war was reshaping their lives. Eventually, the excitement of war preparations was overshadowed by labor demands and growing uncertainty about the future. Part of the shaping of war stories has to do with Micronesians becoming less comfortable with Japanese, as the familiar immigrants and civilian officials were replaced by military troops, then as military rule became harsher and conditions worsened over the months of war. Once Allied attacks began, Micronesians knew they were in danger because of the Japanese presence in their islands. Yet even after the first battles were under way, many Micronesians' sentiments continued to rest with the Japanese.

The sense of danger and oppression heightened as time passed, and the blockade and air war created conditions of near-starvation. While Micronesians continued to work for the Japanese military, they sensed danger in the troops' dwindling morale. In Micronesians' recollection, Japanese propaganda was ineffective or so transparent that it created further doubt about their actual strength.

Late in the war, when military security restricted movement, friendly relations with Japanese could be maintained only covertly. Heightened security measures made Islanders wary of the military. Food scarcity created competition between Micronesians and Japanese troops, forcing Islanders to survive by theft and subterfuge. Micronesians' willingness to die for the emperor could no longer be guaranteed, mutual distrust set in, and rumors spread that the Japanese military planned to exterminate Islanders.

In short, over less than a decade, Micronesians moved from relations so close that their families intermarried with Japanese immigrants to a situation of such fear that they thought the Japanese intended to kill them all.

When Ichios Eas of Chuuk talked about the very start of the war, he recalled what to him was a significant event, an act that struck him as emblematic of the Japanese patriotic ethos, "go for broke." The interviewer is a young Chuukese man who adds his own perspective:

Japanese ships experienced many losses and much damage . . . in the open seas. When I was in Nampo [the main dock on Toloas], damaged ships and submarines came in. One time we went out to bring water to a damaged submarine near Eten. They had to immediately cut off our rope from the submarine as it completely sank. . . . I was on the ship that supplied water then, and was out to provide water for the submarine when it sank. [Q: With the crew?] When it was about to sink, all of the crew members went back inside the submarine and closed it and went down with it. No one was left.

That is the code that the Japanese live by. [Q: Go all the way.] Go all the way! They do not worry about losing their lives, rather than turning back. [Q: It means that if they return they will kill, penalize their families, right?] I do not know the underlying reasons for not worrying about their lives. [Q: No kidding, as their saying goes, "Go for broke." But was there not a chance that the submarine left after it submerged?] No, it is still there today. They have come to dive on it. [Q: Is that the one that many human skeletons were found on?] That's right. That is where human bones were found. [Q: If that were me, I would say, "Wait, let me get out first."] They could have gone to Eten, which was not far at all. . . . The submarine is still there today. They [the crew] could have gone to Eten, which was not far at all. Instead, they cut off our anchor and pushed us away as the submarine was quickly sinking. And everyone got in and went down with it.

Sinino Mateas of Tol in Chuuk describes how, later in the war, this Japanese "go for broke" ethos was occasionally turned against their own soldiers, sparking fear among the Chuukese that it would also be used against them:

If Americans had been late in arriving in Chuuk, we would have been dead, because they had already hauled some people into caves to kill them. Just like those other Japanese who got sick. The commander would come to their house and ask them if they couldn't work. And those [sick] Japanese said no, because they were sick. Then the commander would tell the other soldiers to dig a hole so they could bury that sick man. Yes, they really buried those sick Japanese alive. I swear! This was in Tol.

How are these shifting attitudes toward Japanese reflected in wartime narratives? Rapid militarization and strict security increased Micronesians' sense of marginalization and disempowerment. In contrast to accounts of prewar life, stories from this period contain less personal detail about individual Japanese; instead, the Japanese are referred to by standardized titles. Only Micronesians holding positions in the Japanese colonial order provide more elaborated views. Equally commonly, accounts of the years of military buildup and of the first year of war become progressively condensed, compacted into single events filled with important meanings and moral significance. While there are some exceptions—as we have seen, a recollection of a particularly indulgent officer or an occasional close friendship with an enlisted man—real human relationships with Japanese and significant details about wider events do not reenter most storytellers' accounts until the war is at an end. In other words, the shape of Micronesian stories of the war become increasingly localized and increasingly detached from matters Japanese. In this sense, they are reminiscent of the "citizen as spectator"—as critical observers, but not decision makers.[1]

In these selections from a long interview with Thaddeus Sampson of the Marshall Islands, we see his recollections shift from describing his confidence in Japanese prewar promises to a recognition of how the war changed relations between Japanese and Micronesians:

It was my good fortune with the Japanese, because they still needed me to translate and to tell them the customs of the Marshallese and discuss the needs of the Marshallese. I was highly enough ranked with them that they thought about taking me to stay with the jidi *[chidi, prefectural governor], with the high official, so that I could stay with him in his office, interpret for him, and take care of his needs. So when he made the circuit of the islands, I went with him. [Q: But the thing is, on account of the beginning of the battle . . .] Yes, on account of the beginning of the battle, all sort of things were ruined. Nonetheless, if the war had not begun, I would have been one of the ones who was selected to go to Japan and go to school. . . .*

. . . Before the war, the Japanese were extremely considerate. But during the time when the battle became intense, they were dangerously cantankerous. [Q: And why was that?] Well now, I do not know. They were kind, but if you erred slightly, "There was no excuse." [Q: You would really be harmed?] Die. [Q: But was it because the civilians and the army personnel differed from one another?] Well, the soldiers also had good thoughts amongst them. During the times prior to the battle, they were very kind. But at the time that life changed because we were in the midst of the battle, it was prohibited to commit the slightest error. [Q: You would be hurt?] You would die right in that location. . . .

[Q: Were there people you knew of who went off with the Japanese and served as soldiers with them?] That is correct; there were some who thought that they would stand up against the Americans, because they did not understand the kinds of customs [of warfare] . . . of the arriving Americans. They were taken in by the thinking of the Japanese soldiers. And so they went ahead, and they were hurt. Kwajalein is an example. When they saw the Japanese and the kind

of strength that they were building and the things that they were doing to ready themselves for war, well, they said that they would side with them. But when the Americans landed, then the difficult time arrived and then they did not know what to do. They did not know where their strength and where their best interests lay. And those were the ones who thought they would try to assist the Japanese.

Rutok Ruben describes how food scarcity on Uman in Chuuk Lagoon produced dangerous conditions in which Japanese soldiers strictly monitored resources and punished transgressions. Note that he gives the name of a Japanese soldier who intervened on his behalf:

[Q: Were you ever beaten?] Yes, I was. After work, I went out into the mangroves and took four ripe coconuts. I had three when I returned. The watchman asked me where I took the copra from. "I saw them among the mangrove trees at Nepon [village in Uman]." He told me to give them to him, but I said, "No." They started to beat me with a stick. They might have hit me seven times when a man named Niso, who was a soldier, came. He asked the Japanese, "Why did you beat this guy?" They lied and said, "He stole potatoes." I told Niso that was not really the reason: "They told me to give them the ripe coconuts, but I didn't want to, and they started to beat me." The other Japanese were holding the three coconuts.

Then Niso said, "You'd better give this Kanaka [Islander] his coconuts." The Japanese gave me the coconuts. But Niso took the Japanese soldiers to another place called Monow, where their leader was. Niso told the leader what they had done to the Kanaka, and then, the leader slapped the Japanese. [Q: Were they hungry?] Of course! Yes, because the food was insufficient. . . .

The farms were not for us, but for the soldiers. They nailed up numbers on a piece of board on every coconut tree and breadfruit tree. They wrote the name of their troop. But if we climbed the trees, we would be beaten nearly to death. Yet the trees were ours; they forcibly went in and numbered the trees. [Q: What did they say?] "Don't you guys pick any fruit from our trees." Suppose somebody ventured to speak in opposition, the Japanese would beat him, beat him. But the farms—instead of growing crops, we stole them. The sign of our starvation is that we ate banana root mixed with a bit of rice. They rationed it out in an empty coconut shell. One person, one shellful. But actually, the work was beyond any limit; exhausting.

Chuuk suffered severe food shortages due to the posting of a large garrison in the lagoon and an effective Allied blockade and air war; many Chuukese have tales to tell about harsh military punishments, especially for contravening the strict control of food sources. Here is an account from Osong Seleti, of Romonum:

I was going up to the mountains, and tried to dig up this sweet taro of mine. Just then, a Japanese soldier happened by and asked who I was, and I said I was Osong. He said, "Why are you stealing taicho's [commanding officer's] sweet taro?" I said, no, it belonged to me. He then came and started hitting me. After awhile I ran away to town, away from the mountain. Then he hunted me down until he caught up with me. He took me up the mountains, where he tied my hands and legs and proceeded to hang me about one and a half feet off the ground. Then the officer called his soldiers, and each—with a baseball bat—began taking turns hitting me ten times each. Ten hits for me from all the soldiers. I could not feel any more strength. I was already thinking I was dying.

[Q: Did your bones break?] Here, my bones were crushed into pieces. The flesh was hanging out here. Then the officer said, "If anyone uses that latrine, then he should also hit Osong." So then, one went to the latrine, and on his way he took the bat and hit me. On his way back, he did the same. At that time, I was surely thinking I was going to die. Going to the latrine and back, my life was ebbing.

At three o'clock I was taken down and untied. One brother of mine, Chipen, had to carry me, because I was dying. A Chuukese man came and massaged me. I was vomiting blood while he was doing this! It took him about three months before I could try walking in and out of our house. Then, I was getting my strength back.

Narrators also recount active Micronesian responses to harsh treatment, as in this story told by Aitel Bisalen about his time on Toloas, the center of Japanese rule in Chuuk:

There were many Japanese who beat me or punished me, but I never gave up. They hit me and I hit them back. One time, I was called to the office. I was a bit late after lunch—all the workers went back to work and I was putting the food away. I didn't expect the Japanese to get upset, because I was one of the bosses.

I went down, and my boss [who was Japanese] scolded me, "Why are you late?"
"Because I was putting the food away." I told him, "I don't care whether I'm
late or not, because we both work for money. You work for money, and I work
for money also." And that guy said, "No, that's not the way it's supposed to be,
because we work to help the Japanese so they will win the war." I said, "Do you
mean the few minutes that I was late will make the Japanese lose the war?" Then
my boss came and slapped my face. He grabbed me and pushed me toward the
office, and we both fell down on the boat [they were on the dock at Toloas]. I was
on top, and I was pushing him down into the boat. When I was on top of him,
my uncle (my mother's brother) came—he saw another Japanese coming with a
stick to beat me—my uncle came in time and pushed that other Japanese, and
he fell down. I was lucky; if my uncle hadn't been there, they would have beaten
me up. Some of the Chuukese came and stopped us all from fighting [he and his
uncle were both fighting with the Japanese]. I told that Japanese I was fighting,
"I could take away your life, kill you."

Then that Japanese man went to the office and reported. Then I reported
to the office. They asked me what was the cause of the fight. The Japanese told
me that I was right. Then they told me to go outside, and they started beating
me! One of the ones beating me was a Chuukese, a chingke *[a local policeman].*
The Japanese told him to beat me. . . . After they finished beating me, the Japa-
nese told the Chuukese man to cut my hair like this: [they shaved a swath from
front to back, then one from side to side, shaped like a cross]. Then they sent
me back to work. Then when I walked down, they laughed at me. [Q: Were you
ashamed?] Of course I was ashamed, because of that funny haircut. The next
day, they called me to the office again. They asked me, "Why are you so different
from the other bosses? Whatever I tell them to do, they just do it. But when I ask
you to do something, you never obey." Then my boss came and grabbed me and
beat me. At that time, I was still young, about sixteen or seventeen.

Recall, though, the complexity of the situation in different areas of Micronesia. Palau, civilian headquarters of the Japanese Mandate, had seen inten-
sive immigration and economic development. It was heavily fortified, and
Palauans were asked to express loyalty to the empire by contributing cash and
labor to the military effort. Here, Andres Demei (in a comment collected and
translated by Wakako Higuchi, 1986) describes continued Palauan wartime
loyalty:

In July or August 1944, a squadron of U.S. ships bombarded Melekeok from the sea. Soldiers in Yamomoto butai [work group] ordered us to escape to the mountainous interior. But Lomisang, chutai-cho [squadron leader], refused by saying, "If the U.S. lands [in front of] our forces, we will die fighting alongside the Japanese soldiers."

MILITARY SECURITY AND ACCUSATIONS OF MICRONESIAN SPYING

By the end of the war, with central Micronesia isolated and under siege, security was tight, and the Japanese military were suspicious of Micronesian activities. Rumors created dangerous situations, and Micronesians describe complex currents and changes in their understanding of and relationships with Japanese. Rosete Hebel of Kiti, Pohnpei, recalls friendly relationships with soldiers, but her story also indicates how dangerous interaction with the military could be:

I will say that one time I went to Kiti, and my father's house was a resting place for the soldiers. While I was there, one of the soldiers who was very friendly to us—his name was Suiisang—he came and told me that Miyaka [Miyako, Okinawa?] was captured that night at twelve o'clock. Deniang [Denang, Vietnam?] was also captured by the Americans. And the next day I went to Madolenihmw at Lohd, where one of the policemen stayed, Anton. And I was talking to a woman named Lienweirohi. And she told me that the Americans had dropped bombs on Kosrae and killed those Pohnpeians who were there. Then I told her that I hadn't heard of it. What I heard was that Miyaka was captured at twelve o'clock and Deniang at eight o'clock. I told her that I heard it from the soldiers, and then I left her.

That night, my daughter Kasiko and I were staying at home when the police came and told me to go down to the office. I was walking down the road, and the small sticks scratched my face; it seems like I couldn't feel anything because I was really afraid, because the Japanese said that if anyone talked about the war they would be killed. When I got there the Japanese policeman came; he was a very cruel man. And he told me to come and asked me if I was Rosete. I said yes. He asked if I came from Kiti. And he asked if I said that Miyaka was captured, and I said yes. He also asked who said that, and I told him that it was one of the soldiers. And he said, "A real soldier, or those that were treated as soldiers [mili-

tary workers]?" And I told him that it was a real soldier. I don't know if he was a secretary, but he had a real title. He asked, "What did he say?" I told him that his name was Suiisang and that he said that Miyaka was captured at twelve o'clock and Deniang at eight o'clock, and the war was almost over. One woman, a sister of Joseph Route's mother, asked him why they didn't beg forgiveness [surrender], and he just raised up his hands.

The next day when I left, the man [the Japanese policeman] said thanks and that if I heard that again not to tell anyone. He also asked how come I knew, and I told him that my father's house was a resting place for soldiers. And he told me if I heard it again not to tell anyone, but to come and tell them in the office. When I left there it felt like something moved away from inside of my stomach. I haven't felt that scared again; that was the first time I had it.

My daughter was with me and I said if they were going to kill me, who was going to take care of her? Because they said that one drop of alcohol is more important than the lives of [Pohnpeian] people. I still remember that man Suiisang.

Manuel Hartman of Tatiw was one of several Chuukese whose part-European ancestry attracted suspicion from the military police:

[Q: What was it, what happened? They said you were in jail.] Yes. We were living here, and then it happened, about [a man who] made up a lie, on Uman, so the Japanese came looking for us. [Q: You and your brother?] Me and my father, the Nauruans, the priests. There were priests, also foreigners, one Frenchman and one Swede. We were the ones who were dragged to Toloas. [Q: You mean they just came in and dragged you out?] Yes, they dragged me out and beat me up, until my skull broke. Then my father, they took him and tied him up. . . .

We were still in bed. We were not awake yet, because it wasn't morning yet. We were still sleeping, and we were under mosquito nets, because there were mosquitoes. They walked in and just pulled the nets down. Then they grabbed us and started beating us, me and my father. They took my father and hung him up in a tree. And then I was beaten until I passed out. Then they went and took [their accuser] and brought him over, and they went back to Toloas.

Then it was night. Then the next day came, and they came back again. When they came, our bodies were just swollen from being beaten up. They told us they were taking us to the beach [facing Parem] to execute us. Then they tied our hands, and [when they got there] they tied us to coconut trees. The soldiers who lived there came by and said, "Just tell the truth. Because we never saw you do anything bad—we never even saw you going places; you were with us in our company working all the time. So we have witnessed you are good people." And the officer also told them that we didn't do anything wrong.

So they took us out on a boat and took us to Toloas. We got to Toloas and walked the street with tied hands until we got to the office, where they separated us, but kept our hands tied. When it was time to eat, the police gave us one rice ball each. And then, the second night, they told us to go. "You are free to go back." [Q: Because they found nothing?] Yes.

Sister Magdelina Narrhun and her family of Uman, Chuuk, had a similarly frightening experience when her father was suspected of spying:

During that time, those who were working for the soldiers sent a message to my uncle to prepare all the women to come [to these workers] and dance for them. When my uncle told us, the women didn't want to do it; we escaped or ran away. So he told the men to be prepared, because they were going to do what we were supposed to do. The ladies went fishing, and the men went with my uncle to those workers. The officer asked, "Where are the ladies?" and my uncle said that we were all fishing. Then he asked, why did we go, since he asked for women? Then he started to beat him [my uncle] and cut him with a cutlass, and that's when my uncle told the soldiers that my father communicated with the planes. . . .

At night, while we were inside our house, the soldiers came and gathered around our house, and they brought guns with them. They were already beating my brother. He had just come from Toloas, so when they saw him, they took him and beat him and asked him if it was true that our father had spoken with the planes. [Q: Was it true?] No, it is not true. [Q: Why did they believe it?] My brother escaped. But we didn't know that they had beaten my brother. That's why we were very surprised when they came. They came and woke us up. They got inside our house, took Father and tied him and my little brother. When I went out, I found that they had already tied my father and my brother. But Mother didn't go out, because that was when she was very sick. So they took us, me, my father, and my brother, with them. They asked if we had seen my other brother, but we said no, we hadn't seen him. So they said that they were going to keep us until they saw my brother. But if they didn't see him we would stay there *forever. They tied us outside. My older brother came by and found us, so they took him and tied him also.*

While we were there, they started to beat my father and asked if it was true that he had spoken to the planes. My father said no, it was not true, but they kept on asking him. At that time they took a cutlass and started to scratch his neck and blood started to come out. But it was not a very big scratch. Then they took him to the other side, but I and my two brothers were still there. Then they went to look for the one that they beat up first [the one who had just come from Toloas], and they found him. When they brought him, his other eye had almost fallen out. [Q: Why?] Because they really beat him badly. When they brought him over, we just stared at him, because his body was really black. They brought him over and beat him also. Then that's when they started to beat us all. Then they went and brought Taro and his family [the ones who had said that his father spoke to the planes] and his friends. They took Ropech from Tetiw and took Ananso from the soldiers because he was not eligible to be a soldier, because [they thought] he was a spy. They took us all together and beat us.

One time when we [Sister Magdelina Narrhun and her family] went out to the small uninhabited island, [that] was the time the Americans came in to us [in a submarine] and gave us soap and soft drinks and bread. So that was when my uncle started to think that my father was a spy. But it was not true. So they continued to ask us, but we said no. Those of us who said no, they beat us, but those who said yes, they let them live. They didn't beat them. We stayed for three days, and all those days they beat us. My father told us not to change what we had said in the days before, because they were also writing down what we said on the first day. So the second day we talked again, and they checked to see whether it was the same as what we'd said before. We couldn't talk to each other, but when a Japanese (someone who felt sorry for us) was guarding us, then that's when we could talk, so that's when Father told us not to change what we had said in the days before.

They took my three brothers and laid them down on the ground and put a large [piece of] metal under their neck and they poured water inside their noses—not inside their mouth, but in their nose. But they didn't give up, they just kept saying what they had said before. The days went on and the brother of my mother saw that we didn't change what we said before, so he told his wife that they were going to tell [the Japanese] that he was just lying, that what he said was not true, because he was now feeling sorry for us.

So when they said that they were lying, the Japanese started beating them.
They put us [Sister Magdelina Narrhun and her brothers and father] in a cave.
Then the officers came and said that all of us were going with them, except me
and my three brothers, because we were the ones that hadn't changed what we
said before, and also my father, but they said that he had to go with them because
he was a spy. They took him to Toloas. "They are going before a judge in court,
and if they lose, then you are all going to die." Then my brothers went and asked
if they could substitute for my father to go to Toloas, but the Japanese said no.
"Because this is not a thing, but if it shows that you are a spy, then the families
of Narrhun are going to be assaulted." They had already prepared a hole. [Q: A
hole for what?] For us to be killed inside. . . .

They took them and judged them. We won, but they just kept my father,
they didn't let him go. . . . My father and a priest were the ones in jail. When the
bombing started, that's when they took them out from jail.

THREATS OF EXTERMINATION AND FEARS OF CANNIBALISM

Sister Narrhun's mention of a "hole," a grave already prepared for her family,
is echoed throughout the region in stories of Japanese plans to exterminate
local people. Such accounts express the broken trust between Japanese and
Micronesians near the end of the war[2] and contain other important meanings.
The stories express long-standing fears that the Japanese planned to appropriate all of Micronesia's lands. Given the close interweaving of land and identity
among Pacific Islanders, this is a fear of death twice over. Extermination stories
also express Micronesians' ambivalence about their standing in the empire.
Although ranked low in the ethnic hierarchy, they were expected to display the
unwavering loyalty to the emperor shown by soldiers who committed suicide
rather than admit defeat. Some stories describe Japanese threats of extermination as a way to ensure Islanders' dedication to the cause until the very end.

Extermination represents the darkest, most antisocial element of war. In
the stories, threats of extermination may be overcome through a sympathetic
Japanese officer who protects local people from the abuses of other officers or
the inhumane commands of distant headquarters. In all cases, these stories
construct a view of the world that positions local people, Japanese, and Americans vis-à-vis one another in scenes with moral messages. While the theories
vary depending on the storyteller, tales of extermination always depict the

most extreme limits in terms of which moral actions can be measured. Several examples will indicate the kinds of stories people tell about suspected plans to massacre Micronesians near the end of the war:

They were planning to kill the people. When they told the people to gather at Mutunnea Channel [Lelu] to have canoe races, they [the Japanese] felt that they were going to lose, so that is why they made this plan, to kill all the Lelu people at that canoe race. Some of the Japanese soldiers whispered to some of the Lelu people that they had a plan to kill them. So what the soldiers did was go in among the people and sit with them to watch the race. That is why the Japanese soldiers could not shoot and kill all of the people. (Anna Brightly, Lelu, Kosrae)

During the same years as the war, a plan was set by the soldiers to kill all of the Islanders. This was because their food supplies were very low, and some of their soldiers were dying of hunger, although they stopped the Islanders from harvesting their farms. But the plan was not carried out because the date of the plan was 9/8/1945, which was the date those two American warships arrived on Kosrae. This is why we celebrate September eighth as our liberation day. (Tolenna Kilafwasru, Malem, Kosrae)

There is a place in Sekere where the Japanese had all the people of Sokehs go and dig caves. They instructed us to go and hide in them when the Americans landed and started fighting. Luckily, a Japanese soldier friend of Nahnmadaundehd told him about the plan that the Japanese made. The Japanese had planned that if the Americans landed and started fighting them, they would have us hide in the caves and then kill us all. This was to prevent us from telling the Americans where they were hiding. So our Japanese friend told us never to go there. (Erwin Leopold, Sokehs, Pohnpei)

[Q: How did you know the war was over, and how did you get back to Satawan?] The Japanese ordered the men and women of Satawan to come back to Satawan, with the teenagers to be left behind. There was a secret then. There was one boy from Satawan who worked for the Japanese at that time. He was the one to give the secret to the chief of Satawan, about the Japanese intention for the Satawan women and men to come to Satawan in their best clothes, for as soon as they reached Satawan, the Japanese would slay them all. That was the secret that was passed on to the chief. (Ilar Matafan, Satawan)

I knew the end of the war [had arrived] with denshin-bira *[broadcast leaflets], which were distributed by U.S. planes. I picked them up twice, on July fif-*

teenth and August fifteenth. I didn't believe the news. One Japanese soldier said, "Nothing to be done." Another soldier said, "Stupid. Kill them."

I heard about a plan for mass suicide [shudan-jiketsu] from [my] friend who was hojo-kempei [military police]. I didn't care about it.

The plan was to make a big shelter to put depth bombs there, and choose people over forty-five years old and younger than fifteen years old as victims.

I informed my father. He said, "I'll commit suicide before someone kills me."
(Techitong Rebluud, Palau; collected and translated by Wakako Higuchi, 1986)

A well-known story from Palau is that of the legendary Japanese commander Morikawa, believed by many Palauans to have saved their lives at the end of the war. Yoshiko Ashio gives one account (collected and translated by Wakako Higuchi, 1986):

Morikawa Taicho [commanding officer] was responsible for Palauans. We believe he was a spy and saved our lives. Soldiers in Ngatpang prepared the ground as a bomb shelter. According to someone, Japanese soldiers had planned to order Palauans to go inside. The soldiers would then switch on the bomb. Morikawa Taicho came to our village in August 1945. It was the first time he visited Palauan villages himself. He told us to prepare food and clothes for one week's stay. Also, he said to us, "Take your mattocks. You come to Ngatpang to work on the farms. We must plant food for the soldiers. It is not true that the war is over. Any person who can walk must come to work. Children must stay here." He came to our village with two soldiers. He said, "I will order the day when you come to Ngatpang after I visit all the villages. Maybe one week from now."

We prepared taro and okura [okra?] and wrapped them by cloth after he left.

After Morikawa Taicho left Ngiwal, he was missing for a while. One Palauan saw him climb Todaiyama in Ollei. He saw one light in the darkness. Palauans say that was Morikawa's signal to U.S. ships located between Kayangel and Ngarchelong. Two soldiers were waiting for him. They returned to Ngatpang. Morikawa Taicho asked the kempei-tai [military police], "Please wait one more week before ordering the Palauans to come here." Within this one week Japan surrendered. Everybody said, "Morikawa Taicho saved our lives."

On the morning of about August twenty-fifth or twenty-sixth, which was just

one week later, Morikawa Taicho arrived in Ngatpang. A bell rang in our vil-
lage. We were surprised at it and came from the houses. Shidokan informed us
that the Japanese had surrendered. He said, "Please forget the past and wait for
peace with friendship. Please forgive me for saying severe things to you. Peace
has started." We all cried together.

We believe Morikawa Taicho was a spy. According to my friends, he went to
Koror, but was missing. One Palauan saw him go to a rock island alone and send
telegrams. Soon after, a U.S. submarine came up out of the ocean.

A final group of stories we will consider deals with cannibalism. Like threats
of extermination, stories of cannibalism represent a moral extreme. Recall that
Micronesians had little control over food resources as the war progressed, and
suffered from near-starvation in some regions. Despite these shortages, it was
Japanese soldiers—not Korean laborers or Micronesians—who are accused
of cannibalism in the several sets of stories that emerge from wartime Micronesia. These stories are told about the last, most desperate, phases of the war
and are set in locations with large contingents of Japanese soldiers, where food
shortages were most acute: Chuuk and the Marshall Islands.

In these settings, storytellers depict social relations with the Japanese as
tense and highly contorted by the war. In Chuuk Lagoon, for example, some
thirty-eight thousand Japanese civilians and soldiers were stranded with ten
thousand Chuukese. Under such conditions, local people are depicted as
steadfastly moral (even when faced with starvation), whereas Japanese soldiers are depicted as so desperate that they turn to immoral acts. We should
note, from the point of view of documented history, that Allied accounts based
on postsurrender interviews and studies of Japanese documents indicate that
cannibalism did happen in the Marshall Islands, but there is no indication that
it was widespread or that Islanders were victims.

While these stories are morality tales that highlight power differentials,
they also point out the inherent strengths of Islanders. In some cases, these
stories suggest other forms of local empowerment as well, including the fact
that local people were more resourceful than Japanese under famine conditions. Islanders could not stop the Japanese from participating in these hei-
nous activities. Yet in telling these stories, they recapture some of the control
they must have felt they had lost at the time, by repositioning themselves as
moral social beings.

The World War II cannibals were not the first to travel through these

islands. Most Micronesians also tell stories about ancient times when cannibals terrorized their islands. By setting those cannibal stories in ancient times,
local people distance themselves from such acts. War-era stories of cannibals
reintroduce a model of unenlightened, antisocial, animal-like behavior into
modern times. Yet by distancing it as the activity of foreigners and placing it
in the past (more than sixty years ago), cannibalism as a form of social action
is again safely contained, as an (almost) unthinkable and unspeakable act for
Micronesians.

The clearest set of cannibalism stories comes from Chuuk, where several
people told us that they had heard the rumor that a man named Nekiroch had
been killed for stealing food on Weno and that the Japanese military tried an
"experiment" to see if his flesh would be eaten. Here are some examples of
how this story is told:

It happened. Nekiroch killed a Japanese when he was found stealing in the farms.
A soldier found him and planned to take him to jail, but instead, he [Nekiroch]
turned around and killed him. Our office here [Toloas] went there [Wone] to
help investigate the case. I went there with some officials like Limwick, a keri
[policeman] named Isoda, and the commander of kumpu *[quasi-military con-*
struction workers], named Tatimo. So we went there to investigate, and there the
Japanese found it—they dug up the mud, and they found the soldier's body. Then
that was when they killed Nekiroch. I didn't know that they distributed the flesh
to the soldiers to eat it. I only heard about it, but I never saw it. But I actually saw
the body of the Japanese whom Nekiroch killed. (Sachuo Siwi, Toloas, Chuuk)

[During the war] we lacked everything. There was no more land to farm;
the soldiers took over the land and made their own farms and kept the food all
for themselves. And if they saw someone taking so much as one potato or one
coconut, they would beat him up. They would beat them up, and I know there
was one who died of that in Toloas. That was the place that they repeatedly
stabbed or pounded with a stick [to kill] that guy until he died. Then I heard
that after they killed him, then they broke him apart into pieces and then distrib-
uted it among their groups, and they tried eating it [eating flesh]. And then they
said, "It tastes good." Then after that, they started separating us from them [the
Japanese]. They put us aside in our own holes. And we talked among ourselves,
maybe they were planning to kill us. (Manuel Hartman, Tatiw, Chuuk)

[Q: Do you know if the Japanese killed any Chuukese?] Only one man from
Penia. His name was Nekiroch. We were farming—I worked in the work group

called Kerikumpu—we made miso for the Japanese soldiers. Men and women worked farming potatoes. One day we were farming when the Japanese soldiers came carrying a guy they were going to eat in a sack. They were going to the cafeteria. I didn't see them cut him up. But everybody was talking about it. People said they cut him up alive, like cut off one arm while he was still alive. They were going to distribute it to every group to try—to try the human flesh. Because they said they were going to eat Chuukese people. (Chipun Kom, Wone, Chuuk)

[Q: Do you know if the Japanese ate the flesh of one of those men?] Oooooh, yes, that fellow—Nekiroch. I believe that the Japanese ate his flesh because I was in my work group when they brought us his flesh. I personally ate some, so I knew it wasn't animal meat. I tried and tried to chew on it, but it was different, so I threw it away. When I threw it away, those Japanese asked if I didn't like it, and I said yes [I didn't like it], because I didn't know what kind of meat that was. The Japanese said, "It's your flesh." They told me that it was the flesh of Nekiroch. Eh, in all the work groups, they had told us before that they were going to kill Nekiroch and that we were going to eat human flesh [to find out] if it tasted good. That was how I tasted human flesh. I tasted Nekiroch's flesh because they brought some to our work group. (Kristo Souwas, Neuwe, Wone, Chuuk)

Further east, no Marshallese witnessed any incidents of cannibalism. Nonetheless, there are stories about the Japanese eating Koreans or other Japanese, and some feared that the Marshallese would be next:

[Q: How did the Japanese live?] Well, we do not know, because we had distanced ourselves from them [Japanese soldiers], but we heard that they ate people. They ate the Koreans, they killed the Koreans and consumed them, that's how far it went; their food supplies were exhausted. (Lele Ram, Wotje, Marshalls)

I did not see, but we heard that the soldiers on Imiej [Jaluij], they had begun to eat people. They began to eat the Chosen [Koreans]. There was a large group of Koreans they brought to work for the soldiers during the battle. Well, next, when the war became heated and they were hungry, because now the Americans were coming every day, every day and night they were destroying Imiej. And I heard from some Japanese, and that fellow Nakayama, and he spoke and said that they, the Japanese, said they were beginning to eat people. This fellow, the one between the Marshallese and Japanese [i.e., Nakayama], said they were beginning with the Koreans. (Bwirre Lejmen, Ebon, Marshalls)

WARTIME PERCEPTIONS OF AMERICANS

When Americans are mentioned in Micronesian stories dating to the actual period of the war, they remain somewhat enigmatic. Despite their long presence in the region—as whalers, traders, and missionaries beginning in the early nineteenth century; as colonial rulers of Guam from 1898; as missionaries who remained in some locales even during the Japanese colonial era—most Islanders had little knowledge of or personal experience with them. This fact, combined with the Allies' bypassing strategy throughout the region, led Micronesians to portray them in largely impersonal terms. Americans appear as the operators of sophisticated technology that dropped bombs on or lobbed shells at the islands from afar. Until an island was invaded, American sailors or pilots were only rarely glimpsed, in the distance or, as on Chuuk, as prisoners of war. Stories of the rare moments of interaction with Americans hold an exaggerated place in Micronesians' recollections. In an inversion of the narrative process described above, in which stories of relationships between Micronesians and Japanese became hollowed-out, less personal, and more stereotypical as the tyranny of war gained momentum, Micronesian accounts of their initial interactions depict Americans as impersonal stereotypes, rather than with the personalized knowledge that derives from repeated day-to-day contact. These would be colored in with the details of increased intimacy as Americans became more familiar (see chapter 12).

The Japanese did not leave the depiction of Americans to intuition but attempted to fill the void in local knowledge with propaganda of the American enemy. Looking back on these Japanese depictions of American invaders as incompetent, narrators today often portray the stereotypes as spoofs. Having witnessed the awesome military might of the United States during the war and lived through the era of nuclear testing, Micronesians note that Japanese portrayals of Americans as weak and stupid were often contradicted by the facts. While U.S. troops struggled in their first amphibious invasion in Kiribati, they quickly demonstrated their ability in the Marshalls, obliterating in a few hours installations that had taken the Japanese years to build and replacing them with new operational bases in a matter of days. Marshall Islanders who witnessed these events represent them as evidence of American wealth and might, in contrast to inaccurate Japanese images of Americans. And while Japanese propaganda films during the war showed American slow-wittedness, today's stories recalling the war are more apt to depict Japanese as bumbling and shortsighted.

The atoll of Sapwuahfik, southwest of Pohnpei, was unusual in having limited, positive interactions with American soldiers during the war. Some say these good relations were fostered by the English-based pidgin developed on the island by settlers following the early-nineteenth-century massacre of nearly all the able-bodied men by a notoriously criminal trader, Captain C. H. Hart, then sailing out of Sydney on the *Lambton*.[3] Victor Edwin, the mayor of Kolonia, Pohnpei, at the time of our research, shared stories he had heard from his family and other elders:

The war started when the American planes came. Kalio Edwin could speak and write English. He wrote on the island with coconut palm leaves on the beach, "No Japanese on Island." I don't know how he learned English. He looked American, with cat-eyes, kind of greenish eyes. This came from Kalio's mother. There was an Englishman by the name of Captain Brown, who went to Kiribati. Then there was Lehna and Ehna. Kalio's mother's grandfather was Captain Brown. The teacher at Oa [a school on Pohnpei, also] taught English. My father also spoke English; he learned this during Japanese times at Oa.

American battleships passed Sapwuahfik and came up to Pohnpei. Then, afterwards, the planes started flying. This was when the message was made. The Americans were watching a group of islands—bypassing the islands.

Then the planes started landing. First, they would bomb Pohnpei, then come to Sapwuahfik and land in the ocean. They landed at Wahd, where the water is calm. When they first landed, they went to the island where there was an older Sapwuahfik lady, named Caroline, who said she would act as our spokesperson. She spoke pidgin English. They would give cigarettes and food in return for mats, hats, handicrafts, shells, et cetera as gifts.

The first time they came, the Americans didn't give anything, because they didn't expect to receive anything. Then they brought return gifts. And then, the Sapwuahfik people prepared more gifts; they expected the Americans to return. The Americans brought food, clothes.

On the main islet, from eight to nine a.m., people rushed to their taro patches. Sometimes, the American planes flew over and dropped corned beef. In Sapwuahfik, people made a joke: the planes dropped food at Sapwuahfik; they dropped bombs at Pohnpei.

We were given very different treatment, because there were no Japanese on the island. This was due to the writing on the beach; they saw we spoke the truth. They also wondered why we spoke English. Every canoe that went out to exchange, there were one or two guys on the canoe who could speak pidgin English. This was a result of the experience with whalers, and the massacre on this island. We experienced a lot of language change; people picked up pidgin English. This is why we had good relations.

There was some shooting. My grandfather was on Wahd Island, and he went fishing with some young people. One girl, Freilang, on the way back on the canoe found a piece of a Japanese plane with the symbol of the rising sun on the wing. They put it on the canoe and were paddling, sailing back. One American plane was there and saw the emblem on the canoe and shot; he hit her legs. They really didn't see well.

In most of Micronesia, Americans remained virtually unknown, and were present throughout much of the war only as "the enemy" until the final

Survivors of cave bombing by Japanese with hand grenades, in Marizo, Guam, July 15, 1945. (U.S. Navy photo, National Archives photo no. 331356)

months of the war. Guam, a U.S. possession since 1898, is the exception. This popular wartime song, "Uncle Sam, Won't You Please Come Back to Guam," was composed by Mr. Fultado, a Hawaiian stranded on Guam during the war (his identity was kept secret during the war, for fear of Japanese repercussion); the song was later reworked by Chamorro peoples of Guam. It expresses the continued Chamorro loyalty to Americans during the Japanese occupation and their desire for a speedy return of U.S. rule. During the Japanese occupation, this was one of the songs Chamorro people included in their serenades while away from home, in *mandana* (getting together) fashion. During the Allied recapture of Guam, Chamorros joyfully sang this song all the way to the various American camps on the island (Santos, n.d.).

Uncle Sam, Won't You Please Come Back to Guam
Composed by Mr. Fultado on Guam
(Collected and translated by Carmen Santos, 1989:104)

1. *Early Monday morning*
   the action came to Guam,
   Eighth of December,
   Nineteen forty-one.

Chorus: *Oh Mister Sam, Sam*
         my dear Uncle Sam.
         Won't you please
         come back to Guam.

2. *Nine Japanese planes*
   flew over Guam.
   They dropped their bombs
   right here on Guam.

3. *Our lives are in danger—*
   you better come
   and kill all the Japanese
   right here on Guam.

4. *I don't like saki [Japanese whiskey],*
   I like Canadian [whiskey].
   I don't like the Japanese,
   I like the American.

5.   *Raise up your banner—*
     red, white, and blue.
     People on Guam
     are waiting for you.

6.   *The American prisoners*
     were sent to Japan.
     Only George Tweed[4]
     is safe from the tyrant.

Chapter 10

MICRONESIAN RESPONSES TO WARTIME PRESSURES

MICRONESIAN MEMORIES RECALL not only the hardships of war, but also the strategies used to endure it. They depict themselves as survivors, drawing on a wide array of resources to make the best of tough times. Coping stories constitute deliberate efforts to pass on what elders learned, to teach important lessons about mutual dependence and aid, risk taking, and the importance of their struggles to secure a better life for their children and grandchildren.

Coping stories emphasize decidedly Micronesian responses to challenges. Faced with physical danger, exhaustion, and shortages of food and shelter, they invoked traditional kinship ties that offered nurturance and expanded access to resources controlled by the Japanese. When forced to relocate far from home, people relied on distant clanmates and relatives. Often they forged new relationships, establishing links that continued into the postwar years. Faced with the threat of air raids, they sought sacred protection through divination, traditional magic, and Christian worship. Coping stories also display characteristically Micronesian appreciation of cleverness and trickery in the face of overwhelming odds or powerful opponents. And when all else failed, and opportunity allowed, Islanders attempted daring escapes from Japanese control.

SOURCES OF COMFORT AND RESISTANCE

As we have seen in several recollections, Christian belief was a comfort and assistance to many people, as in this dramatic account by Wendolin Gomez of Kolonia, Pohnpei:

Marshallese arrive in rubber raft at a U.S. Navy LCI, off Majuro, March 11, 1945. (U.S. Navy photo, National Archives photo no. 316734)

One day I went to get another motorcycle. There were many soldiers there. All of a sudden the siren went off, and we ran around looking for what shelter we could find. The place was close to where the nuns lived. I sat down at the trunk of a coconut tree. One Japanese soldier was close by my right, and another to my left. When the bombs started falling, we all bent down and covered our heads. When the bombing stopped, I felt relieved because no shrapnel came my way. When I looked to my right, all I could see were the intestines and other mutilated body parts of what was left of the other soldier. The guy to my left was missing his head.

I stood up and ran like hell to the other soldiers and told them what happened. I never knew what they did, because I left. I don't know whether I became scared or confused. What I remember was that I had pinned inside my shirt a [Roman Catholic] scapular, and this little picture never left me. Maybe that's what brought my luck.

In the face of tight security, Islanders' increasing antipathy toward the Japanese military rarely turned into overt resistance. In a few instances, calculated resistance did take place, as in the Palauan Modekngei movement,[1] the Pohnpeian Typhoon Society, and most dramatically when Marshallese collaborated with Korean laborers in a rebellion on the islet of Jelbon in Mili Atoll. Here is Elson Ebel's account of that uprising:

The Marshallese and Koreans met and talked things over. They [the Japanese] had shot four Koreans under two coconut trees because they caught them stealing, and it was prohibited to steal. They were keeping food from the Marshallese. Now it was the Marshallese and Koreans together, because their low social level was not the equal of the Japanese. After those fellows were shot and killed, the Marshallese and the Koreans met together and said, "Is it a good thing if we just start a war?" and they talked it over and said, "Good." [Q: But what would they fight with, sir?] With knives. Next, they said, "Well, next week we will begin the battle." A week in advance they talked it over.

Next, all of the men prepared red pieces of cloth for the night that they were going to fight. And then afterward, precisely that night at one and two o'clock in the middle of the night, they began to move. There were a hundred and one Japanese on the islet, but [only] fifty-nine Marshallese—and Koreans, four hundred-some, I do not know precisely how many.

The Japanese were asleep, and they went and entered into their houses and they began fighting. They shot many of them. Some few of them were manning the cannon; there were seven men, and they called to them and got them drunk on coconut toddy. Well then, this was fine with those fellows, and so they went ahead and drank and became inebriated, and when they were drunk they killed them. They went into the houses of the Japanese and killed them. The Japanese taicho [commander] they killed; but, you see, his cook escaped. They shot him and he was injured, but he ran off and dove into the water and swam to Lukwōn-wōd, and there he reported, "There are no Japanese. All of the soldiers have died, all of the Japanese are dead."

[Q: Did any Marshallese die during this event?] Mantiera and Larenmij—two of them. The Koreans sliced them up because it was dark and they became confused. Their headbands fell off and they were cut up. They died during the night.

Now, there were some small islets to the west, and their error was that the Marshallese did not run off to those islets. Instead, they remained on the lagoon side of the islet, Jelbon. And that fellow ran off to Lukwōn-wōd, where there were a thousand Japanese, there and on the other islets between there and Enejet. They said, "There are no Japanese left, they are dead, the Marshallese and Koreans have killed them." [Q: And were there people who landed on those places?] Well, there were many small boats (jempan) that traveled back and forth among those islets. So some three hundred soldiers went off that day. They took machine guns and smaller guns and traveled to windward, during the low tide that morning. The islet is like this on the lagoon side [a high flat reef], and I do not know how the other group came on shore and landed, because it was a totally dry reef, flat at low tide, but some of them ran up on the ocean side. Then they started shooting one another. Some shot toward them, some shot away, and on and on things went until the Marshallese ammunition was exhausted.

Then the group [of Japanese soldiers] came up that had run up along the ocean side and shot them, the Marshallese and Koreans. Some of the Koreans escaped while they were fighting. That day, they escaped across the tide flats where water comes into the lagoon, to the small islets and remained on one of the small islets there. [Q: Were there Marshallese who ran off with the Koreans?] None, because they were occupied with the group who was fighting. All of the Marshallese died. After the war when we went there, it was filled with skulls, a hundred-some skulls; we did not know which were Marshallese, and which were Koreans, and which were Japanese. They were all mixed together, and we did not know. [Q: Were there any women?] Yes, there were several Marshallese women. Why was it we could not find their clothes? They died also—there was no one [Marshallese] who lived through this. Eighty-four Marshallese, if we *include children with the adults who died. It was four or five months later when we finally went there, and by the time we got there, there were not clothes on any of them, only bones.*

Then, in 1978, a boat came from Japan and took all of the bones and took them to Mili, and there they set fire to them. The reason they did this is that Korea had sued them in court, because they had taken them [the Koreans] and placed them in conditions of hardship, and greatly damaged them, but they did not pay them anything. And now [in 1990], there is this case between Japan and Korea . . . perhaps Japan feared that they would come and take the remains in order to prove [their case]. Nonetheless, there are many people who can be used as proof.

The reason we knew about the planned movements of the Japanese at that time [was] those Japanese who really cared for the Marshallese on Lukwōn-wōd; they came and informed us. They spoke. . . . One Japanese, they captured [him] because he had given information to the Marshallese. They grabbed him because another Japanese went and told on him. He heard him speaking Marshallese to us, for that fellow also knew how to speak Marshallese. His name was Morita. They said, "This fellow is stealing our secret information and taking it to the Marshallese." When they heard this, they shot him. He died. And also the Koreans who escaped from Jelbon; those that I said had run off to the small islets, they also gave us information, because they knew Marshallese. In the subsequent days, they saw an [American] LCI and they escaped and got on board. . . .

[Q: After this battle on Jelbon, did the Japanese do anything to the rest of you?] Well, then it was tough. After they did battle on Jelbon, it was illegal to come out of the holes [bomb shelters]. It was much more difficult; those who came out of the holes would be jailed. Previously, things were slightly okay, but after Jelbon, then they [the Japanese] hung the shell casings of bullets at the openings to the holes, there where we lived, and when someone came out and moved the shell casings, they would hear the sound and knew that there were people coming outdoors. Previously, they did not do this.

Leban Jorju described a successful instance of Marshallese retaliation against the Japanese near the war's end, with supplies and encouragement from U.S. forces:

There were more than one hundred Japanese on Ronglap—soldiers and coast watchers. The next morning, when they [the Japanese] were going to kill us, the

American ships arrived and killed the Japanese. Some of them [the Japanese]
ran away and the American soldiers were not able to find them, but before the
Americans went back to Kwajalein they gave us some guns and ammunition. We
went and looked for them, to find them [the Japanese] and kill them. Eknilang
was the one who shot and killed them. . . .

They dropped us at Rārōken and we came up in the middle of the islet. We
were looking for them [the Japanese], and when we reached the place where their
houses were, we waited for daylight. When we looked toward the south, we saw
a man who went out to the west from the pastor's house. We ran out along the
ocean side—the island was burned by the bombs and very little vegetation was
found on the island on account of the bombs burning the island. We ran along
the ocean side to where he was at the lagoon side of the islet. We came toward
him, toward the lagoon side, and the Japanese person went off and was north of
the islet. Perhaps he was looking for canoes [that might be] coming toward that
islet. At that time, we did not like each other—there was something between us.
We shot him and ran away from him. And they [the Japanese] told us to come
and take our food that they had prepared—perhaps it was a trick—they wanted
to [trick us] into coming, so they might kill us. We went to look for them during
the nighttime. And we found the guy who was sitting under the coconut tree.
And he came ashore, and then, at the side of the cookhouse, Eknilang shot him
[first], and even though he was hit, he still came toward us. He shot him the third
time and he finally lay down. . . .

After that we went to the north end of the islet and found the other Japanese.
[Q: How many Japanese were there?] About four or five. We went and fought
with them; those were the ones left, the survivors, from the fighting between the
Japanese and Americans. These were the survivors that the American soldiers
told us about when they gave us guns and ammunition to look for them and kill
them, kill those who ran away.

Most opposition took less organized forms. People used quiet resistance, particularly late in the war when oppressive military control had substantial effects on daily life. By the end of the war, individuals began to express resentment among themselves about harsh treatment. Recollections from this time include stories of plotting revenge for acts of cruelty, fighting for personal space, or strategizing ways to acquire the resources closely guarded by the Japanese military. Pohnpeian men sent to Kosrae to work on the construction of a seaplane base and bunkers provide one such example. By this point, Kosrae had become dangerously overpopulated, and the food situation was desperate. The Pohnpeians were particularly vulnerable since they had no resources of their own or close kin as sources of support. In this story, Pensile Lawrence (one of the Kiti men whose experience is commemorated in "Memorial Song of Kosrae," chapter 7) shows how, even under the watchful eyes of the Japanese, he and his compatriots found ways to thwart Japanese plans and ease demands on their labor.

When we started working on [building] the bunkers, some groups cut the mangrove logs, and other groups carried them from where they were cut. Some were responsible for cutting, others for transport to the channel; another group took them to a raft and transported them to another place and left them; and another group then took them. We did this all the way to the other side of Lelu harbor.

Many times, we threw our mangrove logs into the water. We would get up early, earlier than the army men guarding us, jump into the water to wake up, and take our raft into the water, then put it up again and go back to our house and report the number of mangrove we took. But it was not correct. This was many times the case—we reported more logs than we took.

Many times we got up earlier than the army, pulled the raft on the reef all the way to Lelu, and returned. Why we did that was because, usually at eight o'clock in the morning, the U.S. plane would circle the island; that's why we had to get up earlier. Others would carry mangrove to the place near Lelu. . . . We would pull this raft all the way to there waiting for eight a.m. When the sirens and bells rang, we could hear them, and we threw the mangrove into the deep water and returned. And on the opposite side of the harbor, not many logs were placed there.

There were also many [Japanese] army men there expecting mangrove logs. They counted! Actually, whoever cut and carried the mangrove, there would be army men waiting to count it. And from there to another spot, there would be two others. Two army men were with us, but they didn't go along with us on the raft. We took our mangrove logs across the harbor. If we couldn't throw our logs away because we didn't have enough time . . . we would take them across the harbor to the other side. There would be two army men watching, who would count. And from there up to the mountains . . . there were two army men. They were everywhere, counting. They knew that in the water where we usually placed our mangroves after the harbor, there were very few mangroves, and they began to wonder why. You know, a check was made from there to all the way back to where the mangrove was cut, and there was no mistake!

... Some of the small channels going through the mangrove swamp, any of the cut mangrove for making bunkers were thrown [in there]. Those were not found. It's a good thing they weren't found. If they had been found, I don't know ...

Among the most popular coping stories are the amusing ones, still retold long after the war, especially tales of how local people tricked the oppressive Japanese military. Here, Keropin David of Pohnpei repeats what he heard from an older relative:

I heard some funny stories about the war. My mother's first cousin, Dorip Mauricio, I heard this story from him; he talked about it while we were drinking kava. ... During Japanese times he was young, and he wasn't in the group who went to Kosrae. But he used to take [Japanese] people from Wene to Sapwalap by canoe. If a soldier had to deliver a message to the others in Sapwalap, this man paddled him up to Sapwalap. He was not kind to the Japanese soldiers! One time, he and another man took a soldier up to Sapwalap, and while they were coming back they fished for rabbit fish—this fish has a spine that will stick in people's bodies and hurt a lot. When they caught one, he [Dorip] gave it to the soldier to take from the spear. After they caught three fish, the soldier started to scream, because the spines always stuck in his hand.

This was one [story], and another one was about when he [Dorip] and another guy took a soldier to Sapwalap, and when they came back, the soldier wanted a drink from a coconut, so they stopped at one of the small atolls, and he climbed one of the coconut trees that curved over the lagoon. When he was in the tree, he told the other guy to paddle the canoe up so the soldier was positioned under the coconut tree, because he was going to cut the coconuts and let them fall on top of the man. So when the other guy paddled the canoe up, he cut the coconuts, and they fell on the soldier. Some Pohnpeians had a good time doing bad things to the Japanese!

GREAT ESCAPES

The most dramatic form of coping was escape. As Americans invaded select targets, it became possible—though dangerous—to flee to American lines. This happened in the Marshall Islands, where U.S. forces took Enewetak, Majuro, and Kwajalein and kept pressure on remaining Japanese bases while encouraging Marshallese to escape. In Palau, when Americans attacked Peleliu, a few Palauans escaped from Babeldaob to American lines. In both areas, the Japanese military used guards, threats, and reprisals against family members to stem escapes.

Escape stories are set against a background of threat and a foreground of choice: to risk escaping, when the sea or the Japanese might kill you, and you did not know how the Americans might treat you, and when those left behind might be punished or killed for your escape? or choose the path of caution, waiting under conditions of starvation, hard labor, ongoing air raids, and an increasingly violent and unpredictable Japanese occupying force?

In western Micronesia, Itpik Martin Ruwutei of Koror, Palau, describes his escape (collected and translated by Wakako Higuchi, 1986):

I was taking fish with the Japanese soldiers. Their names were Suzuki, Yama-uchi, and Araki. We discussed: "Let's go to [Peleliu] because we have no more food." "No, if we go there by ship, they will attack us." "No, no, if we show a white flag we can do it." Only Araki refused strongly. We almost started to fight. When we were three hundred [sic] miles distant from Aimeliik, Araki insisted on swimming to Aimeliik and jumped into the ocean. We went to Peleliu. One small kuchikukan [destroyer] was near [Peleliu]. We took off our fundoshi [loincloth] and put it on a bamboo pole. We raised it and moved close to the kuchikukan. That night there was a full moon. The sky was very clear, no clouds. It was almost six p.m. We waited in the shadow of a rock island until seven because we were afraid to go out until it was dark. At seven the moon showed light. We waved our flag and moved close to the ship. The U.S. ship showed a sinkaito [searchlight] to us and someone invited us by showing a white flag. We moored our boat alongside the U.S. destroyer. Then the U.S. sailors dropped a ladder, and two of them came down to our boat. Many soldiers held guns at the ready. I was so scared. I thought I would be killed by their guns. I believed I could not oppose them. They checked our bodies, naked except for fundoshi. They gestured us to come aboard their ship. We had only goggles for fishing and piskan [spear]. We didn't have guns. Three of us were disinfected by DDT and were injected into our buttock. I remembered what the sisters in Catholic kindergarten said, "If we surrender, the foreign soldiers will never kill us."

We took a shower. One sailor gave us navy uniforms. The three of us were always together, guarded by two sailors. We went to a waiting room. Two soldiers had carbines. We sat down. Sandwiches, milk, and coffee were served. They gave tobacco. The captain brought a photo of Palau islands and lists of warships, guns, and cannons. A white sailor whose Japanese was perfect pointed to one among the lists and asked, "Where is this located?" We answered all that we knew.

The soldier had attended a university in Japan before the war and could write Japanese characters. He was one of the members of the [American] kempei-tai [military police]. As soon as we appeared in front of them, they called the main office of the military office on the land and some officers came to the ship. After short questions, one military policeman said to us, "You came from Babeldaob, didn't you? You will go to the office of the U.S. military police."

We rode a boat and landed in Peleliu. Their headquarters were stationed next to the present airstrip. We took a jeep. It seemed that more than ten thousand soldiers were there. There were many cars and tents, not barracks. The road and buildings were arranged already. In the headquarters, we were asked by one American, "Why did you come to Peleliu?" "We don't have any food in our place."

We were taken to a prison together. After three days' stay in the prison, we attended a court. A judge said, "You . . . Japanese will be taken to prison, but you, Palauan, should work with the U.S. military policemen."

Clancy Makroro describes a group escape from Mili in the Marshall Islands:

[The] Japanese said that if people ran off from the islet where they resided, they would be killed. There was one time that some people ran off to an islet next to the islet on which I was staying. Afterward they said, all of you, go to that islet. Three men watched us as we went toward the islet. They each had a gun, and they followed behind us as we came to this place. It was evening, when the sun was setting, but it was still light. We were just beginning to land, we were near the interior reef facing windward and [searching out] passages in the reef, and then a ship was traveling toward us. It was a huge ship about the size of the battleships. If we had been thinking then about running off, it would be impossible, because the Japanese were still watching. But we all overcame our fear of death; went ahead; and then when we were near an islet by the name of Nal, the tide was at its highest, and we could not go to Mili because the waves were crashing in so heavily. And they said that we would wait around until dawn.

The group of us waited for daylight there. We did not sleep because we were very frightened, so my [wife] and I, I said we should go to the lagoon side, and *the two of us were thinking about running off, but it was high tide and day had nearly arrived. We thought for a while and said, "Well, there is no use in the two of us running off now, because it is nearly day, and if we run off now and are caught, we will die." So the two of us watched the Japanese, who said for us to go to the house. So we returned and waited a little bit, and then after a bit it was day. Then they took us to Mili, and we went, and when we arrived at the bunker [hole] of the* taicho *[commander], he told us, "Well, you all wait there." So we waited there and the Japanese came. Perhaps they had met in council inside the hole and discussed things [and decided], "We will not kill them but return them so that they can make coconut toddy, so that there will be some value to their remaining [alive]." And the reason they did not kill us [may have been because] our friends [on Jaluij] who escaped in their boat, when they landed on Jabwor, they had seen the others who had landed on Imiej [and had been killed], as well as some others who landed on the ocean side of Jaluij. So, once they returned to the Japanese, then they [the Japanese] said, "The announcement [to kill the Marshallese] was a mistake. You will return [home] and look after the coconut toddy producing trees."*

When they said the Americans were here [on Majuro], I did not believe them. I said that they were lying, but in just a little while the soldiers sailed in our direction and grabbed us all. So we went back to the northward, and after about a week, another [American ship] sailed toward us in a windward direction on the ocean side. They yelled out and said, "If there are any Marshallese on this islet you should all come toward us, for this islet will be [reduced] to only reef once midday has arrived." The commander asked me what they said, and I said, "Well, I do not know, because it was Caroline Islanders speaking to us." But they were speaking Marshallese from the ship, and I think it was Dwight [Heine] who called out to us on the island. I said, "Well, there you see, ma'am, the Majuro people are here. You go oceanside with the other women next to you; they are giving you a chance, because it is the day belonging to Tenno Heika."

But the two women ran to the ocean side, and then when they saw the ship, they yelled toward the islet, and then hid with the other women in the bush. I said to one of the old men, "Well, there you see, sir, do not remain here. Go ahead toward the ocean, and the two of us will seek a position in front [of the others]." But the old man was really unwilling to run off. So when he was reluctant to come with me, I went toward the lagoon side and raced off and sought out the ship that was facing the islet just to the ocean side of the fringing reef, and I shouted to the other folks that we must escape, for there was no time to go back [where we came from]. So the boat faced the islet in that spot, and the rubber rafts were launched, and they came and took us all away to the ship, and also loaded some Japanese who were fishing on the ocean side of the islet to the east, and they came here to Majuro.

[Q: What sort of ship came for you there?] It was an LST. This was how all of the people managed to remain alive. After that time, some other people also escaped, some killed the Japanese and then ran off. Wherever they were, they had to look for a way to escape. But some, well, they simply escaped on the other ships. This was typical of how people sought out methods which would allow us to live.

Luke Lantir describes her escape from Jaluij:

A single plane from America, just one, came at twelve o'clock. We had just returned from the Marshallese mess area. We saw it come toward us onto Imiej and drop a single bomb, and it flew on toward us there where we picked up our tickets, our work tickets. From the time that it dropped the bomb, some time passed, and then [they] came and attacked Jaluij, Jabwor. They did more than a little damage, and on things went, and people died. Well, from that time until the day when the battle was over, [the planes] continued to come, all the time, and damaged the atoll. [Q: Night and day?] Night and day; we did not sleep. . . . Things went on and we, ourselves, ran off. [Q: Why was that?] Because there was absolutely no pause in their bombing.

[Q: But didn't the Japanese stop you from escaping?] They did not. They were going to beat us. Yes, they said we should not run off because they would beat us. So when we ran off, we went and hid in the brush. They came in their boats and began looking for us. It did not matter if you boarded [the boats], they would come and beat you and take you to Imiej and we did not know [what would happen next]. Why was it that the other people disappeared? They took them [to Imiej] and they have not yet reappeared even to this day. . . .

[Q: How did you escape?] We ran off on foot. It was night, and we went along the reef. There where we ran off to, we went there together, and it was there where if the sharks came and bit you, well it was so filled with sharks [that no one would survive]. But that night there were no sharks. Then we swam, because it was not exactly low tide, and it was also nearly day. The daylight was arriving when we landed. We headed out through the surf there at the westward point, that is where we escaped from them, we ran off when they were sleeping on the south [end of the islet].

The Japanese guarded us so we would not run off, but then, that night when we ran off, there were no Japanese. [Q: Why was that?] I do not know, that amazed us. The night we ran off, there were no armed Japanese—[if there had been,] if we had been slow [they would have shot us]. But this was amazing, because the Japanese did not sleep near us. [Q: And where did you go?] I ran off to the small islet where the sharks were. There were many sharks [in that area], but they did not bite me. We swam off from there, and then went to a boat. We selected a rubber boat, and when we were on board the boat, we went to Ekjet.

Nathan Tartios from Maloelap tells of the tragic loss of life during an escape from Airik (the main islet of Maloelap) to Aur:

[Q: And now, when is it that you were going to move from Airik?] Well, a bit further into the middle of the war. We ran off at that time. Those [Marshallese] fellows came and discussed [the situation] among themselves and said, "We should meet here, but should we wait up all night until morning, or go ahead right now, [or what]?" A man came and said, "The soldiers have gotten up." Now those who were mature went ahead and set sail and took on board the people who were their companions. There was no conference, for that fellow came up and said the soldiers had gotten up. And the boat that we were sailing with, when we set sail, the fellow who was watching over the canoe said, "Wait, let us watch who did not get on board." Onward and onward things went and two women did not get on board; the sailing craft belonging to them sailed away without them. He came back and said, "Well, the two of you come ahead, we will go ahead and make [this canoe] even heavier."

The sailing craft of his was way too full. People had to float in the water holding onto the edge of the canoe, for it was over capacity. Now they said, "Throw off the sail" [let it go slack]; the sail was made from Marshallese pandanus matting. "We will go ahead and float downwind from the islet." Another canoe was damaged; it filled with water from the top. Now they again took people from that canoe and placed them upon the other canoe. After that, it became even more overloaded, [beyond] full. The boat could never sail, but at that time, they said, "We'll drift with the surf into Aur."

It did not go toward Aur; it just continued to float about between Maloelap and Aur. Things kept going, and going, and going and what, there were what? Four nights, correct? You were in the ocean, you could not sit [on the boat] like here, you were totally drenched. . . .

Everyone stayed in the water, soaking. There were many children who died.

[Q: But they were still holding onto the canoe?] Yes. No one swam off from the boats. Well, some of them became dazed [crazy], the thing Marshallese call wiwijet, "lost all sense of direction." I do not know what it is in English. Their minds were damaged some from their having been in the ocean for so long. There were many children who were swimming about for awhile and sharks bit them. The sharks were not very large, just nice sized, possibly this length [3–4 feet]. The canoe went ahead and turned upside down, they turned it right side up. Only six people worked on it, righted it, and it was okay. Well, at that time we again stayed put with the canoe, and onward and onward. Then one day we did not get up because we did not sleep, because those folks were so cold that their coldness disappeared. . . .

American planes came and the women waved to them, but they did not see them. We then woke up and we were close to Aur. Now, we drifted downwind right next to Aur. [Q: But were there not paddles or rudders?] No paddles and no canoe bailers. We drifted downwind, drifted further downwind, and then about nine or ten o'clock or so, we drifted ashore on the small islets to the north of Taba. Next to Biken [Aur]. And our canoe, it did not really turn upside down; it turned like this [outrigger down, when it hit the reef]. Now, you see, the women with us fell downward on the outrigger, and some fell down inside [between the outrigger and the canoe], but some fell down in front of it. The two of us, me and a young man, we dragged the women up who were alive, as our women fell to the north and south. Me, I walked [onto the shore], but also crawled on my hands. [Q: So great was your hunger?] I could not do it. I was weak. [Q: You were so cold?] Coldness had disappeared. Hunger had disappeared. Only slightly could you hear . . . [people] speak. Perhaps after only one more night we would have died.

Six of some thirty-two people on that canoe reached Aur and lived. The other canoes that had left with them landed safely on Biken.

PART IV

Cultural Themes in Micronesian Wartime Narratives

PEOPLE IN EVERY CULTURE share a distinctive set of interests. Whether we think of these as key symbols, cultural themes that run through many aspects of life, or structures of consciousness and agency, anthropologists spend much of their time seeking to understand the unique congeries of ideas, values, and symbols that make each culture a separate and to a certain extent integrated entity. While each of Micronesia's many cultures is distinct, as we explained in chapter 1, there are also certain consistencies across the region arising from shared history, philosophy, and style of life.

In part 4, we look at several significant Micronesian preoccupations. Whether people are recounting their legends, composing a song, or engaging in gossip, certain topics are always of interest. By using the term "preoccupations," we do not mean the subjects are trivial. On the contrary, these are the very essentials of Micronesian life: ideas about happiness, scarcity and plenty, and generosity; romance; chiefs; and the arrival and departure of visitors. They are the staples of culture, just as breadfruit and taro are the staples of a meal; these perennially fascinating subjects reflect what is unique and distinctive about Micronesian lives. As we would expect, they appear frequently as themes in recollections of the war years. These enduring cultural preoccupations, furthermore, serve as sensitive cultural barometers of the well-being of individuals and society as a whole during the war.

Chapter 11

SOME MICRONESIAN PREOCCUPATIONS

HAPPINESS IS AN IMPORTANT value in Micronesian cultures, most often taking a form perhaps best translated as psychological and physical contentment.[1] Contentment comes from an individual's social standing—that is, the possession of a certain rank (or position) in the community, which brings acknowledgment of one's worth and respect. It also comes from social harmony, characterized by the absence of public conflict and the presence of sharing, exchange, and working together. Of course, even in the small-scale societies of Micronesia, daily life entails disputes, and island societies have many ways to negotiate, resolve, or bury such conflicts. The modes of resolution form part of the underlying cultural order, the mutual understanding that the desirable state of society is one of harmony, cooperation, and peace. When these taken-for-granted understandings are compromised, as happened in the Pacific War, there is a real threat not only to individual welfare but also to the continued existence of the community.

CASUALTIES OF WAR: HAPPINESS, SOCIAL HARMONY, AND ABUNDANCE

When Islanders talk about contentment, they express the recognition that it also comes from some forms of material plenty, although in these Island cultures the meaning of material satisfaction is somewhat different from its meaning in mass production and consumption societies such as the United States and Japan. The linking of physical objects with well-being does not mean Micronesians are materialistic, but rather that material goods carry

Marshallese boy holding a package of K-rations supplied by U.S. troops, Kwajalein. (Micronesian Seminar: *Transition to Peace*, website album <www.micsem.org>)

strong symbolic weight in island societies. Goods are used for personal consumption and display, but they also play other important roles. Gift giving may be motived by kindness, but sharing an element of one's self with others also extends an individual's social standing. Sharing also creates solidarity within a group, and giving gifts to those outside one's group confers power over them.

Micronesian cultural ideas of happiness, harmony, status, and even physical and mental health are linked to perceptions of abundance and exchange. Material shortages, then, take on the added implication of threats to individual and social well-being. It is not surprising that stories about shortages—especially shortages of food—make up perhaps the dominant theme in describing wartime hardships. Nearly every Islander remembers hardship due to food shortages, though this ranges from a lack of favorite or imported foods (true everywhere), to a lack of familiar staples (anywhere the Japanese controlled taro gardens, breadfruit, and coconuts), to actual starvation (in the bypassed Marshalls and parts of Chuuk, the Central Carolines, and Palau).

On islands where the local population was swelled by civilians or troops, the final years of the war are characterized in memory as times when feeding oneself and one's family was a tense and sometimes dangerous challenge. On blockaded islands targeted for regular bombing raids, the struggle to feed troops, military workers, Japanese civilians, and Islanders became desperate. Recall that in Chuuk Lagoon, for example, the natural resources that had readily supported nine thousand to ten thousand Chuukese in the early colonial era then had to supply as well some thirty-eight thousand military personnel and foreign laborers.[2] The Japanese Army imposed strict control of food supplies and rationing, with rations in some places allotted according to ethnicity. Where the Japanese took over gardens and food trees, Islanders had to steal from their own confiscated lands to survive, often at the risk of their lives. They ate unappealing food, rotten food, famine foods; they ate leaves, tubers, or vines they had thought inedible. They fished despite the danger of strafing, or dynamite, or mines; they waded or paddled out to gather dead and stunned fish after bombing raids. Throughout many parts of Micronesia, the oldest, weakest, sickest, and youngest of the Islanders succumbed, and Japanese troops and remaining civilians also suffered malnutrition and starvation.

But the meaning of food in Micronesian war remembrance goes beyond the very real threat of starvation. Food is a core symbol. As a product of shared land and labor, food carries tremendous cultural meaning, both when used as provisions within a household and when shared with others.[3] Kin may be seen as the product of shared food, as much as of shared biology.[4] Indeed, the sharing of food defines and validates those who are relatives, and food often represents a kin group at community events. Food sharing, like other forms of exchange, expresses solidarity within households, villages, and clans; and it is a fundamental source of power when given to others outside one's group.

Different types of food are ranked within Micronesian societies. Access to varied types of highly ranked food and the capacity to give food without exhausting the supply constitute the means by which Micronesians construct and maintain rank and gain the respect of others.[5] Because foods are central to the domain of exchange and relations of status, any food shortage is perceived as a threat. This short song from wartime Kosrae summarizes the sentiment.

Untitled Song

Unknown Composer
(Collected and translated by Walter Scott Wilson, 1968:35)

Here is our way in that time;
"unable," "busy," day to day;
Cold, thirsty, and hungry
because of the laws hard on us.

Several memories of privation will indicate the depth of concern with this topic. Leon Gargathog discussed some of the extreme measures undertaken by the Japanese to cope with the food shortages on Yap:

We went among fear [lived with fear] all the time. For example, as I said, some people knew their minds, some didn't. Some were stunned with fear [literally, falling down because of something pushing you; in this case, falling down from fear]. So the little we can remember, we talked about it, and we concluded, "So this is what it's like." That's how much deprivation took place.

When the soldiers were all over the island—and it's not even a big island, plus there were so many of them—in each locality there were some of them, so that between them and us, we ate even all the tiny unripe coconut and raw [wild] foods, to the point where they were all consumed. So we suffered from hunger, because the Japanese had also eaten up all their own food. No ships or anything else came. So after we'd all consumed all the food, one of their leaders said, "Those people [Yapese] better work too, because we're going to have problems. Each person will be sent back to his or her village, because there is a group of soldiers there, and he or she will be under that group to work. Because we are going to have problems because of hunger." So some were taken to Nimgil, some were taken to Maap, and Rumung, and they all went back to their homes. [That is, people were sent back home from where they had been brought from all over Yap to work on Japanese projects, such as the airport.]

The first thing we planted was sweet potatoes, because that's the fastest-growing. Luckily, it grew; then our life improved. Then we started uprooting them, even before they were ready, or else we would die from hunger. Because we planted so much, we did that many times, and we were able to eat.

Some people died of fear, some died because they worked with the Japanese and hid with them, and when the Japanese were attacked, they were injured along with them. That's how much suffering we encountered. The Japanese controlled everything: everything we owned, even our taro patches, had guards over them, making sure we didn't get anything. Even when we got something [i.e., stole food from the taro patches], we were not able to cook it, because the smoke would be seen. We had never encountered such impoverished conditions, such extreme lack.

We went through all of those things, and then finally they said, "It's over." We finally had peace of mind, but the soldiers were still here. Then the Japanese came and got their soldiers. Then we really had to work hard, because everything was totally devastated. The taro patches and all were really in bad shape, completely depleted. The coconut trees were cut down and the Japanese ate the hearts-of-palm, and they cut down betel-nut trees to make houses and lampposts.... So that's how much suffering we encountered. They controlled everything, and set guards over everything, so that if one of us took anything we would be put in prison.

Wartime recollections about food are also about social relationships, including those forged with the Japanese. Nobiyuki Suzuki of Chuuk spoke of his father, an immigrant Japanese charcoal maker, whose connections led the young Mr. Suzuki and his friends into exchange relationships with a hospital and with Japanese and Okinawan civilian neighbors:

At that time, food was scarce and people were hungry. [There was] no rice, bread, soy sauce, salt—all the kinds of food the Japanese ate no longer existed. They didn't have food anymore. That's why they really worked hard, farming in the garden. I know, because I ate with them sometimes. They were really suffering at that time. The Chuukese also were suffering, because we didn't have enough food to eat. There were many Japanese, and the food just wasn't enough. There were maybe around ten thousand soldiers who stayed on Wonei, Foup, and Patta. That's why it wasn't enough for us to share our breadfruit, bananas, potatoes, and because they took our land and farmed it. We were suffering at that time.

[Mr. Suzuki's older brother was ill and hospitalized at Wonip.] ... My father went to visit my brother, and when he came back, he told me that the cook for the hospital asked my father if he could help him fish. He wanted to get fish for the hospital.... My father came and asked me to fish for them, and they would bring dynamite. They said every week they would bring the things I needed for fishing. So I went fishing for the hospital's menu. One week I fished for two days. I asked my friends—maybe there were fifteen boys, all around ten years old—then we would bring the fish to the hospital in Wonip.... Then, when we would bring the

fish, we would bring at least five hundred fish. We would work hard to get five hundred fish a day. When we first brought the fish to them, they gave each of us a gift of food, but it was not much. They didn't give us money. Then we would just eat at their cafeteria and come back home. Every week I would go fishing for the hospital, because my father told me to help the hospital. At that time, I was not a man yet, but still maybe in my teens.

One time I caught so many fish, more than the expected amount; I gave away some of the fish to some Okinawans and Japanese, because they didn't have any. Then they presented to my father and me a sack of potatoes from each family. That's how we began to at least have some food, because of what I did. Every week, I would give fish, and they would give us some potatoes.

Some Micronesian leaders organized local production and consumption of what little food was available; here, we see how responsibility for and control over food remained important in status relationships, even where local leaders' power was severely restricted by military occupation. Echen Nakamura, then in Tol, Chuuk, described successful leadership:

After awhile, we started to grow tapioca, bananas, and potatoes. When the potatoes were ready, we started to eat them. But meanwhile, Weno people found something new—apwereka [wild yam]; when we heard about the apwereka, we also tried it and we found out that it was edible. People said, we have to try yams that we have on our farm. When our family leaders found out about the yams, they were relieved and they told us that we weren't going to starve to death. Beside all these, we had a little bit of rice in kamasu [straw bag], the rice they call kemai [donated or collected rice]. Our family leaders had stored it, and they distributed it in a soy sauce container for each house. We mixed the rice with papaya seeds and ate it. When the potatoes were ready to harvest, we harvested potatoes, and again, we mixed potatoes with the kemai. Not long after that, the breadfruit trees were ready to be harvested. Right there, we were very thankful, because we had something to eat; we weren't hungry anymore. Because while we were staying in that place [Tol] we were hungry, but not very hungry. Our leader had done a great job of alternating our [use of different] foods. For instance, when it was time to eat breadfruit, our family leaders would save the rice for future consumption. When the men brought taro or potatoes, our leaders would take a little bit of rice and feed the babies, and let the elders eat either bread-fruit or potatoes. We were also thankful, for the tuba [coconut toddy] that the men had made was good. We also had one particular taro patch that belonged to Taro Mori that wasn't spoiled—because that was another punishment from heaven, the spoiling of our local food.

Managing food resources linked Micronesians with foreigners, as well as with each other. Martina La'ew of Yap explains how some Japanese soldiers tried to protect local food supplies from military demands, and her grandmother's generosity in return:

[Before we began to tape, La'ew described how soldiers in other villages went into taro patches, took their shovels and dug holes in them, or cut down the taro and pulled it out.] If the food was near them [the Japanese], you could not [harvest it], because you might be beaten. If they saw a man walking around, about Fanguchel's age or Chad's age [i.e., an old man], and they told him, "Hey! You climb up and get us some coconuts!" And if he said, "No, I cannot"—they'd beat him. The only village where the soldiers were kind was Toway [La'ew's village]. Just here in Toway, those [soldiers] who settled in Tungun [name of a tabinaw, or patrilineal estate] were kind. They didn't use to beat people like the others. Our grandmother stayed with them inland [i.e., the soldiers lived in the tabinaw of Tungun, and grandmother stayed inland of that place] and provided food for them. The leader of the soldiers told the soldiers not to go in the taro patch, not to go around picking food, because our grandmother stayed there to provide food for them, so they weren't to go around getting food for themselves. So the taro patches were still okay; our grandmother still got taro from them, because the soldiers didn't ruin it. Also, the village [of Toway] was all right. If the leader wanted to eat taro, he sent a message to our grandmother. The messenger would go to see her and say, "You are to pick taro, just two." Our grandmother would pick a whole basket of taro [more than she was asked for]. She would get a basket of food and give it to him [the messenger], and she also cooked some and gave it to him [for the soldiers].

Where friendly relations were impossible, tension was reflected through memories of food. Mieko Nipuk is one of many who explained the need to resort to theft to survive in some parts of Chuuk Lagoon:

When we got to Fefan, I went and stayed with Enis Nipuk [her uncle] at Upwin on Fefan, in a Chuukese house. Then my "mother," named Mocheria, she said she was going to look for me, because she was worried about me. So she found me, and they took me to Tatiw, and that's where I lived until the end of the war. It was miserable. And that's how the Japanese took control of the land, the food, the trees. That's why the Chuukese were starving. The only thing that kept us alive was because I married Este, and he was the one who looked after us. This is when the Nauruans started coming in [transported from Nauru by the Japanese]; they were bringing in one group after another. And then they had them settled in different areas on Tatiw. That's when there was no food at all, on Tatiw. We were really starving, so that's when we went out and started stealing from the farms, and they would bring the food back, and we would eat. The Nauruans also were stealing. And then they distributed them [Nauruans] on Tol, Wone, because we were really starving. That's when five [Chuukese] would go, four would go, dying of starvation [four or five would die of starvation]. The children started eating roots of potatoes and what is left after you squeeze cream from coconuts. We would boil the breadfruit like soft rice, and eat that. If they hadn't started stealing from the Japanese farms, we wouldn't have had anything to eat. And when we cooked, we would go cook in the caves, so they wouldn't see the smoke. If they saw the fire or the smoke, we would get it.

Ironically, the bombing that destroyed food stores and prevented supplies from reaching the islands also produced occasional abundance. Este Nipuk of Parem, Chuuk, is one of many who recalled the unexpected supply of fish produced as a result of Allied bombing in the lagoon:

[Q: You did not eat every day?] Oh, there was no food! Our breadfruit, they took it away. . . . We started eating potato leaves and taro leaves. [Q: How could you eat taro leaves (which are toxic)?] We had to take off the skin down to the white part and cook it; the potato leaves you just cook and eat. They say that this wild yam, they say that Fefan started eating that; but we hadn't yet gotten to that. [Q: Didn't you get sick from not eating anything, or from the water?] Yes, the only thing that made it easy was that we started eating more fish, because of the bombing. After the bombing, the fish would be floating around; we would get on a boat and go out and collect the fish. . . . We'd just eat them fresh or cook them in leaves over the open fire. We'd eat today, there would be bombing tomorrow, we'd eat again, go out and pick up the fish.

Usual forms of fishing were dangerous, since Allied air attacks made fishermen easy targets, as Dione Hatchkawari, Pohrakiet (Kapingamarangi Village), Pohnpei, recounts:

When I worked as a fisherman with the Japanese soldiers, one day I went fishing with a Kapinga and a Japanese. When we were in the sea fishing, an American warplane shot at us. That plane damaged our canoe. I told the Kapinga man to take the Japanese and swim with him to the reef, because I wanted to untie our fishing poles and then swim after them. While I was untying our fishing poles, the American plane came back and flew in low. I hid under the outrigger platform. I swam after them; we swam to Dewak. I told the Japanese soldier that we should bury our fishing lines there and swim to Kolonia. The Japanese soldier didn't want us to swim, because he was afraid of sharks. Then I said, "You're afraid of sharks, but you're not afraid of warplanes?" The Japanese soldier said that he was afraid of warplanes, but when he reached there he was also afraid of the sharks. This was the difficulty that I had during the war.

Many items besides food were scarce during the war, including all imports: medical supplies, tobacco, soap, kerosene, needles, and Japanese foods such as rice and soy sauce. The shortage of clothing, though, stands out in memories. Woven goods are a critical channel of women's power throughout the Pacific.[6] Over the previous century and a half, cloth had become an important item of exchange and control that linked Micronesia with colonial powers. By the time the war began, dependence on imported cloth had replaced knowledge of local methods of production in many locations, making it hard for people to manage substitutes. Sachuo Siwi of Toloas, Chuuk, describes one improvisation:

Some old people had nothing to wear. They cut their mosquito nets and sewed them for clothing. We were troubled because we needed clothes, but we didn't have anywhere to get them. So that was why those old people decided it was better for mosquitoes to bite us and suck our blood than [for us] to walk around naked. That's why they tore down their mosquito nets and made clothes out of them.

Melsor Panuelo, Net, Pohnpei, recalls other makeshifts:

Cloth was a real hardship. People who had stored up clothing for the war were okay, but otherwise.... There were some places in Pohnpei where women would go into the water, take off their clothes, wash them up, and wait in the water for them to dry. When they were dry, they got dressed again. There was a kind of cloth, called houtai, *used for bandages; these were sewn together. Also long stockings, which were cut and sewn together. Some had to use mats. They rolled up inside of these and stayed inside the house all day.*

Kristina Sehna, then a young girl in Kiti, Pohnpei, remembers:

During the war, life was very difficult because we ran out of clothes. I had no clothes at that time. If my mother had died, I could not have left the house [to attend the funeral], because I had no clothes.

Like food, cloth has symbolic meaning as well as practical use. Cloth is inextricably intertwined with missionization. Marshallese still speak of foreigners as "the people of cloth" *(dri palle)*. Missionaries used clothing to distinguish converts. For Islanders who had come to see properly clothed bodies as a mark of the historical shift from the pagan past, the lack of manufactured cloth and clothing during the war became particularly significant. Reverting to old methods of manufacture to replace or repair clothing was a sign of shame, poverty, immodesty, and other degraded conditions.

This song from Palau, sung in Palauan but patterned after Japanese songs, presents wartime deprivation explicitly in a social context, to the point of giving scarcity its own personalized identity:

Untitled Song
Unknown Composer
Ngarchelong, Palau, 1945
(Collected and translated by M. Tmodrang and Wakako Higuchi, n.d.)

Now that we have become friends,
I wish things were the way they used to be.
So when we come to visit here,
 we can also go visit other places.[7]
Poverty and sacrifices in war camps;
people have been starving too long.
Mr. Famine came and put a spell upon us,
so we're eating denges[8] *and* belloi.[9]
If it was up to us to request,
we would ask Mr. War
to stop all his warfare.[10]
Because friends, we've suffered a great deal.

ROMANTIC ENCOUNTERS

Perhaps, as Matsuko Soram on Chuuk commented, it was the scarcity of clothing that led men's and women's thoughts to romance during the war! But though it might seem odd at first, a few moments' reflection will show how closely love and war are linked in many cultural traditions, where people tell, and live, stories of romantic love in the midst of violent conflict. Micronesians, too, speak of romantic experiences when they talk about the war years. Partly this is because the elders we interviewed were recalling their youth when they spoke of that time, but it is also true that Micronesians share a well-established tradition of romantic expression that was, at least for some, heightened by danger. As Pohnpeian Mikel Diana commented,

To me, it appeared that while the war was getting worse, and the laws tougher, the feeling for love was also getting stronger. A man who was separated from his lover during the war seemed to have developed the feeling of greater affection and love for his lover. That's how it seemed to have happened to people.

If life is lived in a much more public arena in the small island communities of Micronesia than in Europe or the United States, romantic love is, perhaps, more highly sequestered. Such sentiments are rarely expressed in public, and remain on the fringe of daily discourse within households. Yet romance fills many private thoughts and shared moments in the lives of men and women of Micronesia. In these cultures, romantic love is potentially very powerful. Indeed, in its most refined forms it approaches obsession, which is said to be dangerous and best avoided. Since love can be manipulated with magic, increased commitment leads to increased risk. Perhaps for this reason, love should be, and often is, somewhat fickle and fragile, especially among the young. Youthful paramours dedicate much energy to discussing and pursuing amorous relationships. Many expect that when lovers are apart, they will seek other partners, and assume that any private encounter will lead to a sexual relationship. Thus, jealousies are common, and it is presumed that a lengthy separation will result in each partner's searching for new relationships.

War proved to be a context filled with the possibility of breaking and mending youthful love matches. Because of the private nature of romantic love, this entire phase of life and important cultural domain is most often publicly expressed through song, rather than personal narrative. Among the surprises of our interviews was the number of love songs—some still well-known—composed during the war. The following two songs were among those composed by two Kiti women working on Japanese plantations in Palikir, Pohnpei. These songs mock the efforts of some very young men from the nearby chiefdom of Uh who attempted to court them. Lihna Lawrence sang them for us:

Untitled Song #1
Unknown Composer

You are a little bit smart,
and have moved up a little to the higher level.
Seems stupid,
you give yourself to me.
I'm sorry,
because [I] don't enjoy you.

Untitled Song #2
Unknown Composer

The men from Uh think they are better
than frogs or whimbrels.
[They are] bragging like herons.

That father is praising
the wild hens.

In a song from Nama, Mortlock Islands, a man returns from his contract labor job with gifts for his lover, only to find that she has betrayed him, despite her protestations of love when he left.

Untitled Song
Unknown Composer
(Sung by Biana of Nama)
(Collected by Rosalinda Walter; translated by Miako Hengio)

Why did I waste my time working for the cost of your dress?
All you strong people who stayed home destroyed the fruits of my labor.
Don't write to me any longer, for I've already taken another lover.
So why did you cry out to me from beside the boat [as I left]?

Another well-known song, composed by a man from Sapwuahfik working on Pohnpei, sings of the power of love, more fearful than the Allied bombs:

Untitled Song

Unknown Composer

Planes flying under the heavens—
I am not afraid.
My love for you—
That I fear.

A final song from Chuuk tells of lovers from different islands who long to forge a lasting bond.

Untitled Song

Composed by Stiven, from Lukunor, who relocated to Sopore,
*   Fefan, after the war*
(Collected and translated by Father Andrew, Catholic Mission,
*   Tunnuk, Weno)*

We're happy and we love one another,
our heart is one and we love one another.
This love will remain between us.

We want to express our gratitude and ask pardon for our shortcomings
in our coming to you today.
We come empty-handed;
we just come that we might join you (in life) once again.

Your island and my island are far apart.
We shall remain together,
we shall speak your language,
we shall be united in one body.

Chorus: Our coming is not like a bomb
*   which destroys island, land, and trees.*
*   I want to seek (and find) the rope that binds us together—*
*   love for your place and my place.*

Let's join together in happiness,
happiness and unity and love for one another.
One true heart,
mutual love and long-lasting relationship
will bind us together as one.

CHIEFS AND LEADERS

The social harmony valued by Island societies derives in part from due recognition for a ranked order. Micronesian communities vary a good deal in how rank conscious or egalitarian they are and in how the chiefly tradition has changed or persisted under modern economic and political conditions.[11] We can say, in a general way, that across Micronesia adults work to maintain and advance their social standing on a daily basis. They think and talk about who should and does manage the decision making in their communities and to what extent individuals or lineages use that power wisely. Most communities include chiefs and commoners, and a title system—a ranked set of identities, like that of the European aristocracy, with its own rules of precedence, obligation, and entitlement. In many islands, this title system allowed people to manage most internal decision making, at least until it was reshaped by severe impacts of colonial rule or Christian mission activity. The disruptions of the Pacific War also had an effect on the form and operation of rank.

Chiefly power had been changing significantly in the decades before the war. More than a hundred years of contact (four hundred in the Marianas) with European, American, and Japanese entrepreneurs, missionaries, and colonial officials had already altered the economic, political, and religious roles of indigenous leaders. A new elite of foreign-educated and mixed-descent people grew up, people who used their personal ties and their linguistic and cultural skills to carve spheres of influence that were separate from, overlapping with, and sometimes antagonistic to the goals of leaders holding traditional titles. And within the title systems themselves, the balance between inheriting a title and competing for one through achievement shifted in response to new opportunities. Access to foreign or imported education, currency, goods, and ideas became part of how one gained status in the indigenous system.

Before and in the first years of war, Japanese-appointed chiefs played a role in the civil administration of the Nan'yō as Micronesia underwent land confiscation, military construction, labor conscription, and new security regulations. The Nan'yō had already gone far in altering indigenous leadership. In some cases, especially on smaller, distant atolls, Japanese officials confirmed the appointments of Micronesian leaders while encasing them in regulations and police oversight. On the more populous islands, Japanese interests more directly shaped Micronesian leadership, with colonial administrators approving and in some cases even naming officeholders. Islander "chiefs" (given Japanese ranks) were paid and were expected to carry out official duties. Other local elites grew or strengthened during this time, including young Islanders who achieved high levels of Japanese schooling and mixed Micronesian-Japanese (or Okinawan) families. During the war, some of these distinctions of rank were emphasized, while others weakened.[12] As Japanese military laborers, and then troops, entered the islands and demands for labor escalated, Micronesians who spoke Japanese were hired as translators and work bosses. This was both a privileged and a stressful position; as conditions worsened, these intermediaries found themselves sometimes able to help their compatriots, but also obliged to enforce military decrees.

Kun Aaron, nicknamed "Ankoa," worked as a boss for a labor group on Kosrae during the war. He recalls that the position was difficult, since local people accused him of being harsh. This song, which Kun Aaron sang for us, was one way they expressed their feelings:

Ankoa
Unknown Composer

Ankoa is enslaving us,
forces us to collect some copra
for the Nistai Ompu[13] *soldiers.*
We are weary and tired.

> Chorus: *A time for picking crabs,*
>   *a time for collecting copra.*
>   *Ankoa is really enslaving us.*

At the height of the war, when military control effaced most civil power, few Micronesian leaders could defend or aid their community. Islanders recognize the powerlessness of chiefs in these conditions, but they also remember chiefs who tried to help. Sometimes they succeeded, as we see in this song from Puluwat (translated by John Sandy). The Japanese military had ordered Puluwat people to leave for Pulusuk and Pulap. A chief named Ikepi objected, saying, "We were born here, we will die here." The armed soldiers lined up; the executioner threatened Ikepi with his sword, ordering him, "You and your people move away." Ikepi replied, "No." Takukuma—the "Tak" of the song—was the executioner prepared to kill Ikepi. Ikepi was saved when his sister's son bowed three times, begged forgiveness, and said he was the successor and had the authority to give the order, so Takukuma returned his sword to its sheath. In the song, the people gather to learn their fate as the Japanese order evacuation; in the end, the young chief's effective intervention preserves them all in safety. The song commemorates the action of Ikepi and his sister's son, leaders of Puluwat, in facing Japanese orders to leave their home. It was sung by two of Ikepi's nieces:

Untitled Song
Unknown Composer

On that frantic day, I was so busy . . .
They sent a letter to Kafakimwen [place name]:
Hurry up, come, women and men—
we will gather in a meeting place to listen.
Let's listen to the words of Takukuma,
speaking harsh words about the southern chief.
His fearful words match the weapon in his hand.
But now here comes the beloved nobleman, the chief's nephew,
interpreting [the chief's] words.
Bowing low, then straightening, greeting Tak to his face.
His smile means there will be no beating.

A common element of colonial policy is to reward native people who acculturate: this is as true of the American era as it was of the Japanese. Those who had attained significant success under Japanese colonial rule talk about this, sometimes recognizing that their investment in the Japanese system was, in retrospect, wasted. For these Micronesians, who lost status in the shift from Japanese to American rule, the war is seen as a threat to social harmony because it destabilized the established social order. Yet the war also presented opportunities for the disempowered. In our conversation with Thaddeus Sampson of the Marshall Islands, he reflects on his confidence in his future had the Japanese continued in power.

They were saying that if Japan wins, they would do many things. They would return the [money from the war] bonds, and they would also give us a new level [of citizenship]. Under the Japanese, there were three levels; well, they would have elevated us to the second level if they had won. . . . In previous times, before the war, they would use the word tomi *[tōmin, third-class citizen]; it was like saying "native," not Japanese. . . . But after the war, if they had won, they would have put everyone in the same category. [Q: And did you believe they would do this?] They told me. They told me, and they said if Japan wins, you can go to school in Japan. Previously, during that era, it was illegal for a Marshallese to go to school in Japan. But if Japan had won, I would have gone to school in Japan, to the high-ranked schools in Tokyo. This is what they told me. . . . During those times, if we had continued to live with the Japanese, we would have been raised to the second level. The Okinawans would have moved up to be at the same level as the Japanese, and we would occupy the second level. It was the same with the war bonds. If they had won, we would have been paid.*

Chapter 12

GREETINGS AND FAREWELLS

ANYONE WHO HAS LIVED on a Pacific Island treasures memories of poignant welcomes and leave-takings. Small islands, by their nature, make vivid settings for ceremonies of arrival and departure. Ships or planes are sighted at a distance and watched into port; songs, dances, and feasts often mark the start and finish of visits. Even the ordinary comings and goings of travel off-island to work, to school, or for medical care are never routine. One never knows—and certainly in the years of war this was even more true—when or whether relatives or friends will meet again. Island songs and stories reflect this uncertainty and the fraught scene of parting.

In a larger sense, the comings and goings of colonial powers mark Micronesia's recent history: first came the Spanish, whose long presence began with the arrival of Magellan in Guam in 1521, extended to other parts of Micronesia, and ended in 1885; then Germans, then Japanese, then Americans arrived as conquerors. These official regime shifts were marked by the ritual of raising and lowering of flags and other ceremonies. Micronesians also note the changing of colonial orders, but with attention to their own concerns rather than the bureaucracy of empires.

HAIL TO THE NEW CHIEFS: THE AMERICANS ARRIVE

As Japanese victory seemed increasingly doubtful, Micronesians had begun to ask new questions. What would happen to them if Japan lost? Would the Americans consider Micronesians to be enemies, indistinguishable from Japanese? Would Islanders be treated as prisoners of war, harmed or exploited by the invaders? Would Americans kill them all, as the Japanese claimed? Such rumors and fears fill Micronesian accounts of this era.

Many stories from this period are devoted to working out what Americans were like, how they differed from Japanese, and why they had come to this part of the world. Several factors shape how Americans are depicted. First, storytellers differed greatly in their familiarity with Americans. Residents of Guam or the Marshall Islands had a longer history of interactions with Americans both before and after the war, whereas people from the Central Caroline Islands had few encounters on which to base their views. Also, many speakers note that their opinions changed during the war, when U.S. military power undermined Japanese claims of invincibility. The exact timings and contexts of Islanders' wartime encounters with Americans are also significant factors. The distribution of much-needed supplies in the wake of battle is routinely

Admiral DeWitt C. Ramsey greets the chief of Ngulu, Yap. (U.S. Navy photo, National Archives photo no. 499123)

mentioned in recollections of early interactions with Americans. The personal fortune of the speaker's family is a major factor in a narrator's assessment of the Americans in relation to the Japanese.

Stories about Americans also reveal how Micronesians understand their recent histories and current political situations vis-à-vis the United States. American governance of Micronesia has had both failures and successes. After sixty years of experience with Americans in postwar Micronesia, many of the elders who told these stories do not see the Americans unambiguously as "the good guys." Yet even when describing how American bombs and bullets killed Islanders (sometimes in deliberate or near-deliberate ways, as in the Marshall Islands or the bombing of Pulap), stories about Americans are interestingly varied and complex; very few blame Americans for wartime destruction.

In their stories of World War II Micronesians frequently express forgiveness toward both the Japanese and the Allies. People say that the wartime activities of both parties were due to the circumstances of war; they were not intended to harm local people; rather, as one resident said, "We simply got in their way." Indeed, in many cases, Islanders excuse the Americans, claiming that they deliberately avoided targeting Islanders, or commenting that harm to Islanders was an accident of war.

Respect and politeness are important elements of the Micronesian social code. Given the face-to-face interaction in these small communities, formal apologies and forgiveness are important components of ongoing mutual respect and a mechanism to both recognize and restore hierarchical status relations. Cultural mechanisms exist throughout Micronesia by which an offending party can and should formally apologize for a wrong. Once an apology has been properly made, there is strong social support for its acceptance. Once a grievance has been formally forgiven, there should be no lingering ill-will. At some level, the past is never entirely forgotten, yet overt retribution is rare, and ill-feelings are usually expressed only in private settings.

American Liberation?

The I-Kiribati people—like Guam's Chamorros, members of former Allied colonies—welcomed the invasion of their Japanese-occupied islands as "liberation." This song from Kiribati reflects the clear sense of relief and the promise of a return to their life before the war:

Untitled Song

Unknown Composer
Lakobo, Kuria Islands, Kiribati
(Sung at a special ceremony on the occasion of the first visit of British District Officer Major F. J. Holland, OBEGM, after his landing on nearby Abemama with counterinvading American forces[1])

We are in merry mood.
The warships are now safely at anchor;
their crews roam our shores.

Chorus: Men, women, and children,
*   fear no more.*
*   All the enemy forces have been annihilated.*
*   A secure life to everyone is now assured,*
*   and freedom is ours.*

The warships are from America,
which is protecting us.
Merrily, merrily they sail along.

(Chorus)

We have heard the glad news,
the capture of Tarawa is confirmed.
Abemama and Makin have been liberated.

(Chorus)

Our friend Major Holland was with Americans,
when they landed at Tarawa.
Be happy! For our cause is victorious.

(Chorus)

The fortifications on Betio were very strong.
Every part of the island guarded.
Coastal defense guns surrounded it.

(Chorus)

The brave Americans made their landing
under heavy gunfire from the beaches.
They fought until all the atoll was theirs.

(Chorus)

Our hearts are filled with joy
because the Allied Forces have come among us.
We thank our liberators a thousand times.

(Chorus)

For Micronesians in the former Japanese Mandate, the transition to American rule, while not exactly considered "liberation," was nevertheless a welcome relief from the hardships of war. Asked what he thought when he first saw the arrival of the first Americans, Bwirre Lejman from Jaluij said, "I was happy, because my worries were gone, and my suffering."

But for some Micronesians who had little knowledge of Americans, their arrival created anxiety. An account by Makino Tariu of Palau (collected and translated by Wakako Higuchi, 1986) provides an example of how widely emotions could range during that period:

One day (probably in August 1945) I went to Taiyo Nojo (Taiyo farm) in Ngiwal, where almost all of the workers were Japanese women. There were twenty-two or twenty-three families, a total of seventy people lived there. When I was halfway there, U.S. planes flew over. I hid under a tree, but they didn't shoot. Many white papers were dropped. I took one of them which said, "The war is over. Saipan, Okinawa, [many place names] occupied by the U.S." Two or three Japanese soldiers came there soon and scolded me. "Don't take and read it." I threw it away. All the papers were collected by the soldiers. I reached Taiyo Nojo and visited the office of the military police. A military policeman was crying and said, "We got an order from Japan to stop the war." I can't describe my mind then. I was rather confused. But I was sure that I was mortified at the defeat by the U.S. I was so afraid that I would have to suffer under the U.S. from that time on.

I returned to my village and called people to rebuild our house, as seinen-dancho *[leader of* seinen-dan*]. Teru Shudan (Teru troop) was stationed one mile from Taiyo Nojo. We took all the materials from the houses that had been* *used by the military, and built our housing in the former place. When I sent Hachisu off near Renraku Doro [present KB bridge], I saw Americans for the first time. I was very afraid of them. Especially Palauan women were in perpetual fear of American men. They believed that our women would be killed by rape. Palauan men felt Americans had no discipline, because they smiled at us without any reason. It was our idea that men should not show their teeth [smile] easily. However, our impression changed, because Americans supplied us with very big cans of corned beef and much food that was transported from Peleliu. We said, "Americans are excellent. They are great."*

Tupun Louis's account also reflects the fear and uncertainty generated by the arrival of American troops in Chuuk after the end of the war:

We didn't know that it was going to be kaijo *[end of the war]. During that time before the* kaijo, *we worked really hard, night and day. Most of our work was cleaning up the bomb craters and dead bodies. And then they said, the war is over,* kaijo. *The Japanese did not tell us it was* kaijo. *We were hiding in the caves, and we didn't know that the noise of airplanes and ships was the Americans. The Americans came on the island. We saw the navy, Americans. We didn't come out; we were scared of them. The leaders said, "Okay, we remain here. If they spray us with poison gas, just stay here. We will die together." And we prayed. Prayed, prayed, and looked out—all the Americans were around. We looked out from inside, and the Americans looked in. And I was thinking, "Maybe the Americans are also afraid that we might hurt them." The Americans spoke to us. We didn't know what they were saying. We were thinking, "Maybe they won't hurt us." That's the time we knew the Americans had won the war. They won— and we lost.*

Among the group in that cave were two oldest men: one old man from Neme, named Damin, and one from Losap, named Sana. There were women and children. The old man from Neme went out. "If they kill me, then you will know that all of us will die." He went out and stood amongst them. They were all looking at him, and shaking his hand, taking out cigarettes, giving him cigarettes, lighting one for him. They put a shirt on him, and a pair of pants. "Wow, lucky guy!"—we were looking out; the Americans actually dressed him. He came back in: "Now we will go out, because Japan lost." Maybe he knew some English, because since German times, this old man had been with foreigners. "We will go out and line up, and I'll teach you a greeting, how to greet these people." And someone inside said, "Why are we going to go out?" The old man said, "Japan lost, and they're taking all the Japanese soldiers, without shirts, wearing only pants. They lost. They gathered all the Japanese officers in Rerre." At that time, we didn't know the war was over. We were confused, without information, we were not informed.

We went out; the old man lined us up. He taught us how to say hello to the Americans. Before we greeted these Americans, we would bow down, and as we rose, we would say our greetings. Everyone would line up—women and children.

[Q: Do you still remember what that greeting was, how you said hello?] Yes. The old man told us, every one of us, one by one, the word we would say. We would bow down, and then as we came up we would say, "How do you do, sir!" [English]. That was the greeting word: "How d'ye do, sir!" He went away from me, and I just repeated the words, "How d'ye do sir, How d'ye do sir," to memorize the words. We were wearing torn clothes. "Okay, get ready—face them now! Then, give the word." We bowed, and then we said the greeting. And the Americans were laughing. They gave us clothes, one by one, they gave us clothes. For the ladies, they gave them the coats [kapa, raincoats], because there were no dresses. They gave us cigarettes, until everyone had everything. And then they distributed biscuits [cookies] and candies. They had four trucks; they got up on their trucks and they left. And we saw Chuukese people riding with these Americans, going around. As we were looking around, we saw these Chuukese on the American trucks, and we said, "What's up?" And they said, "Kaijo! The Japanese are on the American ships, going back." And that was the end of the war.

Other stories reveal a frank mix of feelings about the transition, as in these comments by William Prens of Kolonia, Pohnpei:

When the Americans came, they got the Japanese soldiers and sent them back to Japan. They gave the Pohnpeians some help—cigarettes, food, C-rations, cloth, including old military uniforms. There were no bad feelings toward us; the Americans only wanted to offer help. Nothing really happened among the Japanese. They just got together and gathered their belongings and got aboard the ship. The Pohnpeians were happy because the war was over.

Once the Americans got here, they were kind, helpful, generous. They didn't shoot at anyone. Many Pohnpeians went to work for the Americans at Yasarin. The Japanese had navy quarters there. Some Pohnpeians felt sorry for the Japanese; it was hard to see them go. Pohnpeians are kind, helpful people. They are similar to the Japanese. They [Japanese] are also helpful, respectful, and this made relations between us easy. Other countries are not respectful like this.

I don't know if there was any celebration when the Americans arrived. But Pohnpeians were happy; this was a good era and cause for celebration. This was not because the Americans won and the Japanese lost. Actually, we liked them both. The reason for celebration was just because the war had ended. This is what we really needed [the war to be over].

FIRST IMPRESSIONS

In seeking to understand these newly arriving Americans, Micronesians used what very little they had to go on—mostly their own limited observations. When we asked Nathan Tartios, Maloelap, Marshall Islands, about his first impression of Americans, he said,

I was afraid of them on account of their lying. [Q: Why?] Because they had long noses. And they were giants, very large. I was afraid and then, afterwards, it was fine because they said, "Oh, buddy, buddy," and on things went and my fear disappeared. And then, they gave us stuff—chewing gum and those things. [Q: But at first, you said . . . ?] Eech.

Consider this excerpt from a song composed by Letaweriur, the young wife of an elder schoolteacher, celebrating the arrival of Americans in Ifaluk, Yap. The words express relief and delight at war's end, but note the vague and impersonal references to the early American presence:

Untitled Song
Unknown Composer
(Collected and translated by Edwin G. Burrows, 1963:414; cited in Tammy Duchesne, 2004:81)

Now all our women rejoice;
now the Americans have come.

This is pleasing to the chiefs.
They have given us a paper.

This place is to rise;
this island is to be lifted up.
The chiefs say we are to dance.
We will dance, we will rejoice!
This very month, for this is a good year! Ei!

The chiefs we have are fine men;
it is good that the Americans have come.
They make my heart rejoice.
Oho! My heart is gay.

The Japanese are gone.
We did not like their rough ways.
The gods have been good to us;
now our crops are safe.
The Americans talk kindly.

The people of the Marshall Islands, the first Japanese territory taken by the Allies, were more familiar with Americans than were other Micronesians, largely because of the early missionary presence, the fact that the first invaded atolls received American largesse at a time when it flowed freely, and that the U.S. Navy worked hard to cultivate Marshallese goodwill and rescued Marshallese from the remaining Japanese-held atolls. In their first encounters, some Marshallese tried to establish links with Americans by referring to the earlier American presence in their islands. Daisey Lojkar from Kwajalein Atoll recalled American missionary education and the promise it held for good treatment by these new arrivals:

And then, when the battle arrived, it lasted about three or four days, and then it was over, and then the Americans were there on Kwajalein, at that time. It was not a week, it was not even a single week that the Americans attacked, it was a very short time, and so they were on Kwajalein; this was 1944. [Q: And did the Americans ever come and land on the islet where you were staying?] Yes, they came at the time of the battle, at the time when they conquered, they came to our islets and . . . we came forward and showed them [His] books, the songbook,

*and the big book [the Bible], and read them and looked at them, and we bowed
down, and then we ate together because we had already finished preparing pandanus and coconut and breadfruit. We brought them over and we ate with them,
the Americans, but we were frightened. We were frightened, but they said, "Do
not be afraid," because many Marshallese came with them, and also some of
them knew how to speak Marshallese. And they said, "Do not be afraid of us
because we have really come to watch over you." So then we sat down and ate,
but we were still frightened, because we had just seen them for the first time. And
there was nothing in particular that we did; we just ate. And then there was an
old man who prayed. And then we ate together.*

*[Q: What were you thinking about when you first saw these Americans?]
Well, we were petrified, and this is typical because we just saw them for the first
time, but they were good. The way they came and mixed among us was good,
and then afterward, when the tanks landed and came up onto the islet, we were
amazed. "Why is it that these boats are coming and they continue coming right
up onto the islet toward us?" [Q: You were frightened?] Well, after that we said,
"Umh!" Well, so then, we went ahead and sat down because there was nothing else possible for us to contemplate, so we went ahead and sat down and
waited, and watched to see what [would happen]. And so things went onward
and onward, and they came toward us and kept coming until they were next
to us, and so then when they came and remained next to us; well, we listened
[because] there had once been a missionary who had come to Kwajalein, and
we would go to the church and to Sunday school and they said, "Well, if the
Americans ever come, the way in which they treat you will be really good." And
these sorts of things they said. . . . Some of the missionaries who had come to the
Marshalls had come and taught us English and then returned to America, and
they said, "You guys really look out for the Marshallese because the Marshallese
really know—we have already taught them about the Bible and they really know
it." And so then when they came, we showed them the songbook, the large book
[the Bible]. And we gave them to them and they looked at them.*

In Thaddeus Sampson's description of the early encounter with invading American troops on Kwajalein, he includes details that particularize the
American in the person of a minister and describes one Marshallese response.
By casting the story in this form—with complex moral issues shading each
individual's actions—the encounter on the invasion beach becomes a com-

mentary on past and future political relationships, namely, significant cross-cultural misunderstandings:

There is a story about a teacher or preacher. His name was Doctor Erling [Henley?]. He landed at the time of the [American] conquest of Kwajalein; he was the chaplain. And then when he landed with the American soldiers and placed his foot upon Kwajalein, he knew a little bit of Marshallese, and knew from this and pidgin, the words that were suited for him to use. And the very first word that he spoke was "Aineman"—peace. Peace, peace. That was the word that was appropriate for him to say. And so then when he landed, he went around to the holes where people had hidden themselves and he did not know if there were Marshallese or Japanese inside, but he would call out and say, "Come here, come here. It is fine. Peace has arrived." And he would go to another hole and say, "Come. Come out. It is fine. Peace." And he went to one hole which was precisely the location of a person from these atolls and he called out and said, "It's okay. Peace. Come here. Come here. Peace. Come here. There is no damage." That was how he spoke in Marshallese.

But that fellow responded with a hand grenade. [Q: Who was that?] Lokujo. A man from Namdik. So that fellow pulled on [the fuse of] the hand grenade and looked to see how he would get rid of it. But, you see, in those holes, there were coconut logs about this big around there at the opening of the shelter, and he did not throw precisely out through the door, but it hit that post and bounced back. And it came back and exploded inside. And all of the people inside that hole died. [Q: And that fellow, Lokujo?] Well, he died. Only a few lived, and it's the two of them who tell this story. They were there by the other opening, some other Marshallese. And so this hand grenade came back inside on them and they died, and the minister, he looked inside, and he saw them [dead] inside the hole. [Q: And he knew that they were Marshallese?] Yes, he knew, because he watched them as they came toward him and threw that thing at him. They attempted to throw it at him . . . he [Lokujo] did not know that this fellow was a minister. Perhaps if he had known, he would have been ashamed.

THE SHARING OF RESOURCES

There is a long history of conquering chiefs in the Marshall Islands. When American troops defeated Japanese garrisons at Kwajalein and Enewetak, and when they came ashore without violence at Majuro and the unfortified atolls, Marshallese readily understood the concept of new "chiefs" replacing former rulers. The process was repeated throughout Micronesia, in many places without violence or even drama. In the accounts of American arrival presented below, we see Americans represented as new chiefs, in certain ways—that is, they conquered territory (as chiefs have always done) and followed their victory by offering generous gifts of food, clothing, and other aid. It may be that this welcome generosity, coming on the heels of scarcity and hardship, cemented an impression of Americans as caretakers and chiefs of the region. If Micronesians of the wartime era got that impression from American largesse, it

Men in mess hall chow line, on Falalop, Ulithi. (U.S. Navy photo, National Archives photo no. 347516)

resulted in difficult consequences, since the U.S. government was not inclined to continue its generous ways. In fact, in the first postwar decades, Micronesians found themselves receiving very little in the way of material assistance as they struggled to rebuild a war-devastated economy.

The new American chiefs made perhaps their major initial impression by generously distributing large amounts of food, including new kinds of food, as commemorated in this Kosraean song.

Untitled Song
Unknown Composer
(Collected and translated by Walter Scott Wilson, 1968:36)

[The] American ship came
carrying freedom.
A lot of food they carried.
Everybody lined up for [it]:
tin[s] of egg,
tin[s] of hash,
also cheese and candy inside.
Eat and remember.

Leban Jorju fondly remembers the huge quantities of food supplied by Americans following their victory at Kwajalein, especially the corned beef:

[Q: Were you ever frightened during the battle?] Yes, of course I was frightened, and I will never forget when I was hungry. [Q: But was there anything you remember with fondness during the time of the battle?] Well, I will always remember with fondness the foods of the Americans. We could throw them away, because there was no cost; and one corned beef, iieo! [indicates the length of his forearm]. [Laughs.] A single can of your own corned beef [and that size!]. [Marshallese interviewer: Nearly all of the respected elders say this in their remembrances. They say, "You see, during the battle, they (Americans) came and brought corned beef, iieo! (the length of your forearm)." Long ones, the males of the species. If you opened one, fifty people would have their hunger for meat satisfied.]

Well, that is one of the remembrances the Marshallese will never forget. Yes, we young boys did not know how to open those things at that time. There were cases that these things were in. We took a case and threw it down on the ground

so that one of them would break open. [Q: And when they would break open?]
Then we would eat, along with scraped coconut.

Andonio Raidong, Kolonia, Pohnpei, jokes about his eagerness for
American food, especially canned corned beef, and the translation problems
involved in obtaining it:

At the time that the Americans arrived, I was staying in Net. It was clear that
the Americans had won. They played some sports in Palikir when they landed
[this was several months after the Japanese surrender]. The American soldiers
left their food on the wharf. I didn't know how to speak English. There were Ping-
elapese, their kids, me and my wife. We were going to Net. There were some sol-
diers there. They told them if the soldiers didn't come back, they could have the
food. I fooled the Pingelapese people; I told them not to touch the food. I wanted
to get all the food for myself and my wife. So when the Pingelapese left, I took all
the food home, because the soldiers hadn't come back. They were C-rations. . . .

One time, I was in the municipal office. A ship came in and a captain and his
mate came in. They brought in their lunch. I couldn't speak English. They asked
me what I wanted (I think). I was making coffee (or tea). And my wife asked me
what they were saying. I said, "Maybe they want to eat their lunch and drink cof-
fee or tea. So prepare some." We gave it to them, and they were satisfied.

After awhile one asked me what I wanted. All I knew in English then was
"ship come back." Maybe they would go back to the ship, get what I wanted, and
bring it back. The soldiers used to throw away stuff; we used to go get potatoes
from our garden, and one day while walking by the garbage dump I discovered a
large round can. Some people who went to work on Nauru brought back corned
beef, and this is how I got to like this type of food. So I remembered about the can,
and brought it to the American soldier. The soldier said, "So you want this?" (in
English). The label was still on the can; but it was beans! I knew about beans
because I used to grow them in the garden when I was in school. So I said, "No,
no!" So I put up two fingers, like horns on my head. And the soldier said, "Jesus
Christ." And then I remembered that the Japanese soldiers told us that that was
the sign of the devil! So I felt bad because I thought the American thought I was
making the sign of the devil. So I made the sound, "Moo, moo," and the sol-
dier said, "Corned beef?" and I said, "Yes, yes!" The next morning they came
back and the captain came to me and said, "Moo" (here's your corned beef). He
brought two six-pound cans.

One effect of the self-deprecating humor in such stories is to emphasize the power and wealth of Americans—that is, to represent them as chiefs. And also like good chiefs, the Americans explicitly promised to watch over and take care of Micronesians. Reverend Kanki Amlej, who lived on Wotje and Likiep, Marshall Islands, during the war, recalls,

So, they [Americans] came and asked if there were any Japanese. "None." "Well, all of the people should go to the government building so we can raise the flag." Yes, so the American that I first saw was the commissioner for the entire Ratak chain [of the Marshall Islands], for all of us Ratak people. He was very kind, and it was obvious that he was a Christian, because he did not approach us in a mean way and those sorts of things, but when he saw young children, he would lift them up and place them on iron platforms and give them gum and candy. And as for the respected elders, he gave them his wishes for peace when he spoke to them and gave them words that would make them stronger. And he said [to them], "Do not be worried at this time, because the American flag is sailing above this islet, and if there is an occasion when there is any disruption here, we will watch over you and take care of you to the best of our ability."

In a story from Chuuk, Kimon Phymon depicts a proactive interaction with both Americans and Japanese. The interviewer, a young Chuukese man, begins by referring to a film of the U.S. attack on and occupation of Chuuk that is popular local viewing. Mr. Phymon continues with a story of American generosity and his subsequent switch in allegiance:

[Q: I have seen you in the video cassette when the Americans arrived. Do you remember, when you had a child on your shoulder with many Chuukese lining up beside the road? I do not know which road you were at, with some Americans on their vehicles.] Oh, yes, that's right. That was when the American soldiers arrived. [Q: Where was that?] At Tunnuk. We welcomed them. We said, "Oh, the American soldiers are coming." That's the time the Japanese governor came out, and they asked us what we ate. I raised up my hand with a leaf. The governor said, "Why would we have to give you that?" But one of the American leaders said, "Hey, don't talk."

So I asked one man by the name of Moap [a Mortlockese man who spoke some English], "Translate what I say about our lives." [The American asked,]

"What did you eat?" [I said,] "You tell him that this is what we ate [that is, leaves]." "How did you eat that?" "We cooked it in the pot and we ate it with water." "What about your food?" "They stopped us from having our food. That's how it was during the Japanese administration."

They [Americans] gave us food when I told them about us. And then they told me not to worry anymore, that they were going to give us food, clothing, shoes, and their war clothes. We didn't have anything to wear, only those old clothes. We sewed for our wives' children and loincloths. We had clothes from the Americans when they [also] gave us shoes, food.

[Q: When the American soldiers came, what did you think, were you afraid?] No, I was not afraid. I ran down with my notebook, with English and Japanese language translations written down. For example, "Tapako ippong kudasai?"— "Give me one cigarette." "Good morning"—"Ohaio gozaimas." I walked down and I said, "Give me one cigarette," and they said, "Come, come. You want smoke?" "Yes." So they gave me some [tobacco] in packs, some in sticks. The cigarettes were piled up in front of me . . . the turkey in cans—muaramuareni! [loosely, "My gosh!"]. . . .

[Q: What happened to the Japanese?] They took them to the ships. [Q: Did they hurt them?] They took them to the boat pool. They searched them, those that were carrying knives in their pockets, they took off their clothes, leaving only their loincloths. They stood under the sun. These were the soldiers. But the kai-gun [Japanese Navy] were not hurt, because they were good to the Chuukese. . . . We made a sign to them [U.S. troops] that the Japanese beat us. "Oh, OK, wait." So then, one [Japanese soldier], he was the one that beat me up when we were in Peniyesene when I was a prisoner. They beat us badly with a mangrove stick. [Q: Why were you in prison?] We stole sweet potatoes because we were hungry, and also cigarettes. Here is the damn guy, his name was Nakara. So I told the American Navy, "Hey, see [this] Japanese." "Yes." So I demonstrated it [his previous punishment?]. "OK"; he called the guy to come over here. Then he gave me a stick, and I started hitting him. He started hollering like a small boy. The American was laughing. [I] beat him, beat him [the Japanese]. [Q: Did you hit his head?] No, I was just hitting his behind. So the American said, "Not like that." He really gave him a heavy blow; he was shouting. I said "OK, you run." He ran down to the dock, and they got tired of looking for him. Their leaders, we didn't even consider as leaders. As they went down, we said, "Hey, Tenno Heika bakayaro [you stupid; a rude insult to the Japanese emperor]." They were just *staring at us. [Q: You were brave.] Yes, we were brave; if it hadn't been for the fact that we would get arrested, we would have hit them. The* sambo *[military staff], they were tied up; we said to them, "Hey,* sambocho bakayaro!" *[Hey, you stupid chief of staff!] They just put down their heads.*

Finally, from Utwe on Kosrae, comes Palikun Andrew's account of the favorable impact of American gifts of food, medicine, and, especially, freedom:

September eighth was the day the Americans came. And we were free. A ship arrived in Lelu harbor. The admiral, when he arrived, told all Kosraeans to gather at Inkoeya [in Tafunsak], and he would raise the flag of freedom. I was one of the people who went there. When the people heard this, everyone was strong; even those who were sick recovered enough to walk there. We were really eager to see what Americans looked like.

Some of the people went during the night; they slept at Sansrik and waited for daytime to continue along their way. I was with Isaiah Benjamin, who came the next morning. There was another man who was with us that day; his name was Luk Sanna. We went by canoe from Utwe to Tafunsak, around the other side of the island [east], and the tide was low, so we had to pull the canoe all the way to Mwot. There we went outside the reef and paddled to a small island, then went back inside the reef, and we pulled our canoes the rest of the way to Tafunsak. When we were in Tafunsak, the people were in the church, but we just kept on walking. The three of us got there, and the others went inside, but I kept walking to Inkoeya. I didn't join in the [church] service. I just went to the road and waited for the American admiral, because he said he would be there at one o'clock.

The admiral's name was Woodhouse. There was another American who came with him; his name was Doctor Martin. I was still waiting at the road when someone came running; the messenger came from Insrefusr [in Tafunsak] and saw us there. By the time the service was over and the people had gathered there, he [Admiral Woodhouse] came. Then we saw what Americans looked like. He was very big and tall. We had never seen this kind of man before.

It was a very hot day. When the admiral came, he went up inside the house of the leader of the Malem people; his name was Paul. Some people came inside; some stayed outside in the middle of the road. The people didn't care about the sun; they just sat in the sun. The admiral started to talk. He said, "This day, I will raise the American flag to show that everyone is free from now on." When he raised the flag, everyone stood up, and the admiral told them, "Today you are free, and the Americans are the ones who will take care of you and everything." Another thing he said was, "From now on, you won't see the red eye again." The meaning of the "red eye" was the Japanese flag. And everyone was really happy. The old people who were sick seemed to get well after hearing this.

And then that day I went all the way back to Isra [in Utwe]. I went there to get my family, because the Americans told us that they wanted to give them medicine to cure their sicknesses. Everyone brought their families to Lelu where they were given medicine. They gave out medicine for about one month [because a lot of people were ill]. They were given injections; my family got these, but not me. The first time they got it was really painful. Some people cried. The doctor

U.S. doctor treats diseases among the Islanders of Losap, Chuuk, around January 1946. (U.S. Navy photo, National Archives photo no. 358165)

said the medicine he had given them would prevent a reoccurrence of the illness. He also told pregnant women that their children would not get the illness ruf [an itchy sickness]; the children would be immune. When we got the injection, we felt cured, because we were no longer itchy.

People were really happy, because the Americans treated us well. They even gave us food and whatever we needed. The Americans stayed here for about one or two months. They gave us clothes, food, even cigarettes. This was the first time we felt the American ways. This is what I remember about what happened when the Americans arrived.

MICRONESIANS COMING HOME

One American kindness for which Islanders were especially grateful was the U.S. Navy's willingness to return Islanders home from the many places the war had flung them. The navy expended a great deal of effort, and millions of sea miles, to do this, transporting workers, students, long-separated husbands and wives, children and parents. Pensile Lawrence, one of the men taken from Kiti, Pohnpei, for work in Kosrae (as described in the "Memorial Song of Kosrae" in chapter 7) discussed their emotional return:

At seven a.m. on October tenth, we reached Kolonia. . . . No one knew we were coming. There was a church gathering in Kolonia that day; not on Sunday, but some kind of Protestant and Catholic church gathering. When we arrived in the harbor we saw Timothy of Kapingamarangi. And we also saw another canoe, a Pohnpeian canoe, a man, his wife, and two children, a boy and a girl. The boy is a big man now. . . . He, his sister, father, and mother, they went down to the two ships already anchored in the harbor. They went to the ship carrying a load of bananas. When we saw them, we called their names, and they saw that our ship was different from the other two ships, because it was really a U.S. battleship. On the other side, the crew was really different. Some of us were wearing different uniforms; some of us were wearing Japanese loincloths. No shame. Many of us had no shame.

So after these people [saw us], a boat went out. This was Henry Nanpei and his operator, Felix Janada. They were the ones who came back. They said hello to us and returned. And they told the Pohnpeians that the Kosraeans were already in the harbor. Many people did not believe it. But we stayed there from seven in

the morning until the afternoon, when we were brought in. We came to Carlos
Etcheit, where Etcheit is staying now, at Yasarin. His place was being used as a
U.S. military headquarters, like the administration. Naval station people were
doing governmental work. Leo Etcheit was there; he was the interpreter. The Japa-
nese man, I did not know whether he was a commander, he spoke English, too.
And Carlos Edwin [grandfather of former Kolonia town mayor Victor Edwin],
and a lady whose name was Francisca Eners. She wore a black dress, and she
came when we were still in line and she kissed the face of everyone who had come
from Kosrae whose relatives had died. This gave, I think, some kind of sign to the
Pohnpeians, telling them that they were the ones whose relatives had died.

I saw Louis that day, I don't know how many months after he was born. My
younger brother was carrying him, and I asked him who that boy was and why
he was carrying him. I do not know why I had forgotten the face of my younger
brother. Just two years and two to three months, and I forgot the face of my
younger brother. Hard times.

We got information from the administration. We were told not to harm the
Japanese on Pohnpei. So they divided us into two groups. One group went to
Sokehs and spent the night there. Another group went to Kiti. One group went
on that side; another group went on this side. Some of my relatives were home in
Wene. They had gotten word, I do not know who told them, that I had died. My
adoptive mother cried and cried, until she saw that I was home.

Six men died on Kosrae. One was my brother; one was a guy from Palia-
pailok section, Stamwan; another one was a Mortlockese guy from Pwok sec-
tion, his name was Lens; another one was Kerman, Keropin's father; another
one was Domiko (. . . or Miko?)—this man was the brother of Olter Paul's wife,
his uncle-in-law. They died of sickness. One, the guy from Pwok, was a sick
man when he went to Kosrae. The uncle of Nopuko Paul was also a sick person,
but he pretended he was not sick. Altiano Alphonse became ill when the U.S.
plane first dropped bombs in the ocean, near the harbor, and they landed on
the shore. Maybe he was so scared. He was throwing up; his stomach was bad.
He was sick every day, and he died. Kerman was not sick until sometime in the
middle part of 1944. I did not know what kind of sickness he had. My brother,
he vomited blood from his lungs. The rumor I heard after we arrived on Pohnpei
from some of the others who went to Kosrae, they said that he was poisoned by a
near relative. He was vomiting with blood; this was in the afternoon. It got worse
and worse, and the next day in the afternoon we took him to the hospital. The

following day in the evening, he died. It was fast. From the time he died until sometime at night, from here [chest area] up was blue; after midnight everywhere was blue.

Tadasy Santos, another of the Kiti men sent to Kosrae, adds another dimension to their return, when some men made unwelcome discoveries:

We arrived in Pohnpei early in the morning. Some of our relatives went out in their canoes to welcome us back, but we were not allowed to get in their canoes. We were put into two boats and were brought ashore. There were many on shore waiting to welcome us. We were made to walk in a straight line and not shake hands or touch anyone else. Our relatives were shouting and crying, but we were made to see and talk to the high officials first. Speeches were given in our honor. We were then divided into two groups. All of those from Pwok to Paies were assigned to live temporarily in Sokehs. The rest of us, those who were from beyond Pwok and Roi, were assigned to live in Net. We were not allowed to go

General Blake and party inspecting Japanese troops at Moen, Chuuk, October 5, 1945. (U.S. Navy photo, National Archives photo no. 353893)

home until all of the Japanese were moved out of Kiti. They were thinking that
we might take revenge on the Japanese for sending us away from home. After all
the Japanese left, we were then allowed to go home.

It was good that they [the authorities] took that precaution, for when we
arrived in Kiti, some of us found out that our wives and other relatives were
made pregnant by the Japanese soldiers. They were mad as hell and ready to kill
the Japanese. The big discussion on the ship on our way to Pohnpei was to beat
up the Japanese if we found that they had harmed or abused our relatives. They
were lucky to have left when we got to our homes.

THE END OF AN ERA: THE JAPANESE DEPART

Japan's surrender and the arrival of the Americans was not quickly followed
by significant changes on the uninvaded islands: Japanese troops remained in
place, sometimes for months, until U.S. occupation became effective in late
1945. The eventual departure of Japanese troops created complex responses
among the peoples of Micronesia.

As we have seen, in describing the end of the war and the end of their
military and colonial relationship with Japan, some Micronesian stories and
songs reflect Micronesian anger at their harsh treatment at the hands of the
Japanese. But many others speak of apologies, forgiveness, and farewell. It
may seem surprising, given the many hardships of the war years and the often
harsh treatment by Japanese military, that Micronesians in many places met
the departure of the Japanese with sadness, with commemorative songs and
tears, especially in the most heavily acculturated areas of Palau. But remember
that Micronesians had lived under Japanese rule for decades, that they had
many personal and cultural ties, that the departure of the familiar Japanese
also meant saying good-bye to the familiar forms of daily life.

Many Micronesians felt—and many still feel—close affiliation with the
Japanese. They think that Japanese culture and lifestyle was more in accord
their own, that Japanese sharing was more sincere than American unpredict-
ability. While, in part, these stories inscribe a nostalgia for each narrator's own
youthful past spent under Japanese rule,[2] they also entail some astute cultural
analysis.

This farewell song from Palau, composed right after the end of the war,
tells of sadness felt for the departing Japanese:

Untitled Song

Composed by Shiro Bedul, Ollei village, Ngarchelong, Palau, August 1945
(Sung in Japanese)
(Collected and translated by Wakako Higuchi, n.d.)

Our departure was very sudden,
for us Islanders and our mother country.
We're sad for such sudden good-bye.
Japan, our mother country,
was destined to be defeated.

We won't forget you good people [Japanese]
who were our teachers for thirty years.
My favorite sakura [cherry blossom]—
our relationship with you has ended,
we don't know which direction to go next.

Good-bye everyone, to home you go;
with perseverance do whatever you can.
Perhaps someday we'll meet again.
Please take care,
and let us pray every day.

While some Micronesians lamented the departure of Japanese troops, in other cases their removal signaled a welcome end to hardship. As we see in this account from Kolonia, Pohnpei, sometimes these different views were held within the same population. William Norman reminded us of generational differences in attitudes toward the arrival of the Americans:

Then the announcement [that the war was over] came. Those who had studied with the Japanese approved of them. But the old people, who had heard stories from old people, had told them stories about the American whale ships which had brought salted beef, rice, and strong dungarees. These were given away to the Pohnpeians by the Americans. The Japanese cloth was not good; it was slippery, thin, flimsy, and was rationed during the war. The Japanese were regarded as poor. There was a generational difference, then. The youths liked the Japanese; the older people liked the Americans.

News about the war reached Pohnpei every day and was disseminated to *the Japanese and the Pohnpeians. [Note: Mr. Norman worked as a policeman during the war.] However, the announcement of August twelfth or thirteenth, which stated that the war was over, was not told to the Pohnpeians right away. Perhaps they [Japanese] were afraid the Pohnpeians wouldn't work for them, or would even turn on them. Perhaps they feared fighting would start here. When the Americans arrived, some Pohnpeians went along with the Americans when they started marching. And when they saw the Japanese who had disciplined them, they said, "Now, my turn." . . . Those who had studied with the Japanese were sorry to see them go.*

The U.S. Navy's military government decided to repatriate all non-Micronesians after the war, including civilian immigrants from Taiwan, Okinawa, and Japan—even those who had Micronesian families. This proved to be a very long good-bye, since U.S. policy prevented them from visiting each other for decades. Noriyuki Suzuki of Chuuk lost his father and his brother in the repatriation:

When the war was over, they said that all the Japanese must return to Japan. No one was to stay. . . . They told my father that all civilians must return to Japan. At that time it was cold in Japan. Then my father told me to stay because it was very cold in Japan, and I might go there and freeze to death, because I didn't have the kind of clothes to wear there. But my brother Mori was to go with him, so he [Mori] could take care of him [Father]. But I told him that I didn't want to stay—I wanted to go with him and Mori. But my father said no, I had to stay so I could take care of my little brothers and sisters. And he said there was no use for all of us to go, because we might die, since we were not used to the weather there, and because there wasn't enough food or clothes in Japan. But I had to keep in mind that they would come back when things were all right again in Japan. . . .

When the Japanese were to leave for Japan, we [the family] all went to Toloas to say good-bye to our father and brother. At that time, I saw the American soldiers and their commander standing on the dock waiting for the Japanese to go out so they could check their handbags or suitcases. [Q: What were they checking for?] I really don't know. But before my father went out to the ship, he said to us and to some of the women and children, that they would leave, but they wouldn't forget us; they would come back. Some of the Japanese didn't talk, they just cried.

I thought that they would write as soon as they got there, but for thirty years there was no letter or even communication with my father. At that time I missed my father so much. So then I decided to learn English so that I could learn the whereabouts of my father. I didn't know what had happened to him. Then, maybe thirty years later, my father died. Mori sent a telegram saying that our father had passed away. The telegram was in Japanese and it said, "Chichi uwe si"—which means "Ewe sam a ma" [in Chuukese] or "The father passed away." I heard the bad news from Susumu. He called me and gave me the telegram. When I read it, I was heartbroken, because I hadn't seen my father for years. I went back to Toloas and I decided that I should go to Japan. Then, one month after my father died, I went to Japan. . . .

When we were in Japan, I cried. I remembered my father, now that I had come to his homeland, and he was not here any longer. It brought back memories of my father. Mita-san and Mori came to meet me at the airport. We went on a train and went straight to my father's grave site. [Q: How did you feel when you saw Mori?] I didn't recognize him at first. I recognized Mita-san, but then I recognized Mori, and we shook hands. Then, before we went to the cemetery, we went to a relative's house and they shook hands with me. They called my name—maybe our father had told them about me. When we went to the grave, it brought back all the memories. I just pictured my father's face when he was still alive.

[Q: Did your father have brothers?] Yes, but only his cousins were still alive; my father's real brothers were all dead. When we had a family gathering there in Japan, my relatives just kept looking at me and saying that if I were in Japan maybe I would work harder. I was a little afraid of what they said. [Q: Do you still keep in touch with the family in Japan?] Yes, we write letters to them every New Year. While I was in Japan, I promised Mori that he should come back to Chuuk. I told him that I'd be back after one year to take him back to Chuuk.

A NEW DAY BEGINS

As the thunder of war faded, people began to assess the new situation, to face its limits and seize its opportunities. This sentiment is often captured in Micronesian songs composed at the end of the war. A song composed by Salvador Rebluud, living in the village of Ollei on Ngarchelong, Palau, at the end of the war in September 1945 refers to the pain of acknowledging the loss of family members during the war, once finally returning home, but also of the need to forget the hardships of war.

Untitled Song

Composed by Salvador Rebluud
(Collected and translated by Wakako Higuchi, n.d.)

We cannot really forget,
for when we return we are fewer.
It's hard to think of our missing relatives,
who no longer come with us
to our remote village.

It'll be lasting heartache;
nothing will ever mend it.
We cry hard; nevertheless, war plagued
and disaster came along.
However, it's best we forget everything.

Two songs advise Palauans that the end of the war was no time to lament or to dwell on the sufferings of the past. Instead, they should be thankful for their lives and should work together to mend what had been destroyed during the war.

Untitled Song

by Shiro Bedul, village of Ollei, Ngarchelong, Palau, September 1945
(In Palauan and Japanese, written in Japanese style)
(Collected and translated by Wakako Higuchi, n.d.)

We are lucky—
we have come home.
Let's forget the sufferings of wartime.
With extra care, we took our children
from camp to camp.
I cry for you, and I'll always remember
what you've done.
You're like a true mother, you've saved
my life.

What you've done will die only
when I die.
It will never fade away.

Although I never said anything,
please do not complain.
I depended on you for my life.
So long my friend—
our homes were both destroyed,
and we need each other to put all the
pieces together.

Untitled Song
Unknown Composer
(Collected and translated by M. Tmodrang and Wakako Higuchi, n.d.)

The blue sky has cleared up.
Let's enjoy ourselves.
If I hadn't left home,
I wouldn't have met you.
Now it's hard to think of going back,
because it's hard for us to part.
It's very sad;
it's the dawn of peace.

Rteluul, ours were both destroyed,
but Delbirt [3] was destroyed the most.
The Japanese have failed, and
have no intention of helping.
If the "Newcomers" leave us,
we need one another more than ever.
Let Ngedebuul [4] be. If she cares,
let her come later.
Please don't forget me my friends—
I (Ollei) have very few people.

This is Palau's tranquility,
Which we have missed.
Let's cooperate and help one another.
Let's work hard for the common good.
Let's not ignore the welfare of our villages.
Please remember, always.

John Heine of the Marshall Islands offers a retrospective on the postwar era by describing his experiences, starting with when he worked for the U.S. Navy:

We [workers] lived on Kwajalein, but there was no council, no government for the Marshallese who lived there. We had only a leader, a lieutenant, who was in charge of the labor camp where we resided. The Americans used us to perform assorted menial labor. The labor camp was located on Kwajalein, near where the dump is. The airport had not been enlarged then. Almost all the time, the Marshallese were given the work of pruning and cleaning up the coconut trees, because the trees had been devastated during the war.

... One day a U.S. missionary by the name of Miss Carrie from Boston, Massachusetts, came and tried to preach to us, but no one could understand what she was saying. I was bathing in the lagoon when a deacon came looking for me and said that the missionary wanted to talk to me. I came out of the water, rinsed myself, and put on a pair of khaki shorts, the kind that the U.S. military officers wore, and a tee shirt. When they asked me to go into the church, I felt naked with the clothes I was wearing. Nonetheless, they insisted that I go into the church to assist in interpreting the missionary's sermon.

[Afterward, the missionary asked if John would like to attend college at Silliman University in the Philippines. Even though he had not attended high school, or even primary school, Mr. Heine agreed.] I was the first Marshallese to go to the Philippines. I was given a year and told that if I made it through, I would be provided another year in school. I made it through and was then told to take the GED, the high school equivalency [exam], in order to obtain my high school diploma, since it was a requirement for graduation from the university. It was a very good thing, as I had just completed four years of college, and at that time I was going to take the GED. And so the test, the GED, was very easy. I was also given my college degree. So I became the first person in Micronesia to possess a college degree in 1957. Dwight, my older brother, went to the University of Hawai'i, but almost all of the Micronesians who came to attend school here [in Hawai'i, the location of this interview] were sent back before their fourth year. The [U.S.] government was a bit confused in their policy since they felt that Micronesians should be left alone, as they were happy in their current condition. They believed in the idea that is called the "zoo theory." ... So, they said we should not go [outside of the islands to pursue an education] because we were not suited to college.

Later in the interview, Mr. Heine continued:

I worked on Kwajalein from 1946 or 1947, right after the war, until 1953, with-out taking a vacation or any time to rest. It was just a time of working continu-ously. Afterward, I went to the Philippines. They [the U.S. Navy officials after the war] needed our assistance. However, while they gave the others a time to rest, they did not treat me in this way, because I worked making and disbursing the payroll for the Marshallese, and so my work was nonstop. . . . The other type of work that I did was as a disc jockey. Between nine-thirty and ten o'clock at night I had a radio program in Marshallese. I cracked jokes and played western music over the air. I lived on Kwajalein and moved to Epjā [Ebeye] when the camp was moved to that location [about three years after the end of the war].

Social position continues to constitute a critical factor in Microne-sian wartime stories, even after the war. John Heine's elite status is evident in this account, in which he casts himself as a central figure in the postwar period. Note the personalization of his account: like recollections of the prewar Japanese era, Mr. Heine's postwar memories reflect personalized, rounded representations of his relations with Americans. In contrast, most Micronesian narratives of the first years after the war are much less detailed. They are reminiscent of what Kuipers describes (for an area of Indonesia) as "audience response"[5] by local people who became increasingly marginal participants in public domains as governance of their community shifted from ancestral villages, to the Dutch colonial service, then to the oppressive regimes of Suharto and Sukarno. Public discourse shifted, with these changes in regime, from eloquent displays of verbal prowess toward simple commu-nal responses and ratifications at public political gatherings. In other words, their public speech became simpler, as their power over their community life deteriorated.

Similarly, World War II in Micronesia provided the context for rapid social change in which elites and people who could negotiate between local communities and colonial rulers found themselves in increasingly important social situations while the mass of people were increasingly disenfranchised from participating in public events by their lack of knowledge and control. As the focus of communal life shifts, all but the central figures (such as John Heine) come to rely on increasingly impoverished discourses: they find themselves with less to say about, and less control over, the circumstances of their lives.

As we look back on what happened during the war, and on how the people who lived through it describe their experiences, we see much more than a simple history of combat. We can, in fact, see how Micronesians are building their vision of the past.

PART V

Conclusions

Chapter 13

WARTIME MEMORIES IN THE MODERN WORLD

War shatters communities. Much of history recounts how military conflict transforms the political, economic, social, and physical landscape of contending powers. But wars continue to affect a society long after the obvious damage has been repaired. In this book we have considered one aspect of the long-term significance of war: that is, how the cultural memories of the war years continue to resonate in the minds of survivors and into the next generations.

WARTIME MEMORIES IN MICRONESIAN HISTORIES

Cultural memories, as we have explained, differ from lived experience. They are shaped not only by individual lives, but by social facts and cultural understandings, by the vantage points of persons and groups, and by cultural preoccupations. Stories are the way humans make the past a real part of the present. Once wars end (and even while they are under way), people do a great deal of cultural "work" to wrestle their experiences into a form that makes sense of overwhelming sensations and emotions and that allows the lessons learned by one generation to be passed to the future.

To understand people's stories about the war, then, we must understand more than the simple facts of their experiences, of "what happened to them" during the war years. We must also understand the culture in which the memories were encoded and in which they are recounted. Each culture's ideas about what is most significant and each culture's requirements about how stories are shaped and told intersect in individual and communal memories.

Marshallese children take a great interest looking at *Life* magazine, Majuro, March 15, 1945. (U.S. Navy photo, National Archives photo no. 312661)

In the United States, we might say that the "cultural memory work" of World War II has largely been completed—although it has taken a great deal of effort and time to negotiate how to handle difficult memories such as those of the Holocaust and of internment camps for Japanese Americans. The more recent history of U.S. involvement in Vietnam, however, remains emphatically unresolved as a cultural memory. How to manage it still formed part of public discourse in the rhetoric of the 2004 presidential election campaign. For the Japanese, we have seen, cultural memories of World War II are still incompletely digested.

The situation is far more complicated for Micronesians. They were not Japanese citizens, nor were they necessarily consistently patriotic subjects of the emperor. A few men served with the Japanese military, but even these found their positions and activities of ambivalent worth. In retrospect, by war's end, Micronesians were neither the victors, nor the vanquished, nor the liberated. They were the bystanders—in their view, the "suffering" bystanders. And by war's end they were, in a sense, refugees: though many never left home, their homes disappeared around them.[1]

"It was not our war," our consultants repeatedly told us. In Micronesian cultures, important history is thought to be owned, in a sense, by those who are qualified by inheritance and training to recount it. Because the Pacific War had more to do with foreigners than with their own autonomous action, Micronesians do not usually regard it as a part of Micronesia's own cultural legacy, the sacred history that originates in and connects Islanders with their ancestors. Micronesian histories are carefully transmitted to selected audiences, in private, by experts, in accounts focused on their connection to clan, lineage, place, et cetera. While a few famous wartime stories and songs are treated in a similar manner to such important legacies,[2] wartime history is typically regarded—especially by the elders who experienced it—as more properly belonging to histories of the major combatants—the Japanese and Americans.

Yet stories of "the greatest hardship" are extraordinarily memorable to Micronesian elders, who hope that wartime experiences and the lessons learned will not fade from collective memory. Precisely because they are not typically classed as culturally sacred Micronesian history, wartime stories and songs may be freely repeated. Through widespread recounting in familiar modes of remembrance—landscapes, rituals and reenactments, dances, songs, and narratives—the personal experiences of Micronesian elders have become collective cultural memories. Reflecting uniquely Micronesian perceptions and interests, certain ideas have become part of the cultural corpus of war memories: the unexpected and shocking violence of the war, which arrived as an outside force; the sufferings and hardships that Micronesians underwent; their sensations of powerlessness and marginality and of being bystanders in this global contest; disruptions to happiness, harmony, and plentitude; changes in leadership and colonial rule; and new opportunities for romance all pervade the sensibility and knowledge of the war for modern Micronesians.

As memories are shared, the war is refashioned and relived daily, when elders tell tales and sing songs to children. Rare is the Micronesian youth who cannot narrate a story of suffering under Japanese military rule, name a suspected American spy, or hum a few bars of a war song.[3] Typically, however, knowledge of the war transmitted to those who did not directly experience it tends to be condensed, even truncated and stereotyped. Still, wartime experiences remain a defining feature of the older generation's identity. Reflecting on their ability to endure and survive hardships is a source of individual, generational, and cultural pride.

Memories of World War II are bittersweet; telling these tales allows both the storyteller and the audience to relive a difficult but also proud period of their lives. In fact, it is noticeable that Micronesians become unusually explicit in revealing the emotions they felt during the war. Discussing emotions rarely enters the public realm in Micronesia, but it seems acceptable, perhaps even expected, when talking about the war, and offers elders a chance to garner respect from others. Trading these wartime stories, replete with such strong feelings, among members of their own generation also serves to reinforce old bonds, including those with distant others, even non-Islanders. Telling these stories can create new bonds based on shared wartime experiences, even though the individuals may have only just met.

GLOBAL LINKS AND WIDER VISIONS OF THE WAR

Perhaps because Micronesians had so little access to information about the war while it was being waged, they have an enduring curiosity about what happened in other places. Over the postwar years, this has led to the development of a small, but important, area of new cultural elaboration. New memories of the war also continue to be formed through global connections with other people and other places affected by World War II.

Since war's end, Japanese (both colonial civilian and military) and American veterans have returned to Micronesia for reunion events. Japanese publications, friendship societies, letters, pilgrimages, and tourism reestablish ties to Micronesia. Older Japanese travel to search for the remains of war dead or to hold memorial services. Many wish to reestablish contacts with Micronesians they knew from the past. They want to reconnect and share experiences, to see the changes on the islands, or to right old wrongs. Sometimes they seek out Micronesian relatives left behind in the postwar repatriation. A few who return to their prewar homes elect to remain in the islands.[4] American veterans, too, make pilgrimages, to view memorials and walk the beaches where they offered their lives.[5] When American veterans reunite, however, they usually do so only with each other and usually in the United States. The nature of the war they fought in Micronesia left them with few personal ties to the islands.[6] However, for the fiftieth anniversary of the surrender of Pohnpei, the surviving members of the crew of the U.S.S. *Hyman* were invited to return for the Liberation Day ceremony. The dozen shipmates and their wives who attended the ceremony were presented with a set of limited edition postage stamps, featuring the four U.S. Navy warships that carried out the liberation of islands within the current Federated States of Micronesia.

A few World War II sites, such as those on Chuuk and Saipan, have economic value as destinations for international tourism. Wrecks of Japanese ships sunk in the February 1944 attack on Chuuk Lagoon—creating a "ghost fleet"—today lure recreational divers[7] and constitute one of Chuuk's major tourist draws. And the "mystery" of Amelia Earhart's 1937 disappearance—possibly within the Japanese Mandate—also retains a touristic appeal. Guam's War in the Pacific National Park and Saipan's American Memorial Park draw interested international visitors. And as the potential of war relics to generate tourism interest and revenues is recognized, some sites have been targeted for survey or restoration.[8]

Micronesians themselves have traveled to other World War II theaters, especially in the decades since independence. They have connected with people and places they knew of or heard about during the wartime era, and discovered others new to them. Their expanded visions accompany more than sixty years of schooling in American-style history. This has made them aware of the war's global importance and created a desire to have their stories known as a part of that larger history. In recent years, some Micronesian government agencies have produced videotapes of the war, including interviews with survivors.

While story, song, and dance remain the most dramatic forms of war remembrance, new technologies have given them wider circulation. War songs are recorded and played on island radio. While old songs remain alive, Islanders continue to compose and choreograph new songs and dances on war themes. These are primarily geared to an island-wide, or perhaps a Micronesia-wide, audience. The results of research on the war in Micronesia can be found in libraries and bookstores throughout the region. These works, along with the recent numerous books and especially films about World War II in both the Pacific and Europe, are in demand. Hollywood's versions of the Pacific War, stocked on shelves at video rental stores, are popular family viewing in urban households throughout Micronesia today. (Interest in war movies is long-standing. The favorite film at the Truk Trading Company movie theater in the mid-1950s was the documentary *The Bombing of Truk*, which was shown "once a month, every month, by popular demand.")[9] Graphic artists, too, use war themes, as in Palau on storyboards on *bai* (community centers) and at tourist sites and hotels.[10]

WARTIME MEMORIES AND THE AMERICANIZATION AND GLOBALIZATION OF MICRONESIA

The sharing of stories of their experiences in World War II—among Micronesians and also with others over the years—has increased Micronesians' general understanding of global warfare and awareness of their role in geopolitics and world history. The telling of war stories is meant to provide important guidance for the future and is often accompanied by commentaries that reflect on modern-day implications of war, the pride Micronesians should have in their own traditions, and the wisdom to be gained from them. Wartime experiences and the lessons they hold, whether experienced firsthand and discussed among the elders or overheard by the youth, are often referred to when evaluating changes during the U.S. administration and the future direction of the newly created nations of Micronesia.

The postwar period in Micronesia brought drastic change in the islands' geopolitical role. As we have seen, over the entire historical contact era, most of Micronesia became progressively incorporated into a global economy. Under Japanese colonialism, the islands were a building block of an empire that sought to expand its political, economic, and cultural influence, and Micronesians, although considered third-class citizens, learned to identify with these Japanese goals.

After the war, when the United States adopted a hands-off policy, much of Micronesia was returned to the "self-sufficiency" of a subsistence-level "traditional" life—a lifestyle that most Micronesians had not experienced during their lifetimes. Following hard on top of the destruction they suffered during the war, this radical shift in economic policy caused major difficulties. Local economies—in terms of infrastructure, wage labor, and imported goods—have never returned to the level they grew accustomed to during Japanese colonial times. For the most part, Micronesia became an economic backwater; peoples' standard of living was severely reduced; the region became unimportant and almost unknown on the world stage. A small but positive American presence was felt in the areas of health care, education, and training in democracy, and Americans also offered their Micronesian wards "freedom." Although the meaning of freedom has created its own problems, Micronesians have widely

U.S. Navy enlisted man stops at an Islander home while on an inspection trip, Pohnpei, July 1947. (U.S. Navy photo, National Archives photo no. 497521)

acknowledged and appreciated the opportunities it holds. Otherwise, the Americans remained distant, and used their United Nations–conferred rights of "strategic denial" to minimize the presence of other foreigners.

Micronesian experiences during World War II and during the postwar period have served to heighten their understanding of their strategic position. Here, the potential benefits of maintaining ties to the United States, currently considered the most powerful nation in the world, are well understood. The new Micronesian governments have all, in varying ways, elected to retain an association with the United States, especially for their external affairs. These governments are, furthermore, based in large part on the American ideals fostered in the postwar period. Continued ties with the United States have brought promises of security, economic benefits, and the potential for increased participation in the global economy.

Still, Micronesians remain ambivalent about the Americanization and globalization of their culture. They frequently express the need to strike a balance between this and the perpetuation of their own values. World War II taught Micronesians profound lessons about the high price of foreign dependency, especially dependency on a world power that has shown itself to be prone to war.

WARTIME MEMORIES AND "MICRONESIAN" NATIONALISMS

Continued interest in Pacific War history has played an important role in local Micronesian politics and identity as well. Despite a long colonial history that drew boundaries around the entire area (or large portions of it), people from this part of the world have not seen themselves as belonging to a generic regional culture, nor have they typically referred to themselves by the label "Micronesian." Despite the efforts of American administrators to cultivate national identities in the late postwar period, Islanders have not adopted them wholeheartedly. People's focus remains resolutely local, as they identify themselves with a particular island or local community.

Nevertheless, shared cultural memories of World War II and its aftermath have, on occasion, served as a stepping-stone to a national consciousness.[11] For example, at the 1989 opening of the new capital of the Federated States of Micronesia on the island of Pohnpei, a group from Yap performed a new dance. It was composed by Goofalan, a dance master of Maap, and was introduced in English by the former governor of Yap, John Mangafel, who said,

> This dance is newly composed, composed by an old man from Yap, and it's based on what happened in World War II and on forward to times when we had a good agreement with the United States and word was spread and all the states look at it, read it, discuss it, and like it and finally, they say it's good. And then finally, they sign it.[12]

In this political leader's view, the dance presented the war as the starting point for a unified history of the new nation.

Postwar experiences with Americans and the continuing political, economic, and social ties with them, even after independence, have further developed Islanders' regional and national identities. Young people enlist in the U.S. military services in increasing numbers; some F.S.M. officials think they have been overrepresented in the numbers who served and suffered casualties in the Gulf wars. Elders' memories of World War II became disturbingly relevant during the first Gulf War, as the islands saw tightened postal regulations and customs enforcement, special church services and radio broadcasts dedicated to war news, and a fear that Americans in their midst might bring the war to their islands.

While affiliation with the United States brings safety concerns at home, it has other implications for Micronesians. The political agreements signed in 1976–1994 as part of independence negotiations included a guarantee of free entry into the United States, and migration, especially to Guam and Hawai'i, has dramatically increased in recent years. Like most diasporic Pacific Islanders, Micronesians move to metropolitan areas for access to better education, jobs, and health care. Although Micronesian migrants are typically only a small percentage within their new host population, their departure greatly impacts the small communities they leave behind. And in some cases where Micronesian communities have taken root in urban clusters or in less populated rural areas, their presence has had a substantial effect on those local communities.

This diaspora also reshapes ideas about identity. When they arrive in the United States, immigrants often find that their home region is largely unknown to Americans—despite their wartime experiences, postwar colonial relations, and partial identification with American culture. In attempting to explain who they are and why they have emigrated to the United States, they often refer to the newly formed nations to which they belong. For example, in Hawai'i today, those from the Republic of the Marshall Islands (R.M.I.) are referred to (by R.M.I. citizens themselves, and by others) as "Marshallese." Those from the Federated States of Micronesia are called "Micronesians." While this labeling of national identity could be considered a step forward in terms of recognition by others, it has also created confusion. Many people in Hawai'i do not understand that the "Marshallese" are from a region of Micronesia or that the "Micronesians" comprise the distinct cultures of Kosrae, Pohnpei, Chuuk, and Yap or that each of these contains different islands, islets, or other areas. And how do people from Palau, Guam, and Saipan fit into this scheme? The creation of globally recognizable identities, which travelers will in some way also bring home with them, is still in flux.

In these small and somewhat awkward ways, then, "Micronesians"—who steadfastly maintain their local identities, but who also share experiences of Western and Japanese colonialism, and especially of World War II—are beginning to identify themselves as a part of the wider world, the United States, their region, and their newly formed nation-states.

Chapter 14

"THE GREAT AIRPLANE"

WE END THIS BOOK with the full text of a dance song composed on Fais Island shortly after the war. The song is revealing because it represents the maintenance of an acutely local, but also an increasingly globalized, Micronesian identity. This dance song covers the entire span of Fais Islanders' wartime experiences, both on their home island and on nearby Yap, where they were relocated during the war. It treats the end of the Japanese civilian administration and the military occupation of Fais, and continues through the invasion by American forces at the end of the war.

The song was collected and translated by anthropologist Don Rubinstein, who also provides explanations and background that help us appreciate it.[1] The song is entitled "Waayel" (Airplane) and is in the form of a type of dance called *badug*. (The song has two versions, "The Great Airplane" and "The Smaller Airplane.") *Badug* dances are performed at celebrations marking Fais peoples' return to the island or the arrival of newcomers, at times of harvest, or at other calendrical celebrations. It was sung on Fais as recently as July 2000 to celebrate the return of high school and college students for summer vacation. Although composed soon after the war, "Waayel"—like all the war memories we've discussed—continues as a living memory, helping new generations of Micronesians make sense of their lives.

"Waayel" was composed by Halamar, a man from Limatayfoy house compound in Faliyow village, who was born about 1885. Halamar left Fais during the German colonial era to work aboard German and Japanese commercial vessels. He returned to Fais two decades later, just before the outbreak of the war. Seven other men and women from Faliyow village were involved in composing the song—Lugal, Fasug, Ilechig, Mwaliy, Fichesey, Marulamar, and Utwel. Several other islanders made requests and offered suggestions to this group of composers.

Rubinstein writes that the song "captures the complex mixture of humor, irony, anger, shock and fear that characterizes Fais memories of the war and its surrounding events." He believes that several of the "more worldly and informed observations" in the song probably reflect Halamar's experiences and that the inclusion of English loanwords, at a time when Fais Islanders were generally unfamiliar with English, likely gave the song a sophisticated tone. The song also includes borrowed words from Japanese, Satawalese, Woleaian, and Yapese. Once the verbal composition was completed, dance movements were added, and the entire composition was taught to the men and women who would perform the song (commonly restricted to those who are members of the village of the composers).

U.S. Marine autographs a thousand-pound bomb on an F4U at Falalop Island, Ulithi. The plane is bound for Yap. August 1945. (U.S. Navy photo, National Archives photo no. 347493)

According to Rubinstein, "A prominent theme in the song is the contrast between the security and isolation of the home island, the danger and strangeness of incoming events." As you read it, and refer to the accompanying notes, you will find that many themes discussed in earlier chapters are reflected here. It is easy to see why this song continues to speak to Fais people about their past and their future.

The Great Airplane
Halamar, and others from Faliyow village on Fais, Yap
(Collected, recorded, and annotated by Don Rubinstein, n.d.)

1. *So, clap, and a clap! Clap! Clap!*
    Yuu, Oh, upon our island we were living;[2] *[r1]*[3]
    and then a great shock befell us
    for then came a time of change
    set in motion from America,
    a time that saw our liberation,
    a time gods brought us liberation.
    And our faith will return to our Father
    who art in heaven with the gods,
    who gave us the crucifix
    we wear as our maramar *[floral head garland].*

2. *Clap! Clap! Clap!*
    And so it came to pass[4]
    this time of difficulty. [r2]
    A time the outsiders
    ushered us into
    and we were greatly shocked, unsettled.
    We were sick at heart;
    our boys who'd been close by us
    were now so far apart.
    We were sick at heart.

3. *Clap! Again! Clap and up it goes!*
    Hello! Hello, hello, hello!
    Feefee, feefee no theh! [r2]
    Upon the lone island we were living
    and then it came upon us, [r2]

such a time of difficulty.
The trouble came to us, though
started half a world away.
The Company men⁵ had been here
at that time as our security.
Suddenly the situation turned around,
it blew in from the clear blue sky,
spread to all sides
and turned upon us.
We saw tragedy befall us.
This was the way of Wolofad.⁶
We were in great shock but strove to see
something good come to be.

4. *Clap! Again! Clap and back it goes!*
    Upon this island we were living
    and greatly frightened we were then.⁷ [r2]
    When the ship hove in view,
    came broadside the island,
    and a call blared out [r2]
    a signal to the island chiefs.
    Two sage men they appointed, [r1]
    rose, went out, strode to the guard
    where, as one, they stood erect
    before the captain of the ship.
    In detail they put forth how
    best to provide for the lone island. [r2]
    The message by radio went out
    and reached the battle commander.
    He directed his ship to steam
    toward the lone island. [r2]
    Word was given;
    the day of landing set.
    And they landed and they fought.
    Eey! Yu nguusu huh!

5. *Upon the island apart we were living,*
    the island we so enjoy. [r2]

And then the hour came,
the telegram arrived;
they had radioed from Yap.[8]
The news weighed heavy on our hearts,
so we braided fragrant ginger leaves,
we cried out to all the gods
to join us on our ocean journey,
so they could turn away
the submarines from us
and deflect the periscope's eye,
it should not see us.
After but a single night
the hills of Yap came into sight.
They made their way through
the channel at Rul in Yap.
The flag was unfurled in the wind,
a signal to the island chief.
And they landed and they fought.
Eey! Yu nguusu huh!

6.   I was just worried to death for
the two young men.[9] [And r2]
They rode the fearsome airplane,
traveled great distances across the sky.
They were gazing all about;
the wind was gusting strong
and outside the spray flew by.
Then into their view
rose a mountain range.
They gazed about in shock and fear;
they called out across the sea
to their two guardian spirits
Tarah and Wurusop.[10]
Salapii[11] stood over them, adorning them.
Then loomed Yelimelimal.[12]
They landed on the island
where there is so much to see.

Stop! Ngo hekka, *here's an airplane!*
Ah huu! One that's strange and new!

7.   *In the office they determined*
the conscription and assignment [r2]
of the young men bound across the sea,
who wished to see us once more together.[13]
They were pining away,
thinking how wonderful would it be
if we their parents could come to them.
We felt strange, uneasy,
and we called out to
our guardian spirit Langahiliyol.[14]
Weeks passed, not yet a month
and the leave-taking was so rushed
that our young men could reach their destination.
And the shock lives with us still!
Ah hekka! Here's an airplane!
Ah huu! One that's strange and new!

8.   *We'll never forget that time,*
our time; we, this generation
have seen the most
amazing sights.[15]
That time, a time of gods;
they came down and stood beside us,
told us what would happen.
The telegram arrived,
we had reached the hour of battle,
the time had come.
A fleet of strange ships
were sent in,
ocean-patrolling vessels
for the islands in the war.
They searched and found us,
the people of the lone island,
island of the god Yalusoor.
From the heat of Yalusoor

some small force was given
to put our shelters out of bounds,
to kick away from us
the rockets' bombs, and bullets from the guns.
And the guns, the guns, the guns!
Sootem, sootem, sootem!
March! March!
Eey! Shout it out!
Ah hekka! *Here's an airplane!*
Ah huu! *One that's strange and new!*

9. *Upon the lone island we were living*
    and then it came upon us, [r2]
    such a time of difficulty.
    The trouble came to us, though
    started half a world away.
    The Company men had been here
    at that time as our security.
    Suddenly the situation turned around;
    it blew in from the clear blue sky,
    spread to all sides
    and turned upon us.[16]
    We saw tragedy befall us.
    This was the way of Wolofad.
    We were in great shock but strove to see
    something good come to be.
    Ah hekka! *All different kinds!*
    Hey! Modern food!
    Hey! Makes me hungry![17]
    Ah hekka! *Here's an airplane!*
    Ah huu! *One that's strange and new!*

10. *Oh, upon this island we were living* [r1]
    and we were not worried.
    We did not believe that we would see
    it happen, that orders would come
    for Fais district to be developed.

The administration was really crazy
when they sent into the island
the Company men and those Army men
to survey and divvy up
the soil we lived on,
our livelihood and security.[18]
And how bereft still we feel!
Oh, we were bereaved because
that was the soil we lived on,
soil of rich tobacco.
Those Company men were crazy
when they shoveled away
our sustenance.
How bereft still we feel!
Ah hekka! Here's an airplane!
Ah huu! One that's strange and new!

11. *And so it came to pass,*
     this time of difficulty, [r2]
     a time the outsiders
     ushered us into,
     and we were greatly shocked, unsettled.
     Our boys who'd been close by us
     were now so far apart
     and we were sick at heart.[19]
     Ah hekka! Here's an airplane!
     Ah huu! One that's strange and new!

12. *Oh, upon the lone island we were living,*
     a region so dear to us,
     the breezy lowlands near the beach.
     Our shock and fear were apparent.[20]
     When the Americans arrived
     the submarines' big guns
     bombed the island.
     A strange time it was they came,
     a time we were all asleep.

We were unprepared and we were scared,
gazing about in utter shock,
this generation just come of age;
we were shocked to see these strange events.
Ah hekka! Here's an airplane!
Ah huu! One that's strange and new!

13. *Oh, there was such shock and grief*
     over those two sage men [r2]
     joining a perilous voyage,
     just searching out
     the ship bearing the battle commander.[21]
     The fleet was called together
     in the area of the lone island
     and they prepared to anchor,
     to drop the warship's landing vehicles.
     And the two men came ashore,
     bringing the battle commander;
     they came ashore in front of the men's house.
     Two men were assigned
     to search out the holes where we were buried,
     and to call out everyone.
     They all assembled before the men's house
     for everyone to meet together
     with the young men from the warship.
     And we were all rounded up
     and then it was confirmed
     that Tokyo had lost the war.
     Oh, baa ro poom!

14. *Oh, the young men from far away,*
     they assembled a great force [r2]
     bombs of fearsome big guns.[22]
     They were heading for Germany,
     they would break their way in,
     they shattered the mountain area.
     It is true what had been said,
     the Germans could not defend themselves

against all the ammunition of the battle
and they lost miserably.
Ah hekka! *Here's an airplane!*
Ah huu! *One that's strange and new!*

15.   *Oh, in this area we were living*
      on the island we so enjoy, [r2]
      the place of all our fun.
      We lived without worry,
      then we came under a different flag
      and we were thrown into confusion.[23]
      The men from far away took action,
      streaming in and out,
      the planes flying relays
      up and down the chain of islands.
      We felt in utter shock.
      Ah hekka! *Here's an airplane!*
      Ah huu! *One that's strange and new!*

16.   *Oh, upon this bright island we were living,*
      living here in freedom [r2]
      on this low-lying island
      We just did not believe
      that those crazy Koreans
      would be sent in here,
      would destroy entirely
      the land of our livelihood
      the storeroom of our food.[24]
      That was our sustenance,
      the most fertile foodbasket
      throughout the district.
      But Tokyo lost the war!
      Oh, baa ro poom!

17.   Yuu, *Oh, we were shocked by it, [r1]*
      that time of strange and new events,
      and discoveries that were given us.[25]
      They fired rockets in at us.

For what reason were they angry at us,
when they shattered our island?
Why did they not search out Japan,
Tokyo and Germany,
who were the roots of the war,
who were the ones to make it grow?
But when they removed their uniforms
they were only naked natives. [r2]
So flick a finger in their faces
and make 'em grunt.
Eey, the snorting Mr. Nose-Sticking-Up![26]
Oh, go blow your nose!

18.   *Oh, what sort of vessels are these*
that rammed their way onto our island [r2]
and cut through our burial holes?[27]
And when the soldiers dropped to their knees
and pointed their guns straight at us,
we wept and cried out loud
and we grabbed our mats and wraps
and in a flock we all flew down [r2]
and we settled at the sacred ground.[28]
How many days we remained there, [r2]
while their rations provided our relief!
We were shocked, so skinny and odd we looked.
Hey, Skin'n'bones, Skin'n'bones [r1]
Yah, we didn't even
recognize each other!

World War II was not a Micronesian war. We hope that it is clear, though, why this conflict between outsiders became a major element shaping modern life for Islanders, why the "typhoon of war" was "the greatest hardship" and a watershed event. The dramatic nature of wartime experiences; the resonance, and even the incongruency, of those experiences with local cultural under-standings and values; and the continuing importance of those memories in the postwar period have ensured their perpetuation in cultural memory. The nature of military strategy throughout the region, the vantage points Micronesians were afforded, and the variety of forms available for transmitting their memories have given particular shape to wartime reminiscences. At the same time, war experiences changed Micronesians' lives, their identities and cultures, their position in the world, and their place in history—both in their own view and in that of the wider world.

The process of remembering the war in Micronesia is far from complete. World War II lives on as an important, vital, yet evolving set of cultural memories in Micronesia, as it has lived on in so many other parts of the world.

APPENDIX

List of Participants in Oral History Interviews

FEDERATED STATES OF MICRONESIA

Chuuk State

Achanto (of Fason)
Kan Achew
Anisiro Aninis
Estefania Aunu
Litong Aunu
Aknes Bier
Marusina Bier
Adenis Bilimon
Istor Billimont
Aitel Bisalen
Iteko Bisalen
Nekuun Boone
Finas Bossin
Anton Chipwe
Ichios Eas
Nifereta Eas
Ikeichy Edwin
Sumier Elias
Konstantin Enik
Leon Episom
Masaichi Erimas
Piara Esirom

Eter (of Losap)
Filipos (of Neue)
Sisko Harper
Manuel Hartman
Urur Inek
Kinio Ipon
Antonio Isaias
Umiko Isaias
Topias Isam
Toli Jessy
Iwate John
Simako Joseph
Nikapwut Kachupin
Sontak Kansou
Take Katiw
Kalifin Kofak
Chipun Kom
Litia Kosam
Akki Lorin
Tupun Louis
Kariti Luther
Menas Makimi
Iowanes Manuere
Auchun Marar
Machiko Marcus

Teruo Marcus
Marwin (of Mwaan)
Lucia Masawer
Pius Masawer
Ilar Matafan
Asako Mateas
Sinino Mateas
Mine (of Neue)
Misasi (of Nama)
Akeisuk Mokok
Mine Mokok
Humiko Mori
Masataka Mori
Rokuro Mori
Darshy Nabamura
Echen Nakamura
Parang Namono
Sr. Magdelina Narruhn
Aten Niesik
Nusi Niesik
Miso Nifinifin
Este Puri Nipuk
Mieko Nipuk
Kisiuou Nua
Piriska Nukunukar
Ikefai Onopey
Simako Onusun
Tarup Ounuwa
Anumi Partonome
Faste Petter
Kimon Phymon
Piana (of Nama)
Este Puri
Andon Quela
Kintin Raphael
Akelina Rapun
Kame Rapun
Julio Repwech
Resen (of Mwaan)
Netek Rewein

Saito Rewein
Simon Rewie
Narian Robich
Ropat Romano
Rutok Ruben
Sachiko Ruben
Liwiena Rudolph
Isaac Sakios
Stem Salle
Yuniko Salle
Esperansa Samo
Biloris E. Samor
Anang Samwel
Aikichi Samwen
John Sandy
Okaichi Sapwo
Norimasa Selet
Osong Seleti
James Sellem
Deruko Shirai
Liaf Sigra
Limperta Simmy
Sachuo Siwi
Emwene Sopo
Matsuko Soram
Tomuo Soram
Emilio Sota
Pilar Soumwei
Kristo Souwas
Koko Suda
Ikiuo Sulluk
Weresi Suta
Mori Suzuki
Nobiyuki Suzuki
Keke Tawe
Takis Taylor
Naris Teitas
Soino Tokochee
Nifang Tommy
Saikichi Tommy

Iofina Topich
Likur Uruo
Akena Victus
Wangko Wasan

Kosrae State
Kun Aaron
Austin Albert
Palikun Andrew
Likiak Benjamin
Anna Brightly
Otinel Eddmont
Tulpe A. Jackson
Tolenna Kilafwasru
Kilafwa Likiak
Lupalik Nithan
Osmond Palikun
Milton Timothy
Tulenkun Waguk

Pohnpei State
Carmihter Abraham
Suhlet Abraham
Klemente Actouka
Katarihna Adalpret
Demaunis Adolf
Eperiam Agripa
Isao Aisawa
Paulina Aisawa
Clara Albert
Iosep Aldis
Liwisa Aldis
Marcus Alempia
Isiro Alex
Ludwig Alex
Alfonso Alexander
Ludwik Alik
Alwihs Amida
Manuel Amor
Robino Amusten
Sother Andon

Kaiti Anson
Ciro Barbosa
Alter Bedley
Bernard Behris
Yasio Behris
David David
Eliaser David
Janet David
Keropin David
Mikel Diana
Anastasio Dosoliwa
Victor Edwin
Emensio Eperiam
Regina Esiel
Yvette Etcheit
Ines Etnol
Imanuel Gallen
Mihna Gallen
Robert Gallen
Swingley Gallen
Melsor Gilmete
Wendolin Gomez
Dione Hatchkarawi
Linter Hebel
Rosette Hebel
Etson Henly
Dopias Ilon
Francisco Iriarte
Senoleen Iriarte
Lusios Jak
Andohn Jemes
Mary Jane Jemes
Ainrick Joshua
Masako Luhk Karen
Dobi Kilimete
Peleng Kilimete
Carl Kohler
Melpirihte Konsaka
Iens Lainos
Pernardo Lainos

Lihna Lawrence
Pensile Lawrence
Erwin Leopold
Pelsina Lipai
Benjamin Lopez
Solomon Lorrin
Johna Luda
Ariko Luhk
Hill Manuel
Niemwe Mark
Mikel Marquez
Augustine Mauricio
Johna Melia
Carmen Miguel
Yosko Miguel
William Norman
Bernel Nowa
Eneriko Pablo
Julie Panuelo
Melsor Panuelo
Phillip Patterson
Ignasio Paulino
Elper Penias
Minoru Penias
Sinio Peter
William Prens
Danis Pretrick
Damian Primo
Andonio Raidong
Ela Ringlen
Pretrick Ringlen
Ruben Rudolph
Lusiana Sackryas
Moses Saimon
Iosep Salvador
Edgar Santos
Tadasy Santos
Okin Sarapio

Sekismwindo Sarapio
Kristina Sehna
Oska Seiola
Lotis Seneres
Misko Shed
Konsepsion Silbanus
Pedrus Silbanus
Osei Sohram
Merlusi Stephenson
Ioana Tipen
Julio Vallazon
Nehdo Vicky
Meruse William
Norman William
Takio William

Yap State
Buthung
Mike Faraguy
Leon Gargathog
Gilipin
Vicente Gilwrol
Raphael Gisog
Joseph-Mary Goofalaan
Alvera Guro
Venitu E. Gurtmag
Patrick Hachigelior
Belarmino Hathey
Peter Ianguchel
Ikefai
Martina La'ew
Maria Leemed
Ignasio Letalim
Palagia Mitag
Santiago Sathau
Matthew Yafimal
Francis Yow

REPUBLIC OF THE MARSHALL ISLANDS

Clanton Abija
Klenere Abner
John Abraham
Aili Albios
Ledre Alek
Winnie Amja
Kanki Amlej
John Anjain
Ruth Arelōñ
Limkij Beolu
Anko Billy
Makbi Bokin
Maine Briand
Moody Briand
Kemro Buotwōt
Tibon Buti
Obet David
Onil David
Elson Ebel
Kija Edison
Apinar Edward
Emty Edwin
Jobi Elija
Welli Elija
Joseph Ernej
John Ezekiel
Tira George
Benjamin Gideon
John Heine
Nataniel Henry
Kileon Ijo
Lojan Isaac
Tonki Jabba
Elmina Jahnol
Carl Jelkan
Bellam Jello
Joseph Jibōn
Helena Jitbon
Median Job
Hertes John

Lajiko Jor
Tamar Jordan
Leban Jorju
Kottar Kamram
Aneo Keju
Bobo Keju
Raitu Keju
Labwinmij Laelōñeo
Kobeta Laijek
Taiwel Laimroj
Joraur Lainlij
Aneab Laitak
Tibierke Lakbel
Kilinik Lañejo
Atonej Lang
Keja Laniep
Ato Lañkio
Luke Lantir
Ijimura Lautoña
Yoseph Leban
Ken Lebo
Thomas Lejer
Bwirre Lejmen
Jamba Likinen
Lirio
Bonni Lodrenni
Daisey Lojkar
Manutil Lokwōt
Jabue Lorak
Alowina Lukas
Clancy Makroro
Jomle Malolo
Lombwe Mark
Jacob Maun
Kinoj Mawilōñ
Jimen Mejbon
Don Melon
Akji Menwa
Henry Moses
Arelōñ Nadrik
Balik Paul
Neimon Philippo

Renton Pita   Jabi Tenjue
Lele Ram   Edward Toluwi
Thaddeus Sampson   Eolōt Torelañ
Ateniel Tarki   Kaname Yamamura
Nathan Tartios   Katzan Zion

In addition, we thank our informants' family members who aided our interviews and also those who directed or introduced us to knowledgeable elders.

LOCAL OFFICIALS, INTERVIEWERS, TRANSLATORS

Although we cannot name everyone who helped us, we wish to give special thanks to the interviewers, translators, local officials, and others who gave assistance to our project. We have listed each person's title at the time of our project.

In the Federated States of Micronesia
Baily Olter, President, FSM
Teddy John, FSM Historic Preservation Officer
Jones George, FSM Archives and History

Chuuk State
Office of the Governor
Elvis Killion Osonis, State Historic Preservation Officer
Kaio Noket, Assistant Historic Preservation Officer
Francis X. Hezel, S.J., the Tunuuk Catholic Mission, and the Tol Mission
Graceful Enlet, President, Community College of Micronesia–Chuuk
The Mori Family
George Hartman
Grace Serious
Linda Smith
John Wendel
Richard and Betty Benson
Camy Akapito
Mensi Ifanuk
Kimuo Aisik
Ichios Eas

Interviewers and translators: K.M. Mefy, Jasinto Howard, Nancy Moufa, Frannie Oneitom, Kaio Noket, Linda Mori, Sidro, Matsuko Soram, Ino Oneisom, Francis X. Hezel, S.J., Nick Isaac, Aaron Suzuki, Philip Mwangin, Rosalinda Walter, Miako Hengio, Desder Johnny, Floren Akkin, John Sandy, Minda Oneisom, Basilio Dilipy, Graceful Enlet, Elvis Osonis, Johnson Elimwo, Ioanes Martin, Narcisso Sebastien, Kerio Walliby, Grace Serious, Dersy Erwin, Dolores Roskow, Akiosy Aniol

Pohnpei and Kosrae States
Emensio Eperiam, Pohnpei Historic Preservation Officer
Berlin Sigrah, Kosrae Historic Preservation Officer
Paul Gallen, President, Community College of Micronesia
Tony and Julie Ovella
Assistants for Pohnpei: Lerleen David, Ersina David, Eltes Sehd, Wendolin Lainos,
    Antolin Gomez
Assistant for Kosrae: Kerrick Benjamin

Yap State
Andrew Kugfas, State Historic Preservation Officer
Belermino Hathey, Chief of the Outer Island Council
Lewis Taramweiche, Outer Island Council

Interviewers and translators: John Chodad, Dolores Dinagpitin, Moche'en, Fidelia
Adgil, Robert Kelly, Lewis Taramweiche, Sabino Sauchomal, Tony Marliol, Corinne
Mogon, Lina Ruan, Andrew Kugfas

In the Republic of the Marshall Islands
Carmen Bigler, Historic Preservation Officer, RMI
Alfred Capelle, Assistant Historic Preservation Officer, RMI
Hilda Heine Jetnil, President, College of the Marshall Islands
Oscar Debrum, Chief Secretary of the Marshall Islands
Naptali Peter, Mayor, Enewetak Atoll
Relang Lamari, Chief Secretary's Representative to Ebeye
Alvin Jacklick, Mayor, Kwajalein Atoll
Aeto Bantol and Noda Lojkar, Kwajalein Atoll Local Government
Thomas Keene, Office of Host Nations on Kwajalein Atoll
Enewetak / Ujelang Local Government Council
Interviews /assistants for the Marshall Islands: Henry Moses, Susan Heine
Translation assistance: Neimon, Titus, Joemy

HISTORICAL CONSULTANTS

David Purcell, University of Hawai'i-Hilo
Francis X. Hezel, S.J., Micronesian Seminar

OTHER ASSISTANCE

In Micronesia: Scott Russell, Sam McPhetres, Dirk Ballendorf, Wakako Higuchi, Don
Shuster, the Micronesian Area Research Center, Sr. Alaina Talu, Don Rubinstein,
Micronesian Seminar.

In the United States and Japan: Geoffrey White, Lamont Lindstrom, Gregory Trifanovitch, the East-West Center, Mac Marshall, David Hanlon, Karen Peacock, University of Hawai'i Hamilton Library and Pacific Collection, Hisafumi Saito, Len Mason, Lela Goodell, Mary H. Maifeld, James West Turner, Robert Kelly, Betty Kam, Bishop Museum Archives, Sandy Ives, Northeast Archives of Folklore and Oral History, University of Maine, Colby College, University of Cincinnati, Taft Memorial Fund, University of Wyoming, University of Hawai'i-West O'ahu, Montana State University, National Archives, Navy Historical Center, U.S. Naval Institute, U.S. Army Military History Institute, National Anthropological Archives, Smithsonian Institution.

Suzanne Falgout wishes to thank University of Hawai'i-West O'ahu students Tara Moorman, Kari Lynn Harumi Nishioka, and Jennifer Hackforth. Lin Poyer thanks University of Cincinnati graduate students Lora Anderson, Shawn Barrick, David Conrad, Lori Lamarre, Cay Mateyko, Laura Moll-Collopy, Jennifer Reiter, and Matt Van Pelt. Laurence Carucci thanks Montana State University students Jocelyn DeHaas, Dory Allard, Angela McDunn, Kate Maxfield, and Sara Mansikka. The College of Letters and Science at Montana State University graciously provided funding for Carucci's research assistants.

NOTES

CHAPTER 1 "MICRONESIA"

1. See Hanlon 1989.
2. See Alkire 1978; Bellwood 1978; Carucci and Poyer 2002; Rainbird 2004.
3. See Hezel 1983; Hanlon 1988.
4. See Hezel 1983; Hanlon 1988; also Peattie 1988.
5. See Hezel 1995; Peattie 1988.
6. See Marshall 1999, after Strathern 1991.
7. For summaries of Micronesian prehistory, see Alkire 1978; Bellwood 1978; Carucci and Poyer 2002; Rainbird 2004.
8. Hezel 1995:xiv.
9. See Peattie 1988; Poyer, Falgout, and Carucci 2001:15–32.
10. See Peattie 1988; Poyer, Falgout, and Carucci 2001:15–32.
11. See Falgout, Poyer, and Carucci 1995.
12. See Peattie 1988; Hezel 1995; Poyer, Falgout, and Carucci 2001:15–32.
13. See Peattie 1988:230–256; Poyer, Falgout, and Carucci 2001:33–72.
14. The islands of Micronesia lie on both sides of the international date line. For events affecting a particular location, we use the local date. For events affecting the entire region, we use two dates. For example, the bombing of Pearl Harbor was on December 7/8, 1941.
15. See Peattie 1988; Poyer, Falgout, and Carucci 2001:73–116.
16. Poyer, Falgout, and Carucci 2001:73–116; Bascom 1950:144.
17. See Richard 1957.
18. Peattie 1988; Poyer, Falgout, and Carucci 2001.
19. For more information on the postwar American administration of Micronesia, see Poyer, Falgout, and Carucci 2001; Kiste and Marshall 1999.
20. Meller 1969:26.

21. Falgout 1995; Kiste and Falgout 1999.

22. Kiste and Falgout 1999.

CHAPTER 2 CULTURAL MEMORIES AND THE PACIFIC WAR

1. For an early discussion of cultural differences in the concept of time, see Benjamin Lee Whorf 1988 [1956]. For more recent discussions of differences in the concept of time in the Pacific Islands, see Kameʻeleihiwa 1992; Hereniko 2000; Hauʻofa 2000.

2. Hauʻofa 2000:459.

3. Hauʻofa 2000:459, from Kameʻeleihiwa 1992:22–23.

4. Hauʻofa 2000:460–461.

5. Wendt 2000:35.

6. Connerton 1989 discusses the different modalities of human memory.

7. See Fentress and Wickham 1992:26–36.

8. See Halbwachs 1992 [1968].

9. See Connerton 1989; Finnegan 1992; Fentress and Wickham 1992.

10. See Brown and Kulik 1982.

11. See Neisser 1982.

12. See Irwin-Zarecka 1994.

13. See Connerton 1989; Fentress and Wickham 1992.

14. See Connerton 1989.

15. See Connerton 1989; Fentress and Wickham 1992; Finnegan 1992.

16. Rosenwald and Ochberg 1992:1–2.

17. Hirsch 1995.

18. Fentress and Wickham 1992.

19. Connerton 1989:37.

20. Finnegan 1992.

21. Poyer, Falgout, and Carucci 2001:332–333.

22. See Fischer 1957; Falgout 1984; Petersen 1993; Mauricio 1992; Pinsker 1992; Goodenough 2002.

23. See Falgout 1984; Petersen 1993.

24. For example, see King and Carucci 1984:505; Parker 1985:30.

25. Poyer, Falgout, and Carucci 2001:334. See also Lindstrom and White 1989.

26. Montvel-Cohen 1982:234.

27. Peoples 1977:151.

28. Burns 1997.

29. Carucci 1989, 2001.

30. Rynkiewich 1972:30–32.

31. Moore 1952.

32. Hauʻofa 2000:465–470.

33. See Falgout 1984; Parmentier 1987; Turner and Falgout 2002.

34. See also Kahn 1990.

35. Denfeld 1981.

36. Poyer, Falgout, and Carucci 2001:335; see also Denfeld 1981; King and Carucci 1984:495, 504.

37. Bender 2002.

38. See Poyer 1992; Poyer, Falgout, and Carucci 2001:335–337.

39. Underwood 1994; Diaz 1994. This site was destroyed by a typhoon in 2002; plans for rebuilding are now under way.

40. Reed 1952.

41. See Williams 1973.

42. Connerton 1989:19.

43. See Hereniko 2000; Hauʻofa 2000.

44. See Hirsch 1995.

CHAPTER 3 THE MEANING OF WAR

1. Hezel 1983:197.

2. See Carucci 1995.

3. Fujitani, White, and Yoneyama 2002:4, 7.

4. Watanabe 2001:129.

CHAPTER 4 THE SHOCK OF WAR

1. Presumably, this refers to physically hauling these materials wherever the work bosses told them to go, following along behind the bosses.

2. A rough translation would be to "tough it out" under adverse conditions, especially when there is inadequate food or other compensation.

3. This phrase likely has multiple meanings. Work was clearly the sole obsession of the Marshallese involved in this project, especially given the long hours and adverse conditions. At the same time, many Marshallese songs are forlorn love songs (similar to American country-western songs); this phrase probably also refers to the songwriter's dreams of his love, the sole obsession that allowed him to live through difficult times.

4. Peattie 1988:262–265; Poyer, Falgout, and Carucci 2001:73–83.

5. The first major bombing of Chuuk was February 17, 1944. The date in this song may refer to the small Australian raid in mid-January 1942.

CHAPTER 5 HARDSHIP AND SUFFERING

1. Marshall 1999.

2. E.g., Marshall 1999; Silverman 1971; Schneider 1984; Linnekin and Poyer 1990; Parmentier 1987; Carucci 1992, 1999.

CHAPTER 6   COMBAT EXPERIENCES

1. Morison 1951:278.
2. Davenport 1953:235, in Duchesne 2004:53–54.

CHAPTER 7   "IT WAS NOT OUR WAR"

1. The "open sea of selfishness" refers to the tradition that, in times of danger, a Pohnpeian man's first responsibility was to his brother-in-law, and then next to his close matrilineal kinsmen; he was to think of himself last. However, out on the open seas—a place that land-loving Pohnpeians consider dangerous—each man was advised to think of his own life first. The "authority" translates as *manaman,* "legitimate power." The song questions whether there was genuine authority for sacrificing one's life in this context. The chief who is the ruler of the world refers to God. The shocking news is that of the war's end.

CHAPTER 8   THE TYPHOON OF WAR

1. Rosenthal 1991.
2. See also Leed 1979.

CHAPTER 9   QUESTIONS OF LOYALTY

1. Kuipers 1998.
2. Carucci 1995.
3. See Poyer 1993.
4. A U.S. Navy radioman who survived the Japanese occupation of Guam by living in a cave and with the help of dozens of Chamorros.

CHAPTER 10   MICRONESIAN RESPONSES TO WARTIME PRESSURES

1. Poyer 2003.

CHAPTER 11   SOME MICRONESIAN PREOCCUPATIONS

1. See Lutz 1988.
2. Peattie 1988:304; Poyer 2004.
3. Carucci 1980; Pollock 1992.
4. Linnekin and Poyer 1990; Flinn 1990; Lutz 1988; Marshall 1999.
5. Carucci 1980, 1997.
6. Weiner and Schneider 1989; Kihleng 1996.
7. The song reminisces about the good old days, when Palauan groups would travel

from one village to another for several days of visiting and entertainment. Travel for these purposes was halted during the war.

8. The inedible fruit of the Oriental mangrove, which was eaten late in the war.

9. The fruit of the bitter jam vine, which was eaten late in the war.

10. Palauans here are wondering whether they can stop the fighting simply by asking "Mr. War" to put an end to it all.

11. See Carucci and Poyer 2002.

12. Poyer, Falgout, and Carucci 2001:53–66, 208–215.

13. Possibly *nishitai hombu* (Western unit from headquarters, or headquarters of the Western unit).

CHAPTER 12   GREETINGS AND FAREWELLS

1. From a file of unpublished WWII songs, collected by White n.d.:101–102.

2. Carucci 1997.

3. Names of hamlets in Ngarechelong.

4. Kayangel, a village in northern Palau.

5. Kuipers 1998.

CHAPTER 13   WARTIME MEMORIES IN THE MODERN WORLD

1. Turner and Falgout 2002; Poyer, Falgout, and Carucci 2004.

2. Turner and Falgout 2002.

3. Poyer, Falgout, and Carucci 2001:333–334.

4. Young, Rosenberger, and Harding 1997:33 report continued links between Japanese fathers and their Chuukese sons.

5. See Bahrenburg 1971:187–188; Barnard 1974; Bronemann 1982; Manchester 1979.

6. Poyer, Falgout, and Carucci 2001:339–340.

7. E.g., Lindemann 1987; Poyer 1992.

8. Falgout 1999; Poyer 1992.

9. Trumbull 1959:91.

10. See Nakano 1983:197; Poyer, Falgout, and Carucci 2001:336–337.

11. Jourdan 2004.

12. Pinsker 1992:45.

CHAPTER 14   "THE GREAT AIRPLANE"

1. A few phrases remain untranslated.

2. This opening verse introduces the setting and heralds the ensuing military invasion and eventual liberation of the island, with the divine assistance of the island spirits and the Christian God (Rubinstein n.d.).

3. The bracketed symbols [r1] or [r2] indicate that the particular line is repeated once or twice.

4. This phrase is a formulaic opening in Yap Outer Island songs (Rubinstein n.d.).

5. This refers to the semigovernmental Japanese agency, Nanyo Takushoku Kabushiki Kaisha, responsible for phosphate mining on Fais and the operation of a store that provided the island with basic commodities including rice, sugar, coffee, and cloth as well as alcohol (Rubinstein n.d.).

6. This was the central figure in the pantheon of pre-Christian Fais gods. Wolofad is the god associated with cultural change: the bringer of fire, weaving, and the arts of culture. He is also a trickster hero, associated with trouble and calamity (Rubinstein n.d.; Lessa 1961:15–26).

7. This stanza records an episode that occurred on December 20, 1944. A U.S. naval vessel from Ulithi arrived carrying a Ulithian chief who, using a bullhorn, called the Fais people ashore and asked them to send out a small party of men to inform the naval commander of the Japanese forces defending Fais (Morison 1970:52, in Rubinstein n.d.).

8. This verse recounts the conscription of young men of Fais who were relocated to Yap to work on behalf of the Japanese defense of that island from American bombing raids. The narrative voice is the young men themselves (Rubinstein n.d.).

9. The two young men mentioned in this verse were Hapide and Mul, sent to Guam for medical reasons during the American naval period. Note that the narrative voice shifts from first person plural to first person singular and includes events that occurred after the war had ended (Rubinstein n.d.).

10. Tarah refers to the ancestral spirit Taraguleng from Metaliefang house compound in Faliyow village. This is the spirit name of Buichemal, born around 1865. Wurusop is the spirit name of Lingmar the Elder, from Limatayfoy house compound in Faliyow village, born around 1840. He was the grandfather of Mul (Rubinstein n.d.).

11. Salapii is the spirit name of Laguar, the mother of Mul (Rubinstein n.d.).

12. Yelimelimal is another ancestral spirit of Limatayfoy compound in Faliyow village. This is the spirit name of Ilimalimog or Limalimog, born about 1909, the older sister of Sepwur referred to in the "Smaller Airplane" (Rubinstein n.d.).

13. This stanza returns to events in stanza 5—the conscription of young Fais men to work on Yap; however, the narrative voice here is first person plural, from the perspective of the young men's parents and relatives (Rubinstein n.d.).

14. Langahiliyol is the spirit name of Limalimar, born about 1890, a woman from Faluch house compound in Faliyow village (Rubinstein n.d.).

15. This stanza discusses the impending war as American military ships approached and shelled Fais, while people took refuge in dugout shelters (Rubinstein n.d.).

16. This stanza adds the observation that the Japanese administrators ("Company men") on Fais changed abruptly from a source of security to a threat (Rubinstein n.d.).

17. The tone of the song becomes humorous here, referring perhaps to the large amounts of canned meat and other foods provided by the U.S. military after the war. Despite all their wartime sufferings, Fais people enjoyed "all different kinds of modern food" (Rubinstein n.d.).

18. This stanza protests against the Japanese strip-mining of the central part of the island—the most fertile area for cultivating food and tobacco (Rubinstein n.d.).

19. This stanza again laments the young men of Fais who were sent to Yap (Rubinstein n.d.).

20. This stanza portrays the deep sentiment Fais people feel for their island. It also speaks of the panic and fear they felt over the American shelling of their island (Rubinstein n.d.).

21. Here the song returns to events in stanza 4—the U.S. naval reconnaissance mission to Fais on December 20, 1944, followed by the American invasion on January 1, 1945 (Rubinstein n.d.).

22. This stanza is unique in its reporting of the European theater of war and the Allied invasion of Germany (Rubinstein n.d.).

23. Here the song again contrasts the peaceful prewar Fais with the shock and confusion brought by war (Rubinstein n.d.).

24. Once again, prewar life is contrasted with wartime destruction. And again, the song protests the Japanese mining of the island for phosphate (Rubinstein n.d.).

25. The protest against the Japanese strip-mining and the U.S. invasion of Fais grows more strident in this stanza. The Japanese defending force captured by the Americans is also treated with derision here; once captured and stripped of their uniforms, they became like "natives" (Rubinstein n.d.).

26. This was the derisive nickname for the chief surveyor of the Japanese mining operations on Fais, a man by the name of Honda. In Fais language, this is *gusuru;* it is shouted at the end of the stanza, drawing a great laugh from the crowd (Rubinstein n.d.).

27. The final stanza recounts the American invasion of Fais. The vessels were amphibious tractors. Fais people hid in their shelters and foxholes while American soldiers approached them at gunpoint (Rubinstein n.d.).

28. The "sacred ground" refers to the front of the chief's meetinghouse, where U.S. naval forces assembled the Islanders and raised their flag on January 4, 1945 (Rubinstein n.d.).

REFERENCES

Alkire, William H.
   1978   *Coral Islanders.* Arlington Heights, IL: AHM Publishing Company.

Bahrenburg, Bruce
   1971   *The Pacific: Then and Now.* New York: Putnam.

Barnard, Charles N.
   1974   "Room with a View of World War II: Going Back to Micronesia." *Signature* 9(4):24–30, 50.

Bascom, William R.
   1950   *Ponape, the Cycle of Empire.* New York: American Association for the Advancement of Science.

Bellwood, Peter R.
   1978   *Man's Conquest of the Pacific: The Prehistory of Southeast Asia and Oceania.* New York: Oxford University Press.

Bender, Barbara
   2002   "Time and Landscape." *Current Anthropology* 43(4, Supplement):103–113.

Bronemann, Leroy B.
   1982   *Once upon a Tide: Tales from a Foxhole in the South Pacific.* Bryn Mawr, PA: Dorrance and Company.

Brown, Roger, and James Kulick
   1982   "Flashbulb Memories." *Cognition* 5:73–79.

Burke, Mary Lisa Lawson
   n.d.   "Songs from Kiribati." In a file of unpublished WWII songs, ed. Geoffrey White. Pacific Collection, Hamilton Library, University of Hawai'i.

Burns, Allan F.

    1997   *Micronesian Resources Study: Kosrae Ethnography.* Kosrae Ethnography Project, Federated States of Micronesia. San Francisco: Micronesian Endowment for Historic Preservation, Federated States of Micronesia, U.S. National Park Service.

Burrows, Edwin G.

    1963   *Flower in My Ear: Art and Ethos of Ifaluk Atoll.* Seattle: University of Washington Press.

Carucci, Laurence M.

    1980   "The Renewal of Life: A Ritual Encounter in the Marshall Islands." Ph.D. dissertation, University of Chicago.

    1989   "The Source of the Force in Marshallese Cosmology." In *The Pacific Theater: Island Representations of World War II,* ed. Geoffrey M. White and Lamont Lindstrom, 73–96. Pacific Islands Monograph Series, no. 8. Honolulu: University of Hawai'i Press.

    1992   "We Planted Mama on Jeptan: Constructing Continuities and Situating Identities on Enewetak Atoll." In *Pacific History,* ed. Donald H. Rubinstein. Mangilao, Guam: University of Guam and the Micronesian Area Research Center.

    1995   "From the Spaces to the Holes: Ralik-Ratak Remembrances of World War II." *Isla* 3(2):279–312.

    1997   *Nuclear Nativity: Rituals of Renewal and Empowerment in the Marshall Islands.* DeKalb: Northern Illinois University Press.

    1999   *Ien Entaan im Jerata: Times of Suffering and Ill Fortune.* Majuro: Marshall Islands Nuclear Claims Tribunal, March.

    2001   "Elision or Decision: Lived History and the Contextual Grounding of the Constructed Past." In *Cultural Memory: Reconfiguring History and Identity in the Postcolonial Pacific,* ed. Jeanette Marie Mageo, 81–101. Honolulu: University of Hawai'i Press.

Carucci, Laurence M., and Lin Poyer

    2002   "The West Central Pacific." In *Oceania: An Introduction to the Cultures and Identities of Pacific Islanders,* ed. Andrew Strathern et al., 183–249. Durham, NC: Carolina Academic Press.

Connerton, Paul

    1989   *How Societies Remember.* Cambridge: Cambridge University.

Davenport, William H.

    1953   "Marshallese Folklore Types." *Journal of American Folklore* 66(261):219–237.

Denfeld, D. Colt

    1981   *Japanese Fortifications and Other Military Structures in the Central Pacific.*

Saipan: Historic Preservation Office, Office of the High Commissioner, U.S. Trust Territory of the Pacific Islands.

Diaz, Vicente M.

1994 "Simply Chamorro: Telling Tales of Demise and Survival in Guam." *The Contemporary Pacific* 6(1):29–58.

Duchesne, Tammy

2004 "Micronesian Songs and Chants from WWII: Collective Voices Sing Island Histories." Master's thesis, University of Guam.

Falgout, Suzanne

1984 "Persons and Knowledge in Pohnpei." Ph.D. dissertation, University of Oregon.

1995 "Americans in Paradise: Custom, Democracy, and Anthropology in Postwar Micronesia." Special Theme Issue. Politics of Culture in the Pacific, ed. Richard Feinberg and Laura Zimmer-Tamakoshi. *Ethnology* 34(2):99–111.

1999 "Cultural Tourism in the Federated States of Micronesia." Unpublished typescript.

Falgout, Suzanne; Lin Poyer; and Laurence M. Carucci

1995 "'The Greatest Hardship': Micronesian Memories of World War II." *Isla: A Journal of Island Studies* 3(2):203–221.

Fentress, James, and Chris Wickham

1992 *Social Memory: New Perspectives on the Past.* Oxford, UK: Blackwell.

Finnegan, Ruth

1992 *Oral Traditions and the Verbal Arts.* London: Routledge.

Fischer, John L., with the assistance of Ann M. Fischer

1957 *The Eastern Carolines.* New Haven, CT: Pacific Science Board, National Academy of Sciences, National Research Council, in Association with Human Relations Area Files.

Flinn, Juliana

1990 "We Still Have Our Customs: Being Pulapese in Truk." In *Cultural Identity and Ethnicity in the Pacific,* ed. Jocelyn Linnekin and Lin Poyer, 103–126. Honolulu: University of Hawai'i Press.

Fujitani, Takashi; Geoffrey M. White; and Lisa Yoneyama

2002 *Perilous Memories: The Asian-Pacific War(s).* Durham, NC: Duke University Press.

Goodenough, Ward

2002 *Under Heaven's Brow: Pre-Christian Religious Tradition in Chuuk.* Philadelphia: American Philosophical Society.

Halbwachs, Maurice
1992 [1968]   *On Collective Memory.* Chicago: University of Chicago Press.

Hanlon, David
1988   *Upon a Stone Altar: A History of the Island of Pohnpei to 1890.* Pacific Islands Monograph Series, no. 5. Honolulu: University of Hawai'i Press.
1989   Micronesia: Writing and Rewriting the Histories of a Nonentity. *Pacific Studies* 12(2):1–21.

Hau'ofa, Epeli
2000   "Epilogue. Pasts to Remember." In *Remembrance of Pacific Pasts: An Invitation to Remake History,* ed. Robert Borofsky, 453–471. Honolulu: University of Hawai'i Press.

Hereniko, Vilsoni
2000   "Indigenous Knowledge and Academic Imperialism." In *Remembrance of Pacific Pasts: An Invitation to Remake History,* ed. Robert Borofsky, 78–91. Honolulu: University of Hawai'i Press.

Hezel, Francis X., S.J.
1983   *The First Taint of Civilization: A History of the Caroline and Marshall Islands in Pre-Colonial Days, 1521–1885.* Pacific Islands Monograph Series, no. 1. Honolulu: University of Hawai'i Press.
1995   *Strangers in Their Own Lands: A Century of Colonial Rule in the Caroline and Marshall Islands.* Pacific Islands Monograph Series, no. 13. Honolulu: University of Hawai'i Press.

Higuchi, Wakako
1986   "Palauan Interviews." Typescript. Pacific Collection, Hamilton Library, University of Hawai'i.
n.d.   "Songs from Palau." In a file of unpublished WWII songs, ed. Geoffrey White. Pacific Collection, Hamilton Library, University of Hawai'i.

Hirsch, Herbert
1995   *Genocide and the Politics of Memory.* Chapel Hill: University of North Carolina Press.

Irwin-Zarecka, Iwona
1994   *Frames of Remembrance: Dynamics of Collective Memory.* New Brunswick, NJ: Transaction Publishers.

Jourdan, Christine
2004   "Stepping-Stones to National Consciousness: The Solomon Islands Case." In *Globalization and Culture Change in the Pacific Islands,* ed. Victoria S. Lockwood, 102–115. Upper Saddle River, NJ: Pearson / Prentice Hall.

Kahn, Miriam
1990   "Stone-faced Ancestors: The Spatial Anchoring of Myth in Wamira, Papua New Guinea." *Ethnology* 29(1):51–66.

Kameʻeleihiwa, Lilikala
   1992   *Native Land and Foreign Desires.* Honolulu: Bishop Museum Press.

Kihleng, Kimberlee S.
   1996   "Women in Exchange: Negotiated Relations, Practice, and the Constitution of Female Power in Processes of Cultural Reproduction and Change in Pohnpei, Micronesia." Ph.D. dissertation, University of Hawaiʻi.

King, Thomas F., and J. Carucci
   1984   "The Guns of Tonaachaw: World War II Archaeology." In *Pisekin Noomw Noon Tonaachaw,* ed. Thomas King and Patricia Parker, 467–507. Carbondale: Center for Archaeological Investigation, Southern Illinois University.

Kiste, Robert C., and Suzanne Falgout
   1999   "Anthropology and Micronesia: The Context." In *American Anthropology in Micronesia: An Assessment,* ed. Robert C. Kiste and Mac Marshall, 11–51. Honolulu: University of Hawaiʻi Press.

Kiste, Robert C., and Mac Marshall, eds.
   1999   *American Anthropology in Micronesia: An Assessment.* Honolulu: University of Hawaiʻi Press.

Kuipers, Joel C.
   1998   *Language, Identity, and Marginality in Indonesia: The Changing Nature of Ritual Speech on the Island of Sumba.* Cambridge: Cambridge University Press.

Leed, Eric
   1979   *No Man's Land: Combat and Identity in World War I.* Cambridge: Cambridge University Press.

Lessa, William A.
   1961   *Tales from Ulithi Atoll: A Comparative Study in Oceanic Folklore.* Berkeley: University of California Press.

Lindemann, Klaus
   1987   "Beneath the Waters of Truk." *After the Battle* 57:21–36.

Lindstrom, Lamont, and Geoff M. White
   1989   "War Stories." In *The Pacific Theater,* ed. Geoffrey M. White and Lamont Lindstrom, 3–40. Honolulu: University of Hawaiʻi Press.

Linnekin, Jocelyn, and Lin Poyer, eds.
   1990   *Cultural Identity and Ethnicity in the Pacific.* Honolulu: University of Hawaiʻi Press.

Lutz, Catherine
   1988   *Unnatural Emotions: Everyday Sentiments on a Micronesian Atoll and Their Challenge to Western Theory.* Chicago: University of Chicago Press.

Manchester, William

    1979   *Goodbye, Darkness: A Memoir of the Pacific War.* New York: Little, Brown.

Marshall, Mac

    1999   "'Partial Connections': Kinship and Social Organization in Micronesia." In *American Anthropology in Micronesia: An Assessment,* ed. Robert C. Kiste and Mac Marshall, 107–143. Honolulu: University of Hawai'i Press.

Mauricio, Rufino

    1992   "A History of Pohnpei History or *Poadoapoad:* Description and Explanation of Recorded Oral Traditions." In *Pacific History: Papers from the 8th Pacific History Association Conference,* ed. Donald H. Rubinstein, 351–380. Mangilao: University of Guam Press and Micronesian Area Research Center.

Meller, Norman

    1969   *The Congress of Micronesia.* Honolulu: University of Hawai'i Press.

Montvel-Cohen, Marvin

    1982   "Craft and Context on Yap (Caroline Islands)." Ph.D. dissertation, Southern Illinois University, Carbondale.

Moore, W. Robert

    1952   "Grass-Skirted Yap." *National Geographic Magazine* 102(6):805–826.

Morison, Samuel Eliot

    1951   *A History of United States Naval Operations in World War II.* Vol. 7: *Aleutians, Gilberts, and Marshalls: June 1942–April 1944.* Boston: Atlantic, Little, Brown.

    1970   *A History of United States Naval Operations in World War II.* Vol. 12: *Leyte, June 1944–January 1945.* Boston: Little, Brown.

Nakano, Ann

    1983   *Broken Canoe: Conversations and Observations in Micronesia.* St. Lucia: University of Queensland Press.

Neisser, Ulric

    1982   *Cognition and Reality.* San Francisco: Freeman.

Parker, Patricia L.

    1985   "Land Tenure in Trukese Society: 1850–1980." Ph.D. dissertation, University of Pennsylvania.

Parmentier, Richard J.

    1987   *The Sacred Remains: Myth, History, and Polity in Belau.* Chicago: University of Chicago Press.

Peattie, Mark

    1988   *Nan'yo: The Rise and Fall of the Japanese in Micronesia, 1885–1945.* Pacific Islands Monograph Series, no. 4. Honolulu: University of Hawai'i Press.

Peoples, James
    1977   "Deculturation and Dependence in a Micronesian Community." Ph.D. dissertation, University of California, Davis.

Petersen, Glenn
    1993   "Kanengamah: Pohnpei's Politics of Concealment." *American Anthropologist* 95(2):334–352.

Pinsker, Eve
    1992   "Celebrations of Government: Dance Performance and Legitimacy in the Federated States of Micronesia." *Pacific Studies* 15(4):29–56.

Pollock, Nancy
    1992   *These Roots Remain.* Laie, HI: Institute for Polynesian Studies.

Poyer, Lin
    1992   "Defining History across Cultures: Islander and Outsider Contrasts." *Isla: A Journal of Micronesian Studies* 1(1):73–89.
    1993   *The Ngatik Massacre: History and Identity on a Micronesian Atoll.* Washington, DC: Smithsonian Institution Press.
    1997   *Ethnography and Ethnohistory of Taroa Island, Republic of the Marshall Islands.* Micronesian Resources Study: Marshall Islands Ethnography. San Francisco: Micronesian Endowment for Historic Preservation, Republic of the Marshall Islands, U.S. National Park Service.
    2003   "Revitalization in Wartime Micronesia." In *Reassessing Revitalization,* ed. Michael Harkin. Lincoln: University of Nebraska Press.
    2004   "Dimensions of Hunger in Wartime: Chuuk Lagoon, 1943–1945." *Food and Foodways* 12(2–3): 137–164.

Poyer, Lin; Suzanne Falgout; and Laurence Marshall Carucci
    2001   *The Typhoon of War: Micronesian Experiences in the Pacific War.* Honolulu: University of Hawai'i Press.
    2004   "The Impact of the Pacific War on Modern Micronesian Identity." In *Globalization and Culture Change in the Pacific Islands,* ed. Victoria S. Lockwood. Upper Saddle River, NJ: Pearson Prentice Hall.

Proust, Marcel
    1919   *A la recherché du temps perdu.* Paris: Gallimard.

Rainbird, Paul
    2004   *The Archaeology of Micronesia.* Cambridge World Archaeology. Cambridge: Cambridge University Press.

Reed, Erik K.
    1952   *General Report on Archaeology and History of Guam.* Santa Fe, NM: National Park Service.

Richard, Dorothy
    1957   *U.S. Naval Administration of the Trust Territory of the Pacific Islands.* Vol.

1: *The Wartime Military Government Period, 1942–1945.* Washington, DC: Office of the Chief of Naval Operations.

Rosenthal, Gabrielle
  1991   "German War Memories: Narratibility and the Biographical and Social Functions of Remembering." *Oral History* 19(2):34–41.

Rosenwald, George C., and Richard L. Ochberg, eds.
  1992   *Storied Lives: The Cultural Politics of Self Understanding.* New Haven, CT: Yale University Press.

Rubinstein, Donald H.
  n.d.   "Oral Literature: A Song Text from Fais Island." Unpublished manuscript in the files of the author.

Rynkiewich, Michael A.
  1972   "Land Tenure among Arno Marshallese." Ph.D. dissertation, University of Minnesota.

Santos, Carmen I.
  1989   "Guam's Folklore." In *Umatac by the Sea: A Village in Transition,* ed. Rebecca Stephenson and Hiro Kurashina, 87–112. MARC Educational Series, no. 3. Mangilao: Micronesian Area Research Center.
  n.d.   "Songs from Guam." In a file of unpublished WWII songs, ed. Geoffrey White. Pacific Collection, Hamilton Library, University of Hawai'i.

Schneider, David M.
  1984   *A Critique of the Study of Kinship.* Ann Arbor: University of Michigan Press.

Silverman, Martin G.
  1971   *Disconcerting Issue: Meaning and Struggle in a Resettled Pacific Community.* Chicago: University of Chicago Press.

Strathern, Marilyn
  1991   *Partial Connections.* ASAO Special Publication, no. 3. Savage, MD: Rowman and Littlefield.

Trumbull, Robert
  1959   *Paradise in Trust: A Report on Americans in Micronesia, 1946–58.* New York: William Sloane Associates.

Turner, James W., and Suzanne Falgout
  2002   "Time Traces: Cultural Memory and World War II in Pohnpei." *The Contemporary Pacific: A Journal of Island Affairs* 14(1):101–134.

Underwood, Robert
  1994   "The State of Guam's Agenda in Washington." Speech by Honorable Robert A. Underwood, delivered November 13, 1995, in chamber of Guam Legislature. *Isla: A Journal of Micronesian Studies* 4(1):109–130.

Watanabe, Morio
2001   "Imagery and War in Japan: 1995." In *Perilous Memories,* ed. Takashi Fuji-
       tani, Geoffrey M. White, and Lisa Yoneyama, 129–151. Durham, NC: Duke
       University Press.

Weiner, Annette, and Jane Schneider, eds.
1989   *Cloth and Human Experience.* Washington, DC: Smithsonian Institution
       Press.

Wendt, Albert
2000   "Inside Us the Dead." In *Remembrance of Pacific Pasts: An Invitation to
       Remake History,* ed. Robert Borofsky, 35–42. Honolulu: University of
       Hawai'i Press.

White, Geoffrey, ed.
n.d.   File of unpublished WWII songs. Pacific Collection, Hamilton Library,
       University of Hawai'i.

Whorf, Benjamin Lee
1988 [1956]   *Language, Thought, and Reality: Selected Writings of Benjamin Lee
       Whorf,* ed. John B. Carroll. Cambridge, MA: MIT Press.

Williams, Raymond
1973   *The Country and the City.* New York: Oxford University Press.

Wilson, Walter Scott
1968   "Land, Activity and Social Organization of Lelu, Kusaie." Ph.D. disserta-
       tion, University of Pennsylvania.

Young, John A.; Nancy R. Rosenberger; and Joe R. Harding
1997   *Ethnography of Truk, Federated States of Micronesia. Micronesian Resources
       Study. Truk Ethnography.* San Francisco: Micronesian Endowment for His-
       toric Preservation, Federated States of Micronesia, U.S. National Park Ser-
       vice.

INDEX

Vallazon, Julio, 76
vantage points, 4, 101, 120, 219

"*Waayel*" (Airplane), 228–238
Walter, Rosalinda, 180
war, concept of, 39–41
war from the sand spits, 120–123
war of mobility, 120–122
war preparations, 16, 44–45, 52–59, 63–64
war relics, **21**, 32–34
war remembrances: books and movies, 223–224; forms of, 28–32; reunion events, 222–223. *See also* songs, chants, and dances
Wendt, Albert, 22
Weno (Chuuk), 66–68
"What a Surprising Day This Is," 86–87
White, Geoffrey M., 42
Wickham, Chris, 23
Wilson, Walter Scott, 172, 198
Woleai (Western Caroline Islands): Allied bombing of, 96–97; relocation of Islanders to Ifaluk, 85–86

"Work at Sirebu" ("Tiger Group"), 109–110
World War II: "it was not our war," 103–107, 221; meaning of, 35, 41–43; Micronesians knowledge of, 44, 49–50, 121–123, 124–126, 208–209, 214–215; overview, 16–18; typhoon analogy, 119–120. *See also* Allied bombing; Allied invasions; coping strategies; end of the war; hardship and suffering; postwar period; roles of Micronesians; start of war

Yafimal, Matthew, 85–86
Yap: Allied bombing of, 95, 97–98, **229**; arrival of Americans, **187**, 193–194; colonial period, 11; end of the war, 124; feelings of powerlessness, 104–105; food shortages, 172–173, 176; "The Great Airplane" (Halamar), 228–238; map, 58; start of war, 68–69; war as typhoon, 119; "Work at Sirebu" ("Tiger Group"), 109–110
Yoneyama, Lisa, 42

ABOUT THE AUTHORS

All three authors are anthropologists with many years of Micronesian experience. Suzanne Falgout of University of Hawai'i–West O'ahu has conducted research on Pohnpei and with Pohnpeians now living in Hawai'i, and on the history of anthropology in Micronesia. Lin Poyer of University of Wyoming has conducted research on Sapwuahfik and wrote *The Ngatik Massacre* (1993). Laurence M. Carucci at Montana State University has worked in the Marshall Islands and with Marshall Islanders now living in Hawai'i and is the author of *Nuclear Nativity* (1997). Together, the authors conducted research throughout the islands of Micronesia and co-authored *The Typhoon of War: Micronesian Experiences of the Pacific War* (2001).

CPSIA informatio
Printed in the USA
LVOW06s213804
452673LV0